A Tapestry of Global Christology

Weaving a Three-Stranded Theological Cord

Isuwa Y. Atsen

MONOGRAPHS

© 2022 Isuwa Y. Atsen

Published 2022 by Langham Monographs
An imprint of Langham Publishing
www.langhampublishing.org

Langham Publishing and its imprints are a ministry of Langham Partnership

Langham Partnership
PO Box 296, Carlisle, Cumbria, CA3 9WZ, UK
www.langham.org

ISBNs:
978-1-83973-236-2 Print
978-1-83973-794-7 ePub
978-1-83973-795-4 Mobi
978-1-83973-796-1 PDF

Isuwa Y. Atsen has asserted his right under the Copyright, Designs and Patents Act, 1988 to be identified as the Author of this work.

All rights reserved. No part of this publication may be reproduced, stored in a retrieval system or transmitted, in any form or by any means, electronic, mechanical, photocopying, recording or otherwise, without the prior written permission of the publisher or the Copyright Licensing Agency.

Requests to reuse content from Langham Publishing are processed through PLSclear. Please visit www.plsclear.com to complete your request.

All Scripture quotations, unless otherwise indicated, are taken from the Holy Bible, New International Version®, NIV®. Copyright ©1973, 1978, 1984, 2011 by Biblica, Inc.™ Used by permission of Zondervan.

Scripture marked (NASB) taken from the New American Standard Bible®, Copyright © 1960, 1962, 1963, 1968, 1971, 1972, 1973, 1975, 1977, 1995 by The Lockman Foundation. Used by permission.

British Library Cataloguing-in-Publication Data
A catalogue record for this book is available from the British Library

ISBN: 978-1-83973-236-2

Cover & Book Design: projectluz.com

Langham Partnership actively supports theological dialogue and an author's right to publish but does not necessarily endorse the views and opinions set forth here or in works referenced within this publication, nor can we guarantee technical and grammatical correctness. Langham Partnership does not accept any responsibility or liability to persons or property as a consequence of the reading, use or interpretation of its published content.

This book is an ambitious undertaking. By engaging the resources of contextual theology, analytic theology, and the theological interpretation of Scripture, Atsen adroitly draws together strands of theological discourse which have proceeded all too often in isolation from one another. The result of the inquiry is a robust and richly integrative contribution to the church's reflection upon the doctrine of Christ. Atsen's proposal is essential reading for all students of Christian thought, and especially for those who lament the phenomenon of fragmentation in contemporary theology.

David Luy, PhD
Associate Professor of Systematic Theology,
North American Lutheran Seminary, Pennsylvania, USA

"A cord of three strands is not easily broken" (Eccl. 4:12). This may not be an African proverb, but in Atsen's hands it becomes a compelling image for doing theology – for reading Scripture theologically – that is simultaneously catholic, conceptually precise, and sensitive to cultural context. Especially important are Atsen's explanations as to why neither creedal Christology or ontology are examples of Western theological colonialism. Here is theology that is as biblical as it is global, which is to say, a theology for the church today, and tomorrow.

Kevin J. Vanhoozer, PhD
Research Professor of Systematic Theology,
Trinity Evangelical Divinity School, Illinois, USA

Isuwa Atsen's *A Tapestry of Global Christology* demonstrates faithfulness to orthodox Christianity and incredible knowledge, wisdom, and insight. Astute in the way he engages the task of Christian theology from a Majority World perspective, Atsen develops a Christology that is canonical, catholic, analytic, and contextual. It is filled with fresh insights and opens new vistas of theological engagements. This book is a breath of fresh air in Christological analytic theology. It will be useful to Western and Majority World theologians alike. I highly recommend this book.

Bulus Y. Galadima, PhD
Former Provost, Jos ECWA Theological Seminary, Nigeria
Dean, Cook School of Intercultural Study,
Biola University, California, USA

This book is a theological response to Christological controversies tormenting the African Church. It provides a theological treatise to answer the catalogue of Christological misinterpretations, misrepresentations, misapplications, and misleadings. The author provides a sure way through these errors by using Scripture as the standard of our faith and authority. The book concludes with a pragmatic application of Christology to our worship and confession in the midst of danger and violence. I strongly recommend this book.

Rev. Gyang D. Pam, PhD
Provost, Gindiri Theological Seminary, Nigeria

To Anya,
who now beholds Him face-to-face

Contents

Acknowledgments xi

Chapter 1 1
Introduction
    Problem and Thesis 4
    The Thread of the Theological Interpretation of Scripture 6
    The Thread of Analytic Theology 9
    The Thread of Global Theology 13
    Rethinking the Western Versus Non-Western Bifurcation 16
    Scope and Delimitation 21
    Significance of the Study 22
    Summary of Chapters 23

Chapter 2 27
Use of Scripture and the Nature of Christian Theology
    The Idea of Using Scripture in Theology 29
    The View and Use of Scripture in Christian Theology: A
        Historical Survey 33
        The New Testament Use of the Old Testament 33
        Scripture and Its Use in Premodern Theology 37
        Reformation and Modern Uses of Scripture in Theology 45
        The Bible as the Scriptures of Believing Communities:
            Postmodern Approaches 57
    Construing and Using the Bible Theologically 62
    Situating Scripture and Its User within the Divine Economy 63
    From Theological Interpretation to Theological Theology 68
    Conclusion 70

Chapter 3 73
Using Scripture in Analytic Theology
    Understanding Analytic Theology: Its Story 74
        From Analytic Philosophy of Religion to Analytic
            Philosophical Theology 76
    Understanding Analytic Theology: Its Nature and Method 77
        Non-Substantive and Substantive Analytic Theology 80
    The Use of Scripture in Analytic Theology: Revelational Control 82
    Explicating the Person of Christ in Analytic
        Theological Discourse 87

- Oliver Crisp on the Anhypostasia and Enhypostasia Distinction 87
- Thomas McCall on the Relation of Christ in the Trinity 95
- Between Analytic Theology and Theological Theology 99
- Analytic Style and Scriptural Form 102
- Philosophical Versus Theological Reason 104
- Accessibility of Content and Attention to Context 107

Chapter 4 111
- *Christ in Global Theological Perspectives*
- From Context to Text: Method in Global Christology 113
- The Quest for an African Christology: An Overview 116
  - Missionary Christology as Deficient 118
  - Christologies of Liberation: Jesus "for" Africa 119
  - Christologies of Inculturation: Jesus "of" Africa 121
  - Christologies of Reconstruction: Jesus "in" Africa 124
  - Other Christologies in Africa 126
- Some Constructive Christologies in Nigeria 129
  - The Guest Christology of Enyi Ben Udoh 130
  - The Revealer Christology of Victor Ezigbo 139
- Decolonization as De-Missionarization: The Final Word 147
- Conclusion 149

Chapter 5 151
- *Toward a Global Analytic Christology*
- A Theological Analytic Contextual Approach to Christology 153
- Scripture as Canon 153
- Tradition as Guide 156
- Context as Theater 159
- Conceptual Analysis as a Tool 164
- Conclusion 170

Chapter 6 173
- *Christ in the Context of Violence*
- Encountering the Son of God in an African Windstorm 177
  - Plot and Structure 178
  - The Absence, Presence, and Worship of Jesus 179
- Confessing Jesus Christ as Lord of and in All Contexts 190
  - Divine Self-Emptying and Human Self-Humbling 191
  - The Exaltation and Lordship of Christ 198
- Conclusion 201

Chapter 7 203
    Summary and Conclusion
        Summary..203
        Conclusions and Recommendations...................................205
Bibliography 209

Acknowledgments

This book is my doctoral dissertation submitted to the faculty of Trinity Evangelical Divinity in Deerfield, Illinois, USA. The work has gone through moderate revisions based on the recommendations of my dissertation committee and the peer reviewer of Langham Publishing. I wish to begin by thanking Langham for accepting my work for publication. I deeply appreciate the efforts of Vivian Doub, who was my primary contact person at Langham, for her timely responses to my initial inquiries and subsequent exchanges. Many thanks to Dr. Mark Arnold who took over from her and continued working with me to this stage of the project. I especially and sincerely thank Langham's peer reviewer for pointing out quite a number of issues related to both substance and style that I needed to revise. Their work has helped to improve mine significantly.

My doctoral journey was tortuous both for me and for my family. But at the same time, it was a wonderful opportunity for intellectual and spiritual growth. I wish to acknowledge all the people who, at different stages of the journey, helped me with their intellectual, financial, moral, and spiritual support. Without them, I would not have made it to the end. First, my dissertation committee – it has been the privilege of my academic life to have worked on my dissertation under the expert and kind supervision of Dr. Kevin J. Vanhoozer. I have learned so much and have been changed in many ways through my interactions with him, thus enriching this study from its conception to its delivery in the present form. In addition, his incisive and multiple feedback, and usually in a very timely manner, have helped to make this work better than what it would have been. Dr. David Luy was not only my second reader, but also graciously gave me the opportunity to serve as his Graduate Assistant for more than four years. I have benefited immensely from this relationship with him. A number of the lectures I gave during some of his classes were portions of this dissertation and that provided me with an avenue for feedback, which informed some revisions of my earlier submissions. My third reader, Dr. Tite Tiénou, completely transformed my understanding of Africa and the practice of global Christianity and Christian theology. His influence has made me a better thinker, particularly with respect (but not limited) to contextual matters. I could not have asked for a better dissertation committee, which also included my Program Director, Dr. Richard Averbeck. I thank them all most sincerely.

Finances were always a challenge for me from the beginning to the end of my program. But the Lord was faithful through it all and raised many financial supporters along the way, which are too numerous to mention here. However, I must mention Calvary Orthodox Presbyterian Church, La Mirada, California, together with Immanuel Church, Gurnee, Illinois, for consistent monthly support to my family from 2014 to 2019. I must also mention the "above and beyond" generous support of my dear uncle, Maj. Gen. D. A. Bako and of my older cousin, Hon. Bitrus B. Kaze, without which our situation would have been much worse. The support of these friends and churches at different points in the journey is also much appreciated: Patrick and Sarah Dakum, John and Angel Ayuba, Jude and Janet Habu, Simon and Chancit Bunshak, Atang Augustine Azi, COCIN LCCs Rahwol Kanang, Karu Phase II, and Garki, as well as COCIN RCCs Fobur, Jos Jarawa, Maijuju, Karu, and Abuja.

During times of discouragement (and there were so many of them) throughout my program, the Lord used a number of people to renew my faith and hope through their prayers, counsel, and financial gifts. Many thanks to my mentors and encouragers in life: Drs. Bulus and Rose Galadima, my discipler Evang. Judah Bedimma Gonzwak, Dr. Garrett DeWesse and his wife Barbara, Rev. Markus D. Atsen, my mom Elizabeth Yohanna, my siblings, and my wife's family. These people believed in and stood by me at very crucial points in my life. I also wish to thank my church denomination, the Church of Christ in Nations (COCIN), Nigeria, for letting me pursue doctoral studies.

Finally, I thank my wife Esther who endured this journey with me as a doctoral student herself, while also being the spouse of a doctoral student. Our children, Atsen, Abi, Arum, and Anya, added to both the stress and the pleasure of going through my doctoral program and dissertation writing.

However on 9 April 2020, nine months after we returned to Nigeria, our last daughter, Anya, went to be with the Lord. My life has never been the same since then and I cannot say at this point if I will ever recover from this broken place. Therefore it is to her memory that I dedicate this work!

CHAPTER 1

Introduction

The centrality of Christ to Christian theology is undeniable, and this explains the church's preoccupation with Christology from the earliest days of her birth and everywhere Christianity makes an entrance. Christology is reflection about the person and work of Christ that often produces an understanding of the Christ in one's own ecclesial and social context (e.g. cultural, political, economic, etc.). We can think of this understanding as a tapestry, which is a textile fabric that uses natural (and/or cultural) resources to produce a "covering" (for walls, floors, or furniture) with a design or picture on it. In this sense, Christology may be construed as a tapestry with Jesus's image on it that adorns particular rooms in the church (the house of God), shaping the christological imaginations of its occupants. Given this imagery, the task of Christian theology may be likened to the art of weaving, which brings together a variety of individual threads into a coherent, attractive, and useful whole. The art of weaving is a common craft in many parts of Africa. I grew up in the Nassarawa Gwong neighborhood of Jos, Nigeria, where I witnessed first-hand the skills of these artisans (mostly of the Yoruba ethnic group). I was captivated daily by their work of weaving the traditional *Ashoké* (lit: top cloth), something they often carry out in a community of weavers – a significant issue in doing theology.

The craft involves the use of many threads, usually three or more, placed about ten feet away on large rollers and linked up to the locally-made weaving equipment where the craftsman sits to ply their trade. The artisan uses both hands to throw another thread (placed in a small roller) from side to side across the stretch of larger threads and presses them together intermittently. At the same time, they use both feet to pull down two rope-like parts

1

of the weaving equipment in order to give the piece being weaved firmness and texture as a single and unified piece of cloth – one that is not easily broken (cf. Eccl 4:12). In addition, the cloths are not only weaved in different combination of colors but also with different designs and, sometimes, images. This ability of the artisans to come up with beautiful designs and images on hand-weaved cloths, dexterously using both hands and both feet at once and bringing many threads together, is simply breathtaking; one cannot adequately describe it in words. Obviously, this skill is not something that someone acquires in a day, or a week, or even a month. It usually takes many months, even years of apprenticeship to master the craft. Not only that, but weaving a piece of cloth is also not something that can be started and completed in a day or two, no matter a person's mastery of the craft. It takes many weeks or months, depending, not only on the worker's skills, but also on the complexity of the design or image that is being weaved into the cloth. This seems like a helpful metaphor for doing theology, particularly with respect to christological reflections.

Today, many have and are still making efforts to weave the image of Christ into newer contextual cloths. Christ is constantly being "re-imaged" in the diverse constructive Christologies that continue to emerge from different parts of the world where the Christian faith is being professed. This ongoing work around the globe is being instantiated primarily by the massive growth of Christianity in what is referred to as the Majority World (or Global South), that is, the continents of Africa, Asia, and Latin America. It is also widely acknowledged that this growth in the Majority World has coincided with a decline of the faith in most of the West (Global North) where it was once vibrant and much at home for about two millennia.[1] It is therefore unsurprising that hitherto, Christianity has been identified with the West, rightly or wrongly, and as a corollary, Christian theology has been (and is still being) queried to have taken on distinctly Western characteristics.

However, given the oft-repeated shift in Christianity's center of gravity, it is natural that a redefinition – some would say recognition – of the character of Christian theology as "contextual" has been anticipated, encouraged, and

---

1. For discussions about this shift in Christianity's center of gravity, see Sanneh, *Encountering the West*; Walls, *Missionary Movement*; Jenkins, *Next Christendom*; and Kim, *Rise of the Global South*.

pursued. Stephen Bevans asserts that all theology is and has always been contextual. For him, "One can even say that there is no such thing as 'theology,' because there is only contextual theology: African American, Latino/a, Asian, Liberal Protestant, Neo-orthodox, Congolese, feminist or womanist, Thomist, White U.S. American or European."[2] Bevans also comments on the scope of contextual theology when he says:

> Theologians use other terms to speak of the contextual nature of theology: incarnation, inculturation, local theology, indigenization, intercultural theology. While these terms are certainly valid and acceptable, the term "contextual theology" has the advantage of pointing to the fact [that] the particularity from which theology must be done today is more than a consciousness of culture, place or ethnicity, but includes every aspect of life.[3]

It is with this key that earnest constructive theological work is being carried out in and from the various regions where Christianity is presently enjoying very visible vitality. Perhaps, this is a moment of prophetic fulfillment – the earth being filled with the knowledge of the glory of the Lord as the waters cover the seas (cf. Hab 2:14).

With respect to context, this work focuses on explicating who Christ is for Christians in northern Nigeria who continue to experience deadly violence from their Muslim attackers. As a victim of these attacks myself, I find the idea of imaging and understanding Christ in this context to be both important and urgent. On Friday 7 September 2001, rampaging Muslim mobs began attacking Christians, Christian businesses, houses, and places of worship in the city of Jos in North Central Nigeria (also known as the Middle Belt). This was the first of such crises to break out in the city. Over a thousand people were killed in the immediate conflicts that followed, which lasted for six days.[4] On just the second day of this bloodbath, my father was shot in front of our house and he later died. To add to the pain, I could not attend his funeral, which was hurriedly done the following day to avoid letting his corpse be mass-buried by the government. So many Christian families in northern

---

2. Bevans, "Contextual Theology," 1.
3. Bevans, 4.
4. Human Rights Watch, "Jos: A City Torn Apart," https://www.hrw.org/report/2001/12/18/jos/city-torn-apart.

Nigeria have gone through similar or worse experiences as mine. Such an experience / context definitely shapes, or reshapes, one's understanding of Christ, and we shall return to this setting in chapter 6. However, does one's contextual understanding need guidance or should it be left unchecked to birth a new image of Christ?

Problem and Thesis

While theology is being carried out in diverse contexts and addressing a variety of Christian doctrines, Christology has featured most prominently thus becoming the touchstone doctrine of global Christian theologizing.[5] But how well is this endeavor being carried out? The task does require, as will be argued, the skillful use of some crucial threads if the identity of Christ is to be understood and stated correctly amid diverse contextual realities or experiences. While the focus on using contextual realities and cultural resources in this enterprise is not only necessary but also commendable, many of the Christologies that emerge from this approach often exclude and/or limit certain threads and principles that are necessary if we are to engage robustly in global Christologizing.

The use of Scripture is the first critical thread that we need to take into account. David Kelsey notes that, "Virtually every contemporary Protestant theologian along the entire spectrum of opinion . . . has acknowledged that any Christian theology worthy of the name 'Christian' must, in *some* sense of the phrase, be done 'in accord with scripture.'"[6] However, what does it really mean to do theology in accord with Scripture? The mere fact that Scripture is used in theology, though necessary, is not in itself sufficient to guarantee that the said theology is in accord with Scripture. Therefore, the way in which Scripture is read and used seems to be as important as the very fact that it is used. Indeed, Scripture would need to be used in a way that is canonically consistent, sensible to the catholicity of the Christian faith,

---

5. The notion of global theology vis-à-vis contextual theology will be defined shortly in this chapter. The centrality of Christology however has been noted by Hans Frei in his claim that the different understandings of the identity of the person of Christ are the basic determining factors for the types of Christian theology seen in Western contexts, particularly in England and Germany. Frei, *Types of Christian Theology*. See also Niebuhr, *Christ and Culture*.

6. Kelsey, *Proving Doctrine*, 1. Emphasis in original.

contextually relevant or meaningful, and without violating certain basic laws of logic (e.g. the law of non-contradiction – that is, that no claim can be both true and false at the same time and in the same sense). This is the conviction that underlies this study.

Our goal in this project is to orient Christology in the direction of a global analytic theology, that is, the interaction of the theological reading of Scripture, analytic theology, and global theology (these will be defined shortly). But what might this interaction look like? How will it help us speak more adequately about Christ in the diverse contexts of world Christianity? It is to these ends that this study develops and defends the thesis that a truly global understanding of Christ would take seriously the canonical writings and use those writings in sync with the early Christian tradition encapsulated in the creeds (e.g. Nicaea and Chalcedon), while at the same time using contextual realities and resources with the help of analytic tools to portray the very same Christ of Scripture and of the Christian tradition with precision, clarity, and consistency. Our proposal therefore is the deployment and interaction of these hermeneutical approaches that include the theological interpretation of Scripture, analytic theology, and contextual theology for global Christologizing.

We will argue that analytic theology holds promise for benefitting the practice of contextual and global theology, on the condition that it (analytic theology) interfaces with the theological interpretation of Scripture. Indeed, analytic theology would be strengthened through an apprenticeship in theological modes of reading Scripture just as theological readings of Scripture would find some dose of analytic theology (i.e. the critical moment) beneficial. Similarly, contextual theology that is inclined to both theological interpretation and analytic theology will help these practices avoid mere discussions of scriptural and logical theological ideas that may have no bearing to real issues faced by the local church. On the other hand, contextual theology would also benefit by being safe-guarded from a theology whereby context alone determines truth claims and overrides any other concerns. This interaction, as already hinted, should yield a theology that exemplifies canonical fidelity, catholic sensibility, contextual sensitivity,[7] and conceptual clarity,

---

7. Kevin Vanhoozer advances canonicity, catholicity, and contextuality as constituting his canonical-linguistic approach to doing Christian theology, which this study appropriates.

thus instantiating the capacity to benefit the church in its quest to better understand and follow Christ in diverse global contexts.

This study therefore focuses on interlacing the three threads of theological interpretation of Scripture, analytic theology, and global theology as the means to making possible a global Christology that adequately exemplifies the principles of canonicity, catholicity, contextuality, and conceptuality. It is the interaction of these principles and threads that should undergird the practice of global Christian theology in general and Christology in particular. But we may ask at this point, what do these threads represent individually and why are they important for global Christologizing? We will briefly introduce each thread here as a means to defining some key terms, while a more detailed treatment will be undertaken in the main body of the study.

The Thread of the Theological Interpretation of Scripture

What exactly is the theological interpretation of Scripture? According to J. Todd Billings, it is simply interpretation of the Bible as God's word with and for the church as God's people.[8] He thinks of it as "a multifaceted practice of a community of faith in reading the Bible as God's instrument of self-revelation and saving fellowship. It is not a single discrete method or discipline; rather, it is a wide range of practices we use toward the goal of knowing God in Christ through Scripture."[9] Daniel J. Treier points out that this way of reading the Bible is not really new but an old Christian practice (particularly in patristic and medieval eras) that is now being recovered. This recovery, he notes, began with Karl Barth and has now blossomed in the intellectual climate of postmodernity.[10] As a way of reading the Bible, it differs from biblical interpretation as a purely academic discipline (i.e. historical-critical hermeneutics), an approach that became dominant due mainly to the quest birthed by the Enlightenment – that of making biblical theology *Wissenschaftlich*.[11]

See *The Drama of Doctrine: A Canonical-Linguistic Approach to Christian Theology*. Louisville: Westminster John Knox Press, 2005..

    8. Billings, *Word of God*.
    9. Billings, xii.
    10. Treier, *Introducing Theological Interpretation*, 11–36.
    11. Treier, 13.

Treier further identifies three major features of theological interpretation of Scripture that mark it as a unified school of thought. These features include the practice of imitating patristic hermeneutics, interpreting Scripture by the "rule of faith," and participating in and with the community of other faithful interpreters.[12] First, proponents of theological interpretation affirm the pre-critical practice of reading the Bible as God's authoritative word for Christian faith and practice. It recognizes and seriously takes into account, not only the literal sense[13] of the Bible, but also its spiritual sense. This simply means that the reading of the text is undertaken as piety (i.e. in a contemplative, prayerful, and typological manner) rather than as a mere academic or intellectual activity. The theological interpretation of Scripture affirms this practice and seeks to retrieve it as a truly legitimate way of reading the Bible.[14]

The second feature of reading by "the rule of faith" acknowledges the fact that we all inevitably come to the Bible with interpretive lenses. The ideas of absolute objectivity, methodological neutrality, and impartial inquiry as purported by modernist thinkers is in reality elusive. To this extent, says Treier, theological interpreters consider as cogent the postmodern critique of universal reason (i.e. the view from nowhere). The Bible then as Christian Scripture is to be read in light of the core beliefs of Christianity as circumscribed in the "rule of faith."[15] This "ruled" reading privileges the final form of the Bible as a single Trinitarian story (or drama) such that one part of Scripture is understood in light of the whole canonical storyline.

Finally, theological interpretation emphasizes reading the Bible together with the church both past and present as opposed to claiming intellectual autonomy from ecclesial authority. This practice of communal reading takes seriously the reality of human fallenness or fallibility and finitude, which

---

12. Treier, 34.
13. Fowl, "Importance of a Multivoiced Literal Sense," 37. Fowl argues that, in Thomas Aquinas for example, the literal sense is not single but multi-layered or multi-sided.
> Thomas thinks that a many-faceted literal sense of Scripture is needed because of the Christian doctrine of God; because it helps to foster and maintain Christian community and, in particular, the communion of saints; because of his views about the dignity of Scripture and the place of Scripture in Christian life and that his students and all people grow into an ever-deeper friendship with God.

(Fowl, 37). This point will be very significant to the interaction of theological interpretation and analytic theology given the fact that the former prioritizes univocal expressions.

14. Treier, 44–45.
15. Treier, *Introducing Theological Interpretation*, 59.

means that interpretative vices and blind spots are ever present with every reader of Scripture.[16] In this sense, reading with the rest of the church empowers each reader to see more and not less – more clearly and more correctly all that the Holy Spirit has illuminated other believers (past and present) to see in Scripture. This underscores the need for certain interpretive virtues that the reader should possess for the right reading of Scripture, virtues such as humility, honesty, submission, and diligence.[17]

As a movement though, "theological interpretation comes in many forms and is practiced by Christians across the denominational spectrum."[18] A number of its key proponents, (e.g. Stephen Fowl, Francis Watson, A. K. M. Adam, and Kevin Vanhoozer) employ different approaches to their theological reading of the Bible and disagree among themselves over how best to approach the project.[19] Vanhoozer alleges a near dismissal of theoretical endeavors by his colleagues whom he thinks "display a number of telltale symptoms of contemporary theory-phobia."[20] He then argues that theological hermeneutics can be theoretical, "if by theoretical we mean giving some explanation or account of why we read the way we do."[21] Because some of these other advocates of theological interpretation tend to place communal or ecclesial practices in opposition to theoretical concerns, Vanhoozer further notes that theological interpretation ought to focus on both *scientia* and *sapientia*, (i.e. *explaining* what the gospel is and *performing* it in the everyday life of the church in different contexts).[22] Such theological interpretation of Scripture is attentive to the reflective, worship, and mission life of the church, thus making possible a theology that is at once theoretical and practical, explanatory and evocative, even propositional and phronetic (i.e. practical wisdom for Godly living in a given context).[23]

---

16. Treier, 80.
17. Treier, 95–96.
18. Bartholomew and Thomas, *Manifesto for Theological Interpretation*, 2.
19. See for example: Fowl, *Engaging Scripture*; Adam, *What is Postmodern Biblical Criticism?*; Watson, *Text, Church and World*; and Vanhoozer, *Is There a Meaning*.
20. Vanhoozer, "Four Theological Faces," 133.
21. Vanhoozer, 134.
22. Vanhoozer, *Drama of Doctrine*, 18.
23. Vanhoozer, 362.

How does this relate to doing contextual theology well? As already hinted above, the pursuit by some practitioners often displays certain signs of, what we may call here, theological anemia – a condition of insufficient canonical and catholic orientation. This condition is often seen in the wholesale characterization of the Christian tradition as the mere reflections of a particular culture(s), thus providing justification – at least from a postcolonial standpoint – for the outright dismissal or a subtle degrading of, say, creedal Christology.[24] On this basis, the Christian tradition is made dispensable for readers of Scripture in non-Western contexts. However, what might a theological, as opposed to a merely cultural or historical, construal of the creeds mean for reading Scripture in a global context? While it is true that christological reflections in Africa, Asia, and Latin America have produced helpful Christologies, emphasizing different dimensions of our understanding of Christ and his relevance to human life from those in other parts of the world, the major concern with some of these efforts is whether they are still speaking about the same Christ of Scripture and the Christian tradition. The issue is critical due to the fact that one can easily end up creating a different "Christ" and a different gospel altogether (cf. Gal 1:6). This underscores the need for a global theology that is deeply immersed in the canonical and catholic considerations that constitute the theological use of Scriptures, thus summing up our first thread. We may now turn attention to our second thread for christological reflection, analytic theology.

The Thread of Analytic Theology

Analytic theology is growing significantly on the Christian theological landscape. An increasing number of Christian theologians, particularly in the Anglo-American context, now self-identify with the broader analytic tradition in their approach to theology. This means that they undertake the task of doing theology with "the *ambitions* and *style* of analytic philosophy."[25] In other words, they treat particular Christian doctrines (or some aspects

---

24. See for example: Mbuvi, "Christology and *Cultus*." Mbuvi categorically argues that the "creeds themselves were prompted by the encounter of Christianity with Greco-Roman culture and religion," which means that it cannot dictate christological reflections in non-Western contexts. Mbuvi, 161.

25. Rea, "Introduction," in *Analytic Theology*, 7. Emphasis added.

thereof) with the tools of analytic philosophy, hence the designation analytic theology. Several contributions that reflect this approach to theology are published all year round, especially since the establishment in 2013 of the online *Journal of Analytic Theology*.[26] The field has and continues to make helpful contributions to theological discourse by way of bringing much needed clarity and precision to certain complex theological topics and concepts. Some of these topics include the Trinity, the atonement, perichoresis, hell/eternal punishment, the hypostatic union, the anhypostasia/enhypostasia distinction, and others.[27] These successes have encouraged analytic theologians to start exploring additional topics and areas of study such as prayers (Oliver Crisp) and the relation of analytic theology to other theological and biblical sub-disciplines such as exegetical theology (Alan Torrance) or biblical studies (Thomas McCall). The progress is massive such that "Analytic theology is no longer a research program that needs to apologize for itself."[28] It has come of age, it seems.

Nevertheless, the discussion on how analytic Christian theologians actually use Scripture in their project needs further treatment. In practice, are analytic tools deployed in reading the text of Scripture, or are these tools fit only for analyzing concepts? How might an analytic theologian read biblical texts, which are written in literary forms that differ from the analytic style?[29] For example, can the Gospel narratives be used in analytic christological discourse, and if so, how? These are important and indeed urgent concerns if analytic theology is to be practiced as Christian theology. This study will help us see that while analytic theology has a potential contribution to make to reading Scripture theologically, it seems to have trained its critical focus elsewhere,[30] which raises some questions. Is analytic theology really theology *qua* theology or is it merely a subdivision of analytic philosophy of

---

26. See *Journal of Analytic Theology*, http://journalofanalytictheology.com/jat/index.php/jat.

27. See for example: Crisp, *Divinity and Humanity*; McCall and Michael Rea, eds., *Philosophical and Theological Essays*.

28. Crisp, Arcadi, and Wessling, *Nature and Promise of Analytic Theology*, 66.

29. See Vanhoozer, "Love's Wisdom," 247–75.

30. See Johnson, *Biblical Knowing*, 181–86. Johnson is of the opinion that analytic theologians have not brought to bear the claims of scripture and the Christian tradition on the underlying philosophical assumptions of their discipline. But it must be noted at this point that this state of affairs is, roughly speaking, a generalization.

religion?³¹ Should it be categorized as simply philosophical theology (albeit Christian), or does it qualify as actual Christian theology, that is, (borrowing from John Webster) a theological theology?³² Embedded in this idea of theological theology is the centrality of Scripture (i.e. its ontology and teleology) in Christian theological discourse. So, is analytic theology theological? This question seeks to probe the position of analytic theology as a theological discipline. Webster notes that, among other things, one of the key factors for determining the theological status of any discourse is its principles of theological knowledge. He notes that the cognitive principle of theology is grounded in God's knowledge of himself and of all things relative to him, which he (God) has communicated a certain share to humanity in the Scriptures.³³ Thus, the triune God, according to Webster, is the ontological principle of theology from whom and about whom theology's cognitive principle is realized.³⁴ What this claim entails for analytic theology should be obvious; besides the significance of Scripture's role in establishing the status of this endeavor as a truly theological enterprise, the characterization of human reason and its epistemological function in analytic theology are central to any discussion about its status as Christian theology.

On this note, it seems analytic theology will benefit from interacting with Webster's idea of Christian theology as biblical reasoning (i.e. exegetical and dogmatic reasoning)³⁵ as opposed to merely philosophical reasoning. Such a theology, according to Webster, "is the redeemed intellect's reflective

---

31. Baker-Hytch, "Analytic Theology," 347–61. As it currently stands, the dividing line between the two disciplines is extremely faint. Max Baker-Hytch has suggested that the most crucial difference-making element between analytic theology and analytic philosophy of religion is the additional appeal that analytic theology makes to Scripture and ecclesial tradition. The extent of such appeal determines the degree to which the two disciplines differ, such that "several forms of analytic theology" can be exemplified, "each of which differ from one another with respect to the epistemological status that they accord to scripture and tradition." Baker-Hytch, 359.

32. Webster, "What Makes Theology," 17–28. Here, Webster makes the case that for any theology to be considered truly theological it must meet certain criteria that comprise the nature of theology. These are: "an account of theology's object, its cognitive principles, its ends, and the virtues of its practitioners." Webster, 17.

33. Webster, 20.

34. Webster points out elsewhere that theology's cognitive principle is twofold. Scripture is theology's "external or objective cognitive principle" while "redeemed intelligence of the saints" is theology's internal or subjective cognitive principle. See Webster, *Domain of the Word*, 135.

35. Webster, *Domain of the Word*, 129.

apprehension of God's gospel address through the embassy of Scripture, enabled and corrected by God's presence, and having fellowship with him as its end."[36] This should take theological discourse farther in the direction of what Kevin Vanhoozer calls *theo-ontology* (as opposed to ontotheology) – using philosophical concepts "in a non-totalizing manner in order to clarify the divine ontology implied by the words and acts of the triune God."[37] In reflecting on the status of analytic theology as a theological discipline therefore, we need to ask whether "created intellect" in and of itself suffices for purposes of Christian theology. Is Scripture necessary for doing analytic theology as Christian theology or not? If it is, then how have analytic theologians used it in their actual practice of doing analytic theology? It is expected that the dialogue being proposed here will on the one hand bolster analytic theology by theologically drawing upon the Bible for analytic theological discourse, and on the other, the theological interpretation of Scripture will be more conscientiously attentive to the critical (or analytic) moment in theological reading and discourse. One may rightly ask at this point how we intend to go about relating these two disciplines. What factors should determine the relationship? Moreover, should this relationship be entirely ad hoc or somewhat systematic? These important questions will be addressed in chapter 3.

In the meantime, another important question to consider is, given its Anglo-American roots and coloration, how might analytic theology actually benefit the endeavor of global theology in a way that is non-paternalistic and non-imperialistic? So, while I agree with McCall that analytic theology holds promise for fruitful work in global Christian theology, we need to explore the modalities of this *promise*. Before now, we have dwelled on two other related needs – (1) *position*: identifying and establishing the nature and status of analytic theology as a theological discipline; and (2) *practice*: defining and strengthening analytic theology with respect to its use of Scripture. The appropriate conversation partner in addressing these two needs, as I see it, is theological interpretation of Scripture. However, the third need of exploring the promise of analytic theology for global theology clearly requires a different conversation partner and that for me is the field of global or intercultural theology itself. This is the third and final thread to consider – the very note on

---

36. Webster, 128.
37. Vanhoozer, *Remythologizing Theology*, 104.

which we began our discussion. We now return to it with the aim of making finer distinctions and providing additional explanations.

The Thread of Global Theology

Just as analytic theology is growing, the practice of global theology is also growing – as many times as much because of its global spread. Interestingly, Thomas McCall (himself an analytic theologian) has called for the extension of analytic theology into newer geographical, cultural, and ecclesial locations (i.e. in non-Western contexts). He suggests that the "work of *global analytic theology* might be both beneficial and indeed urgent."[38] This suggestion is grounded in the fact that analytic theology offers clarity in conceptual analyses that transcend the context-specific limitations of social scientific approaches that currently dominate the project of global theology. But what exactly is global theology and how does it differ from contextual theology? According to Gene Green, "The characteristic feature of global biblical interpretation and theology is the unyielding commitment to understand the faith from and to a particular social context, always with self-awareness of the interpreter's place and a celebration of the fact that the faith is translatable into the languages of the world."[39] Someone may wonder here why it is called global if the commitment is to a particular local context rather than the entire world. This is because the assertion of and attention to their own specific contexts by global voices is done in resistance to the hegemonic and racializing tendency of modernist Western theology and philosophy with its presumption of theological universality and cultural supremacy over others.

Therefore, the suggestion, however "modest" as McCall is keen to note,[40] that analytic theology might be beneficial to global theology engenders the question as to *how* this might be pursued in a manner that is not counterproductive (i.e. coming across as alien or even imperialist). It is one thing for a Western analytic theologian to opine that analytic theology might benefit the task of global theology, and a different thing altogether for global theologians to share in that opinion. So, is McCall's call legitimate and is it realizable?

---

38. McCall, *Analytic Christian Theology*, 159. Emphasis added.
39. Green, "Challenge of Global Hermeneutics," 52.
40. McCall, *Analytic Christian Theology*, 171.

Will analytic theology truly benefit global theologizing, assuming the project is possible? How might such an ambitious proposal be pursued and what might be the obstacles that must be surmounted? To begin with, one of the fundamental contentions of non-Western theologians generally speaking is the idea that, for the most part, Christian theology has been held captive by Western culture and thought forms laying claim to universal applicability, and that this alleged captivity limits its impact on the task of global theology. It is therefore asserted that Christian theology needs to be freed from this unnecessary Western, and some would say White, cultural captivity by recognizing the contextual nature of all theologies.[41]

Indeed, from economics to politics, religion to culture, and intellectual life in general, almost everything in the contemporary world is differentiated by virtue of what is "Western" and that which is "non-Western," or as Meic Pearse renders it, between the West and the Rest.[42] This differentiation has been shown to be problematic based on two major factors. (1) The West is not so much a geographical demarcation as it is political, economic, cultural, and religious. (2) The differentiation is usually not construed as something between equals, but one in which the West, by default, exemplifies certain dominance over the Rest. In view of (1), it is now commonplace to speak more in terms of the Global North and South as opposed to East and West or, the more commonly, Western and non-Western respectively. Nevertheless, the Global North is often used as synonymous to Western just as the Global South (Majority World) is generally representative of non-Western.[43] On the basis of (2), the West has succeeded in arousing widespread global opposition and rage against it, thus an ever-increasing demand for and assertions of distinctly non-Western self-identities both at home and abroad. In this regard, Pearse rightly notes that "anyone who cares about their culture, and has enough exposure to us and our way of doing things to be affected by us, will feel threatened."[44]

---

41. See for example, Rah, *Next Evangelicalism*.

42. Pearse, *Why the Rest Hates the West*.

43. For more on this, see for example Lamport, "Preface," *Encyclopedia of Christianity in the Global South*, xix–xxii; Mahler, "Global South"; and Wolvers, Tappe, Salverda, and Schwarz, "Concepts of the Global South."

44. Pearse, *Why the Rest Hates the West*, 12–13.

Christianity and Christian theology are not exempt from this rather convenient (or heuristic) categorization and its attendant "dominance versus resistance" dynamics. Lamin Sanneh points to a certain "misconceived dialectic" by writers, that is, the tendency "to polarize the issue between a Christianity that is opposed to culture and a Christianity that is culturally determined."[45] This way of thinking, he believes, led to a situation whereby converts

> ipso facto capitulated to Western cultural imperialism, and that their sins have been visited on their children who are condemned to an ambiguous identity, being born, as it were, with a foreign foot in their native mouth. Converts may, for that reason, be considered cultural orphans and traitors at the same time.[46]

The non-Western encounter with the West therefore (whether in the form of colonization or Christianization) meant that an "us versus them" perception inevitably emerged, further complicating the idea of Christian identity and theology in non-Western contexts. But now that Christianity is demographically post-Western and the West post-Christian,[47] the reversal of this identity problem is currently being witnessed. It is against this backdrop that many, like Stephen Pardue, insist on the need for "renovating theology in light of global Christianity."[48] He suggests that this renovation is necessary because the cultural context of Christian theology has shown "more historical continuity with Western ways of thinking about the world than with the conceptual frameworks that are familiar in the places where Christianity is currently growing."[49]

Therefore, before beginning to talk about analytic theology benefiting global theologizing or vice versa, we must first establish the very possibility of this interaction – more so, when the practice of theological interpretation of Scripture is added to the equation. To this end, we must turn a corner and provide grounding for the proposal to be pursued in this study, that of bringing together these three diverse threads for global Christologizing. At

---

45. Sanneh, *Encountering the West*, 16.
46. Sanneh, 16.
47. See for example: Walls, "Demographics, Power and the Gospel"; and Jenkins, *God' Continent*.
48. Pardue, "Introduction," 4.
49. Pardue, 4.

the core of this grounding is a crucial question about the very idea of what is Western and non-Western, particularly with respect to the development of culture and intellectual practices. What exactly determines what is and what is not Western, say for example African? Is there a method of discourse and reasoning that is essentially Western and another that is, for purposes of this study, African or Nigerian? In addition, if a Westerner were to use African modes of thinking or vice versa (assuming these exist), would that make them African or "Africanized" and *mutatis mutandis* Westernized? This concern will resurface in chapters 4 and 5. However, it is necessary that we consider an initial response that addresses (perhaps, redresses) certain presumptions that carry deep methodological implications for our study.

Rethinking the Western Versus Non-Western Bifurcation

Earlier on, we noted the widespread acceptance of the distinction between things Western (say, theologies, politics, economies, modes of reasoning, etc.) and those that are non-Western. In the Enlightenment framework of modernist thought, steeped in evolutionary anthropology, this distinction was always value laden with Western ways considered reasonable, superior, developed, right, and good, while non-Western ways were construed as nonsensical, inferior, primitive, wrong, and bad. This persuasion was quite prevalent in modernity with Lévy-Bruhl's anthropology, Hegel's philosophy, and Darwin's evolutionary science among some of its most prominent proposing and promoting forces at different times and to varying degrees.[50] This was a major ideological underpinning of Western colonialism that, rather unfortunately, made its way into the theories and practices of Christian mission.[51] Western culture was portrayed as a higher culture with all others following in middle (e.g. Chinese and Japanese) and lower (i.e. African and black) level cultures. The idea that there is an *essentially* distinct way that Westerners think from

---

50. Irele, Introduction to *African Philosophy*, 11.

51. Tite Tiénou articulates this point as follows: "When one looks for an epistemological-linkage between missions and colonialism, one should examine the literature on mission theory and strategy. It is here that one finds that both colonial doctrine and Christian rationale for mission involve 'a sense of mission, of spreading a nation's vision of society and culture to an alien, subjected people.'" Tiénou, "Which Way for African Christianity," 4.

the way that non-Westerners (say, Africans) do was then postulated as evidence (among other things) for the difference and superiority of Western people and their ways to non-Western people and their ways. Some African thinkers and sympathizers towed this line of thought, identifying Western culture with rationality or rationalism, while African culture was associated with emotivity or emotivism.[52]

However, in *Theories of Culture*, Kathryn Tanner shows that a theoretical shift took place sometime in the 1920s from modernity's static, evaluative, and sharply-bounded view of culture to a postmodern "anthropological sense as a group-differentiating, holistic, nonevaluative, and context-relative notion."[53] What this meant was the possibility of acknowledging every culture's right to being different and not having to conform to any presumptive standard or higher culture. But even this anthropological view of cultures has now been questioned due to the fact that, "It seems less and less plausible to presume that cultures are self-contained and clearly bounded units, internally consistent and unified wholes of beliefs and values simply transmitted to every member of their respective groups as principles of social order."[54] Some of the indicators of this implausibility include the complexity, dynamism, and similarity within and between cultures. Therefore, Henning Wrogemann's view of culture and its implications for intercultural hermeneutics seems quite attractive here. He articulates an eclectic construal that sees culture both from a cultural-semiotic perspective and from a discourse-theoretical approach. In this sense, "*cultures are to a certain extent delimitable spheres containing those things taken for granted within one's own lifeworld; yet at the same time, they are conceptual formations of social cohesion oriented toward certain publicly communicated identity markers.*"[55]

---

52. See Appiah, *In My Father's House*.
53. Tanner, *Theories of Culture*, 24.
54. Tanner, 38.
55. Wrogemann, *Intercultural Theology*, 155. Emphasis in original. Before settling on his proposed view of culture, Wrogemann provides a treatment of six different conceptions of culture which include: the diffusionist concept, postulates a common origin of all cultures; the functionalist concept and its claim of similar structures in all cultures; the evolutionary concept, portrays culture as a universal process of progress; the relativistic concept, thinks of cultures as discreetly separate entities; the semiotic concept, considers culture as a text which is decoded; and finally, the discourse-theoretical concept, sees culture as a field of discourse and dynamism. Wrogemann then brings together the last two in order to articulate a view of culture that takes full account of how both understanding and identity formation take place.

In this sense therefore, the idea of an authentic Western or African culture (or any culture for that matter) is problematized. To further appreciate the problem, let us consider the findings and claims of Martin Bernal, who provides such historical data as to question the notion that Western civilization is the sole creation of the West itself. In *Black Athena: The Afroasiatic Roots of Classical Civilization*, Bernal points out that there are two explanatory models for the origins of Western civilization, and these are the Aryan and the Ancient models.[56] The Ancient model holds that "Greek culture had arisen as the result of colonization, around 1500 BC, by Egyptians and Phoenicians who had civilized the native inhabitants."[57] Not only that, but Bernal also shows that the Greeks continued to borrow heavily from Near Eastern cultures and most early Greek intellectuals traveled to Egypt for their education. This view, Bernal notes, was widely accepted and was never questioned by anyone before AD 1600.[58] In the Enlightenment however, the Aryan model emerged claiming that "there had been an invasion from the north – unreported in ancient tradition – which had overwhelmed the local 'Aegean' or 'Pre-Hellenic' culture. Greek civilization is seen as the result of the mixture of the Indo-European-speaking Hellenes and their indigenous subjects."[59] This model therefore denies the Egyptian and Phoenician roots of Greek civilization in order to situate it within and among Western peoples and boundaries. The reason for that, as Bernal points out was not factual or logical, but ideological.

> The Ancient Model had no major "internal" deficiencies, or weaknesses in explanatory power. It was overthrown for external reasons. For eighteenth- and nineteenth-century Romantics and racists it was simply intolerable for Greece, which was seen not merely as the epitome of Europe but also as its pure childhood, to have been the result of the mixture of native Europeans and colonizing Africans and Semites. Therefore, the Ancient

---

In keeping with these aspects of cultures, intercultural theologies for Wrogemann therefore must "be understood from the perspective of local sign systems, on the one hand, and to what extent they remain inseparable from their discourse location, on the other." Wrogemann, 155.

56. Bernal, *Black Athena*, 1.
57. Bernal, 1.
58. Bernal, 121.
59. Bernal, 2.

Model had to be overthrown and replaced by something more acceptable.[60]

Bernal goes into great length to trace the indicators of the Ancient model in antiquity from Greek sources in particular, and then develops what he calls the Revised Ancient model in the second volume of his work.[61] We do not need to go any further in discussing Bernal's work, not only because we lack the time and space to do so, but also in view of the fact that the point needed to be made for purposes of this study has already been made. If the West is not the sole creator of Western civilization and intellectual ideals, then the claim that some approach should be excluded from some non-Western intellectual and theological inquiry simply because it is Western is a misinformed and mistaken move.

Similarly, the claim that there is a *distinctly*, say, African way of reasoning and an *authentic* African culture for doing theology becomes problematic and leaves open the deployment of whatever is true and useful without exclusion on the basis of its cultural background. This is the idea that Ngugi wa Thiong'o expresses with the term *globalectics* where he speaks of culture-contact or exchange as the oxygen of civilization and (for his purposes) literary theory.[62] In a subversive appropriation of Hegel's dialectics, Thiong'o thinks in terms of a reorganization of literary space such that different perspectives are accommodated rather than excluded, thereby making literature "a collective contribution of the human."[63] The quality of each contribution he claims is dependent on placing it "in a more catholic space," thus his belief in "the liberation of literature from the straightjackets of nationalism."[64] In this sense, "Globalectics combines the global and the dialectical to describe a mutually affecting dialogue, or multi-logue, in the phenomena of nature and nurture in a global space that's rapidly transcending that of the artificially bounded, as nation and region."[65] To read and reflect globalectically therefore is to embrace

---

60. Bernal, 2. Original italics removed.
61. Bernal, *Black Athena*, vol. 2.
62. Thiong'o, *Globalectics*, 2.
63. Thiong'o, 8.
64. Thiong'o, 8.
65. Thiong'o, 8.

"wholeness, interconnectedness, equality of potentiality of parts, tension, and motion."[66] One may call this a non-theological construal of catholicity.

However, in view of the theological catholicity of the Christian faith – grounded in the Trinity and the oneness of the body of Christ (Eph 4:4–6) – as well as the present reality of world Christianity, the submission above seems more apt for the practice of Christian theology as global theology than it is to just reading literature. Consequently, this project pursues an interdisciplinary approach for christological reflection, one that appropriates elements from both Western and non-Western worlds (or from both the Global South and Global North), a move akin to what Paul Hiebert describes as going beyond anti-colonialism to globalism.[67] While contextual theology is opposed (and rightly so) to the hierarchicalization and universalization of theology and cultures, it can get stuck in the anti-colonial mode or moment. However, it can also be pursued as a first step in an aspect of globalizing or global theology – that is, doing theology with the contextual awareness that recognizes one's own particularity while at the same time intentionally taking into account the interconnectedness of other diverse particularities to one's own. More importantly, this should translate into the practice of global theology in a way that connects organically to a theological theology (i.e. biblical and dogmatic).

As a consequence of the foregoing, global Christology (analytic Christology as well) will be strengthened by an emphasis on exegesis of biblical texts as the primary task of christological reflection – the kind of exegesis that is served by Christian dogma in a global context. This way of doing theology is in tandem with Vanhoozer's canonical-linguistic approach which *"has as its goal the training of competent and truthful witnesses who can themselves incarnate, in a variety of situations, the wisdom of Christ gleaned from indwelling canonical practices and their ecclesial continuation."*[68] This is much needed in

---

66. Thiong'o, 8. This point of view is consistent with the broad definition of globalization expressed by George Thomas. He says,
> When scholars, journalists and individuals use the term globalization in every conversation, they tend to focus narrowly on economic interdependence, but it is better understood more broadly. Globalization refers to the increasing complexity and interdependence of the world as a whole and to the process and mechanisms involved. These changes undermine stable, taken-for-granted identities, both individual and collective (national, ethnic, religious).

Thomas, "Cultural and Religious Character," 35.

67. Hiebert, "Beyond Anti-Colonialism," 263–81.

68. Vanhoozer, *Drama of Doctrine*, 25. Emphasis in original.

the enterprise of contextual Christologies as it will enable the body of Christ in one geographical location to be both enriched and corrected by insights from the body in another location.[69] What should ensue is a truly global theology (as opposed to being merely contextual) in the sense noted by Thomas McCall when he says: "If this theology is truly global, it will not be – and cannot be – reducible to what 'Westerners' say about 'global' concerns. At the same time, however, if it is truly global, it will not remove or ignore insights and contributions from Europe, North America or Australasia."[70]

This study is one such approach to global christological reflections and makes a proposal that is interdisciplinary, integrative, and interactive in order to guide global theology in the direction that it is able to say more about Christ – more and not less than what the church has historically professed about him. In this sense, this may be understood as a cumulative case approach whereby the different methodological concerns and insights of the diverse threads being brought together are taken into account for christological reflection. However, this approach does not claim to be the only one that accomplishes this goal, even if the particular threads it appropriates have not been brought together in any work known to the author. To further clarify this last statement, we will need to spell out not only the scope and delimitations of this study, but also its anticipated contributions and significance.

Scope and Delimitation

While at various points the present work explicates and appropriates the multiplex field of theological interpretation of Scripture, it does not provide a complete and systematic discussion of the discipline as a whole. Instead, the study engages particular aspects and proponents of theological interpretation of Scripture. More precisely, attention is given to the New Testament use of the Old Testament and the history of biblical interpretation in general as premises for embracing some form of theological interpretation. The primary form that this study adopts is John Webster's exegetical and dogmatic reasoning,

---

69. The Majority World Theology Series also takes this stance as clearly stated in its first volume: "In learning what it means for Jesus to be Lord in other places, we often grasp the gospel more fully for ourselves and are more able to see the blind spots of our own locally embodied versions of Christianity." Pardue, "Introduction," 2.

70. McCall, *Analytic Christian Theology*, 158.

but certainly Kevin Vanhoozer's canonical-linguistic approach as well. This should become clear as the study progresses.

In addition, the study investigates the use of Scripture in analytic theology and engages the discipline primarily through some christological texts of select evangelical analytic theologians. Although it attempts to characterize the enterprise of analytic theology in general, such characterization is neither comprehensive nor exhaustive, but simply illustrative of how Scripture is construed and deployed in this way of doing theology. The goal is to present an adequate representation of theology in the analytic mode, particularly with respect to the doctrine of the person of Christ. Given this goal, the project interacts only with analytic theologians who use Scripture in their work and have written on some aspect of Christology. In this sense therefore, the work does not attend to purely philosophical christological discourses, albeit one or two receive a cursory mention.

Similarly, with respect to global theology and Christology, the study is delimited by attending to: (1) the broad categories by which christological discussions have so far been carried out in Africa; and (2) the Christologies of two Nigerian evangelical theologians. This move is intended to help explicate in greater detail the desideratum of contextuality in theological discourse by providing a focused discussion on a specific context. It is important therefore to note that these Christologies are merely illustrative and not representative of global theology in general or Christology in particular.

Significance of the Study

In the past, the theologies of Africa, Asia, and Latin America have largely been ignored by the disciplines of biblical studies and systematic theology and have been left, almost entirely, to intercultural theologians or missiologists and some church historians. The discussions have been mostly confined within the departments of intercultural studies and the study of world Christianity – the only exception, in some instances, being discussions on Latin American liberation theology. While this situation is gradually changing, it remains the general state of affairs.[71] The present work however proposes that the serious

---

71. In the area of biblical studies for example, the field of postcolonial biblical criticism, which started in the late 1990s, continues to grow through increased membership of the

engagement of these theologies in the practice of systematic theology is a much-needed conversation, one that might be approached as the interaction of contextual theology, theological interpretation of Scripture, and analytic theology. This tripartite interaction has great potentials for the task of global Christian theology.

The major contribution of this study is this attempt at interlacing the theological use of Scripture, analytic theology, and contextual concerns in doing theology. The outcome, it is anticipated, would advance the discussion on global theological methodology in general and christological reflections in particular. In addition, it is hoped that all three disciplines will be mutually enriched through this interaction. While Thomas McCall mentions the intersection of analytic theology and theological interpretation along with that between analytic theology and global theology among his "modest suggestions,"[72] there is no existing evidence in the literature that such work has been attempted by anyone. This study is therefore a first step in this direction. The study also provides increased clarity to how appeal is made (or can be made) to Scripture to authorize theological claims in analytic as well as global theology. In this sense, the study will show how both analytic theology and the theological interpretation of Scripture might engage with and be appropriated in a global theological context.

Summary of Chapters

Chapter 1 serves as the general introduction of the entire work and introduces the reader to the three threads to be weaved into a single theological cord for christological reflection. The chapter spells out the main thesis of the study, its scope, anticipated contributions, as well as its methodology. Chapter 2 focuses on the idea of using Scripture in doing Christian theology. It makes a case for the theological interpretation of Scripture on the basis of the New Testament use of the Old Testament and the history of biblical interpretation generally speaking. The chapter gives a historical survey of the views and uses

---

guild and new publications in the field. See for example: Sugirtharajah, *Exploring Postcolonial Biblical Criticism*, and *Postcolonial Biblical Reader*; Moore and Segovia, *Postcolonial Biblical Criticism*; Liew and Segovia, *Colonialism and the Bible*; and Dube, Mbuvi, and Mbuwayesango, *Postcolonial Perspectives*.

72. McCall, *Analytic Christian Theology*, 174–75.

of Scripture in Christian theology, noting the major shifts that produced the current dominant positions, and pointing out implications for theological practice.[73] It then explicates and extends John Webster's biblical reasoning as a compelling view and use of Scripture – one that accounts for both canonicity and catholicity. In general, the discussion in this chapter is shaped by an emphasis on viewing theology theologically, the idea of Scripture as divine address, and on the church as the primary context for the reception of the Bible.[74] It concludes with an attempt to show what makes for an adequate view and use of Scripture for the kind of theological discourse that serves the Christian church and its life of the mind – a reiteration of the case, as it were, for viewing and reading the Bible theologically.

In chapter 3, I attempt to characterize analytic theology, situating it within the broader tradition of analytic philosophy, yet noting what makes it different from that tradition. The chapter also probes the status of analytic theology as a theological discipline or, so to speak, a *theological* theology. More importantly, it investigates the use of Scripture for Christologizing in analytic theology by analyzing select christological texts of two analytic theologians – Oliver Crisp and Thomas McCall. The choice of these analytic theologians is informed by the fact that they are not only leading voices in the field, but also trained theologians who carry out their work within the broader evangelical tradition. This move enables us to trace what concerns are being addressed, how theological proposals are authorized, as well as whether and how Scripture is viewed and used in this mode of doing theology. The primary goal here is to find out how each analytic theologian uses Scripture and in what way such uses informs their christological constructions and conclusions. We conclude the chapter by providing a theological assessment of analytic theology in terms of its use of Scripture, particularly in the light of Webster's biblical (i.e. exegetical and dogmatic) reasoning,[75] and also with

---

73. Those who are conversant with the history of the interpretation of Scripture may skim through much of this section that simply rehashes the story. However, those who do not have prior knowledge of this history will find my narration to be helpful.

74. See Webster, "What Makes Theology"; and Bartholomew and Thomas, *Manifesto for Theological Interpretation*.

75. John Webster never self-identified with the theological interpretation of Scripture (TIS) movement, but on occasion made pronouncements as to what TIS is or should be. In addition, given his discussions about Christian reasoning and the created intellect, he is a potential bridge figure between the two movements of TIS and AT.

respect to the possibility (or otherwise) of its being beneficial to the practice of global theology.

Chapter 4 attends to the work of global theology in general, but focuses more precisely on the christological conversations in Africa. After presenting an overview of the more prominent christological discussions in Africa, the chapter then considers two concrete constructive Christologies in Nigeria (the author's context). These are Guest Christology by Enyi Ben Udoh and the Revealer Christology of Victor Ezigbo. After engaging these Christologies, the chapter concludes that both are not only functionalist Christologies, but that they also lack what can be described as theological comprehensiveness. This theological comprehensiveness is explained in chapter 5. The chapter steps back and articulates the main proposal of this work by drawing from the discussions in chapters 2 to 4, to succinctly present four major principles for doing Christology, that is, the principles of canonicity, catholicity, contextuality, and conceptuality.

Chapter 6 proceeds to put this proposal to work in the context of the experience of Christians and churches of northern Nigeria – an experience of following Christ in the midst of hatred and violence from the Muslim majority, as well as considering the very possibility of following Jesus's Lordly example. The discussion draws from the best of both analytic theology and theological interpretation of Scripture for purposes of engaging christologically with this context. Two passages of Scripture, Matthew 14:22–33 and Philippians 2:5–11, are used toward this end in a way that reflects and facilitates our proposal. It presents theological readings of two passages of Scripture with analytic sensibilities. The goal is a Christology that is biblically theological, historically catholic, contextually relevant, and logically coherent – thus taking into account biblical claims as well as contextual concerns.[76] The chapter seeks to proffer ways in which the doctrine of Christ may be performed by the church in northern Nigeria.

Chapter 7 is the general conclusion of the study and provides an overall summary of the work, restating our main claims, drawing final conclusions, and posing some questions for potential further research.

---

76. See Vanhoozer, "Christology in the West," 11–36.

CHAPTER 2

Use of Scripture and the Nature of Christian Theology

The place and use of Scripture in theology is a complex issue and the conversation has a very long history that remains relevant for the theological task today. While most Christian theologians will agree that the Bible should be used in theology, why, when, and how this may be done is a matter of much disagreement. Kevin Vanhoozer rightly points out that "The real problem of 'Scripture and theology' only arises . . . when interpreters disagree about what God is saying. Whose reading or use of Scripture counts, and why?"[1] David Kelsey seems to think that such disagreements are not necessarily problematic since he affirms a variety of legitimate ways that Scripture may be used in theology to help authorize theological proposals, "each of which brings with it a different concept of 'authority.'"[2] However, Gerald O'Collins and Daniel Kendall believe it to be quite clear (and painfully so for them) that in theology's present state, "the scriptures are often used *incoherently* or at least *inconsistently* and *inaccurately*."[3] In other words, it is one thing to use Scripture in theology, and another to use it rightly.

The issue is even more pertinent with the emergence of relatively newer approaches to doing theology, particularly (and for purposes of this project),

---

1. Vanhoozer, "Scripture and Theology," 143.

2. Kelsey, *Proving Doctrine*, 3. Kelsey makes it clear that his is a descriptive project, that is, he offers a study of theologians' methods rather than one in theological methodology. In this sense, his work simply devises "a way of commenting on quite different theological procedures without relying on a general theory about the nature of theology." Kelsey, 8.

3. O'Collins and Kendall, *Bible for Theology*, 6. Emphasis added.

analytic theology and global or intercultural theologies. Such theologies, like any theology undertaken as Christian theology, would not only need to define their notion of what the Bible is, but also demonstrate in practice how it functions *as such*. This is because, "Practicing Christian theology demands that we give an account of what Scripture is, what it is for, and how to read it."[4] Generally speaking, every type of "Christian" theology is inextricably tied to the particular view and use of Scripture it adopts – the kind of thing that Scripture is taken to be (its ontology) and the kind of function that one thinks or makes it to serve (its teleology) – whether these are made explicit or not.[5] To put it another way, every type of theology instantiates a particular view/use of Scripture. However, the question again is whether every instance of Scripture's view and use is equally valid.

This chapter therefore examines, albeit briefly, what it means to use Scripture in theology both in a theoretical sense and from actual practice in the history of theology. This approach to the topic is intended to orient our study to the way Scripture has functioned in historical Christianity so as to discern important shifts that will both explain contemporary uses of Scripture and inform our judgments for a normative approach. More importantly therefore, the chapter wrestles with the question of what it means to, not only use Scripture, but to use it rightly (i.e. coherently, consistently, and accurately). In addition, it considers how the use of Scripture affects or shapes the nature and practice of Christian theology, more precisely, Christology.

In pursuit of these aims, the chapter first discusses the concept of using Scripture in theology as a necessary first step in terminological specificity and clarity. This is followed by a descriptive or historical sketch of the various ways in which Scripture has been construed and used both within Scripture itself (the NT's use of the OT) and in the history of Christian theology. In doing this, we will note the shifts in the ways Scripture has been perceived and used during the different eras in the history of theology and what exactly informed those shifts. The doctrine of the person of Christ will serve to demonstrate how these different attitudes to and uses of Scripture shaped theology. Finally, the chapter draws from this descriptive work and

---

4. Vanhoozer, "Scripture and Theology," 142.

5. While this has implications for the nature of theology in general, our discussion will attend primarily to the use of Scripture as an activity in theology.

probes the question of whether there is (or should be) a normative way to use Scripture in Christian theology. If there is, what would (or should) it look like? And what factors should inform its characterization and practice? The normative position defended at the end of the chapter is an appropriation of John Webster who argues that the biblical economy must be situated within the divine (triune) economy for Scripture to be rightly used in theology. Its alternative is "a privileging of the elements of the biblical economy, and a reluctance or inability to trace those elements to their cause in the fullness of God's own life."[6]

The Idea of Using Scripture in Theology

John Webster opines that we need "to move away from pressing concerns about the proper 'use' of Scripture, the nature of biblical authority or the practice of theological interpretation."[7] This suggestion seems counterintuitive since Webster himself acknowledges, and quite rightly, that these concerns are pressing (i.e. fundamental or *prolegomenal* to theology). However, Webster thinks that "Widespread confusion, and impatient and incoherent debate about these matters should alert us to the need to push back, and to question the adequacy of the terms in which the debates have been conducted and the concepts through which matters have been framed."[8] This underscores the importance of making explicit what we mean by the phrase "the use of Scripture in theology" and why it is important.

Simply put, the use of Scripture in theology refers to that movement or passage from biblical text to Christian doctrine – a passage that O'Collins and Kendall believe "is not being negotiated skillfully."[9] According to David Kelsey, it is the process of appropriating Scripture to show how some text therein informs or supports a given theological claim (in Kelsey's words, authorizing theological proposals). For him, "Scripture fills the function of 'authorizing'

---

6. Webster, *Domain of the Word*, vii–viii. In a similar remark, Kevin Vanhoozer and Daniel Treier note that we ought to treat "theological prolegomena, the biblical gospel and the church together by situating all three within the triune economy: the 'collected works' of the triune God." Vanhoozer and Treier, *Theology and the Mirror*, 14.

7. Webster, *Domain of the Word*, 116.

8. Webster, 116.

9. O'Collins and Kendall, *Bible for Theology*, 6.

a particular theological proposal when it is used to fill some role in an argument designed to make a case for the proposal in the face of objections to it."[10] To use Scripture in theology therefore is to appeal to it (in whole or in part) as a basis for the authorization of the truth of one's theological belief or opinion.[11] But how is this carried out in actual practice?

Kelsey argues that "'Scripture' is not something objective that different theologians simply use differently. In actual practice it is concretely construed in irreducibly different ways."[12] This claim is one of the conclusions that Kelsey arrived at after sampling the use of Scripture of seven modern theologians: B. B. Warfield, Hans-Werner Bartsch, G. Ernest Wright, Karl Barth, L. S. Thornton, Paul Tillich, and Rudolph Bultmann. To help analyze the works of these select theologians in a non-biased way, Kelsey advanced and used four diagnostic questions as follows. (1) What aspects of Scripture are taken to be authoritative? (2) What is it about this aspect of Scripture that makes it authoritative? (3) What sort of logical force is ascribed to the Scripture to which appeal is made? And, (4) How is the Scripture that is cited brought to bear on theological proposals so as to authorize them?[13] At the end of his analyses, Kelsey concludes that before using Scripture, theologians have to first decide the telos of the texts, then construe Scripture in a certain way, and finally ascribe a certain logical force to it. He summarizes his analyses as follows:

> If the texts serve to teach, then when used in theology they are construed as a text-book of doctrine having the force of *asserting* (infallibly) some eternal truths about objective states of affairs (Warfield); or the logical force of *proposing* a set of concepts by which to reform the conceptual schemes we hitherto have used to order experience, either in the form of a lexicon (Bartsch); or

---

10. Kelsey, *Proving Doctrine*, 212.

11. This way of explaining the idea may suggest that one already has their theological proposal in place and only needs Scripture to support (or authorize) it. This raises the question of how a theological proposal is arrived at or formed in the first instance. If Scripture is not used at the level of forming the given theological proposal, then is it not suspect to use it afterwards for authorization? Perhaps, some underlying ideology (political, cultural, economic, etc.) might have informed this theological proposal that Scripture is now being used to authorize or justify. More will be said about this later in the chapter.

12. Kelsey, *Proving Doctrine*, 2.

13. Kelsey, 2–3.

in the form of a historical narrative that uses concepts to "interpret" events (Wright); [or narratives that render the person of Christ (Barth)]. If the texts serve to "express" and "occasion" something, then when used in theology they are construed as having the *expressive-but-non-informative* force of certain kinds of poetry (Thornton); or religious symbolism (Tillich) or as having a *self-involving* force with abstractable content that sometimes is straight-forwardly descriptive and sometimes expressive, using mythic language (Bultmann).[14]

Kevin Vanhoozer draws from Kelsey's work and helpfully charts these different uses of Scripture into four quadrants. The first quadrant consists of theologians who consider biblical *propositions* as the authoritative aspect of Scripture, which they then use "as higher, theoretical or timeless truths that may be systematized."[15] However, they suffer from a pathological extreme he calls metaphysicalism (i.e. extratextual philosophy). Those in the second quadrant take the *images* (e.g. symbols, metaphors, types, etc.) of biblical narratives as the authoritative aspect of Scripture and use them to both express and experience "the revelatory and redemptive significance of the event of Jesus Christ."[16] The pathological extreme of this group is liberal revisionism whereby these images are transmuted to suit non-biblical frameworks. The third quadrant has theologians who take the *testimony* of biblical narratives to be authoritative, particularly with respect to the history of redemption. However, in a naturalistic mode, it suffers from the pathological extreme of historicism (using Scripture merely as evidence for the history of religion). Finally, Vanhoozer's fourth quadrant consists of theologians who (like those in the first) also take propositions to be the authoritative aspect of Scripture, but they focus on *data* or empirical information to be gleaned. The pathological extreme here is "a kind of positivism in which discrete packets of biblical data are affirmed in isolation from the broad narrative sweep of Scripture and without regard for the results of modern learning, including biblical scholarship."[17]

---

14. Kelsey, 100. Emphasis in original.
15. Vanhoozer, "Scripture and Theology," 149.
16. Vanhoozer, 150.
17. Vanhoozer, 150.

Given that all four quadrants have something important to offer, Vanhoozer proposes an all-round use of Scripture whereby the positive or virtuous practices of each quadrant are appropriated. These diverse virtuous practices will cancel out the collective pathological tendencies of all the quadrants. In this sense, "To be biblical is to be sensitive to the variety of biblical discourse, acknowledging statements as statements and stories as stories. Being biblical means avoiding the trap of thinking that *all* of Scripture should be used in one way only (e.g., as propositional information)."[18]

One final thing to note regarding the idea of using Scripture is its relation to interpretation. Again, Vanhoozer points that "It is one thing exegetically to determine what a text meant, quite another to say what it entails for the Church today."[19] The distinction here is that while interpreting Scripture seeks to establish textual meaning, using Scripture aims at establishing Christian doctrine. Thus, the use of Scripture necessitates its interpretation, but its interpretation may or may not entail its use. In other words, one may interpret Scripture without using it, but one cannot use Scripture without first interpreting it, whether explicitly or implicitly. Similarly, and as noted earlier, the manner in which and the ends to which one uses Scripture supervene on how one views Scripture, that is, the use of Scripture is intertwined with what Scripture is taken to *be*, what it is taken to be *for*, and what it is taken to *say* or *mean*. Therefore, in order to get at the question of how Scripture is used in theology, the questions of how Scripture is viewed and what informs a given view, as well as how Scripture is interpreted and what informs a given interpretation must be understood. The discussion that follows further highlights this claim. In considering how Scripture has been viewed and used, both within Scripture itself (the NT use of the OT) and in the history of Christian theology, an unbreakable cord emerges (Scripture's ontology, teleology, and interpretation).[20] Although our focus will be on the first two strands, the third (quite inevitably) will be hovering over the discussion all the time.

---

18. Vanhoozer, 149.

19. Vanhoozer, 142.

20. The cord is not unbreakable in terms of a logical possibility but a theological one, which means one cannot break it without, at the very least, some unhealthy theological outcomes.

The View and Use of Scripture in Christian Theology: A Historical Survey

The use of Scripture to formulate or authorize theological proposals is a practice that has been with Christianity from its inception. It is pertinent then to know how and why it has been practiced. Has there been one particular approach to it, or several at once, or perhaps several over time? For heuristic purposes, we shall approach this survey through the major epochs (or turning points) in the history of Christianity commonly used by church historians – i.e. New Testament, patristic, medieval, Reformation, modern, and postmodern eras. In each era, I will provide a general overview of the dominant way Scripture was viewed and used in theology, using the thoughts and practices of some key contributors as examples. Where possible, I will briefly highlight how such dominant approaches in each epoch inform the understanding of the person of Christ.

As an overview, this is simply a sketch for purposes of reorienting our study to the different approaches and attitudes to the Bible over the years and the underlying assumptions that informed them.[21] Following these historical accounts, this chapter will end with a consideration of certain conceptual or theological principles that ought to direct our use of Scripture for Christian theology.

The New Testament Use of the Old Testament

Many biblical scholars and theologians have been fascinated, disturbed, and at times confused by the New Testament use of the Old Testament for different reasons. There are those who think of it as totally arbitrary, lacking any form of coherence, and simply driven by the apologetic agenda of the earliest Christians amid disagreements with Jews over the messianic identity of Jesus.[22] Others see it as a variegated approach to the Old Testament with an inherent controlling element – an approach that may or may not inform contemporary

---

21. This chapter is basically my retelling of the story of biblical interpretation or (to put it another way) the use of Scripture in Christian theology. Those who are familiar with this history may elect to skip this part, although the reader might be keen to know how I have construed this oft-told story.

22. See for example Erhman, *How Jesus Became God*, 116–17.

hermeneutical practices.²³ In any case, the dominant and controlling idea in the New Testament use of the Old Testament is that Jesus of Nazareth is construed as Israel's prophesied Messiah whose identity is united to that of the one God of Israel.²⁴ But *how* the New Testament accomplishes this has been understood quite differently.

Walter C. Kaiser Jr. argues that the NT simply cites the OT accurately and authoritatively to communicate the single meaning and unified referents of the OT texts. He claims that the NT writers do not give any new meaning to the texts of the OT they employ, because with careful exegetical analysis we will see that the NT meaning given to any OT text is already there in the original text. For him, this is possible because, "Given the 'generic wholeness' of the divine promise-plan of God, the prophets were divinely enabled to see 'near' fulfillments, as well as some of the more 'distant,' climactic fulfillment of those same near fulfillments."²⁵ Kaiser therefore claims that it is not "legitimate to find a meaning that goes beyond the 'authorial will' of the OT human writer, especially if that meaning exceeds the grammatico-historical process of locating that sense."²⁶

Darrell L. Bock agrees with Kaiser on the idea of the OT text having a single meaning, but disagrees with him on the nature of its referents. Bock theorizes that the NT use of the OT involves both the original OT context of the passage and the immediate NT context within which it was used. He calls his position "the one meaning, multiple contexts and referents view."²⁷ This view holds that meaning is unchanged at one level and fresh at another, or that "a text can 'deepen' in meaning *without departing from its inherent sense.*"²⁸ For example, the use of Psalm 2:1–2 in Acts 4:25–26 where the referents in the original text are Gentile nations and Israel, but in Acts the referents are expanded to include the nation of Israel and Jesus. Therefore, "The hermeneutical key in describing the use is to pay careful attention to each historical

---

23. For a more detailed work on this topic, see Beale and Carson, *Commentary on the New Testament.*

24. See Bauckham, *Jesus and the God of Israel*; and Hays, *Reading Backwards.*

25. Kaiser, "Single Meaning, Unified Referents," 65–66.

26. Kaiser, 60.

27. Bock, "Single Meaning," 106.

28. Bock, 125. Emphasis in original.

context and a range of meaning that the original utterance can tolerate at the level of its sense."[29]

Peter Enns advances a third view on the use of the OT in the NT by situating such use within its Second Temple hermeneutical-historical context. He notes the existence of "interpretive activity on the OT long before the NT was written, and the fruit of such interpretive labor came to circulate among interpreters of the time."[30] Enns acknowledges the diversity of Second Temple literature but quickly notes that they are unified by a certain "*hermeneutical posture* that seeks (1) to mine Scripture (by applying conventional hermeneutical strategies) for hidden, richer meanings in order to hear God speak once again in a community's present circumstances, and (2) to preserve these interpretive traditions for successive generations."[31] The difference of the NT use of the OT from its use in these other literatures does not lie in their hermeneutical techniques, but in the fact that NT writers directed their use on testifying about the identity and works of Jesus Christ. Enns also notes that the use of the OT in the NT needs to be understood under a bigger umbrella, that is, the presence of the OT in the NT. He writes:

> The OT *permeates* the NT because the NT describes how Christ and his work are the realization of God's purposes throughout Israel's history as recorded in the OT. At times this is seen in direct, explicit, and straightforward ways, while at other times the matter is more subtle and difficult to explain. Either way, the pervasive presence of the OT in the NT should balance any temptation to think of citations of the OT in the NT as a phenomenon to be explained independently from a larger theological program of the NT writers.

This theological program is also described as the Christotelic principle, that is, reading the OT "*already knowing* that Christ is somehow the *end (telos)* to which the OT story is heading; in other words, to read the OT in light of the exclamation point of the history of revelation, the death and resurrection of Christ."[32]

---

29. Bock, 132.
30. Enns, "Fuller Meaning, Single Goal," 175. Emphasis added.
31. Enns, 177.
32. Enns, 214. Emphasis in original.

To summarize, it seems one might explain the apparent difference in meaning or alleged inconsistency in the NT appropriation of the OT either by denying it (Kaiser), diminishing it (Bock), or radicalizing it (Enns).[33] Although Walter Kaiser holds that NT authors "used a plain, simple and straightforward hermeneutic" (something he argues we should do today), even he needed to give extended and not quite convincing explanations of what makes their use of particular OT texts unproblematic.[34] It is hard to see how Kaiser's exegetical analyses would have been the same reasoning operational in the minds of NT authors when they used an OT text to reach the conclusions they did.[35] Bock acknowledges but limits such new meanings to the referents (not the original sense) of the texts used; thus, he seems to operate with a restricted, only the semantic, theory of meaning.[36] The position advanced by Enns goes farther in allowing for a radically new, namely Christotelic, meaning in the NT use of the OT, and this use models "for us a hermeneutical 'attitude' that is authoritative for us, even if that authority does not function as a five-step hermeneutical guide."[37] Enns however, may have overstated the identification of NT use of the OT with Second Temple Jewish uses, the only difference being the theological function of Christ.[38] The truth

---

33. Steve Moyise, in a related but narrower study, notes that there are three major approaches to assessing Jesus's use of Scripture in the Gospels. The first is a minimalist approach, which holds that the early church substantially and invalidly changed the message of Jesus as the tradition developed over time. This group therefore acknowledges a change in meaning when the NT uses the OT but denies that it originated from Jesus. The second approach is a moderate one and it also acknowledges a change in meaning but neither sees it as an invalid move nor untraceable to Jesus. Instead, it sees it as emerging from Jesus's first-century hermeneutical context as well as a kind of narrative theology. Moyise calls the third approach maximalist because it not only affirms that the Gospels express Jesus's original message but it also denies any change in meaning between the OT texts and Jesus's use of those texts – a move that coincides with Kaiser's solution as seen above. Moyise himself identifies "most with the 'moderates.'" Moyise, *Jesus and Scripture*, 121.

34. Kaiser, "Single Meaning, Unified Referents," 72.

35. See for an example Kaiser's treatment of James's use of Amos 9:12 in Acts 15:17. Kaiser, 65–72.

36. Besides the fact that Darrell Bock fails to take into account a foundational theory of meaning, even his appropriation of the semantic theory of meaning is rather simplistic since he offers no assessment of the view. For a nuanced treatment of both views, see Speaks, "Theories of Meaning."

37. Enns, "Fuller Meaning, Single Goal," 217.

38. Donald Juel affirms the same position by noting that "the particular investment in Israel's heritage and Israel's Scriptures suggests that *the most helpful* analogies for our study will be other Jewish scriptural interpretation, as practiced, of course, in the Hellenized world." Juel, "Interpreting Israel's Scriptures," 285. Emphasis added.

of this claim is not what is contested, but the fact that it does not tell the whole story of what was going on in the NT appropriation of the OT understood within the divine triune economy rather than a mere biblical economy.[39]

This last claim anticipates our discussion in the second major section of this chapter; that the NT is actually a particular reading of the OT, shaped by the transforming experience of the reality of Christ as both human and divine. However, this discussion must wait as we turn our attention to the use of Scripture in theology during the two major eras that constitute the premodern phase of Christian theology.

Scripture and Its Use in Premodern Theology

Scripture as the Word of God: Patristic Practices

By the time of the apostolic fathers,[40] many of the books that constitute the New Testament were well known, albeit not widely regarded as Scripture until the time of the Apologists.[41] Therefore, "To speak in generalities, the Apostolic Fathers understood the books of the New Testament as part of the kerygma or proclamation, and not as Scripture with definitive authority, while the Apologists were beginning to understand the books of the New Testament as Scripture."[42] This shift is rooted in the fact that the NT as kerygma of the Christ event experienced by the apostles was taken to be revelatory just as the OT. Ignatius, for example, understood "the gospel to be grounded not in the Old Testament but in the church's experience of Jesus Christ."[43] Frances

---

39. See Webster, *Domain of the Word*, vii–viii.
40. Joseph Trigg notes as follows,
    The term "Apostolic Fathers" has served since the seventeenth century as a classification of convenience for some of the most ancient Christian literature outside the New Testament canon. It includes works, such as the Ignatian letters, about which we can be fairly confident in ascribing authorship; works, such as the *Didache* (see Draper 1996), that are anonymous; and others, such as the *Letter of Barnabas* (see Hvalvik 1996), which are pseudonymous . . . the Apologists wrote, for the most part, a generation later. They are known as such because their principal surviving works seek to clear Christianity of charges thought to justify persecution of Christians. The Apologists include [among others] Justin Martyr, his pupil Tatian, Athenagoras, and Theophilus of Antioch.
    Trigg, "Apostolic Fathers and Apologists," 304–5.
41. This is often deduced in the way they used quotation formulas when citing the OT but conspicuously leave out such formulas when referencing the NT. Both Ignatius and Clement of Alexandria exemplify this practice in their letters and/or homilies. Trigg, "Apostolic Fathers."
42. Hauser and Watson, "Introduction and Overview," 40.
43. Hauser and Watson, 40.

Young notes that we see in Ignatius, "As already in Paul and the Epistle to the Hebrews, [that] *Christ has become the hermeneutical key which relativizes the texts*, even as they confirm the Christian testimony."[44] Irenaeus also affirmed this principle in *Against Heresies*.[45]

With the proliferation of "Christian" writings in the first to third centuries, this conviction – that Jesus Christ, as experienced and testified by the apostles, is the self-same God and Messiah revealed in Israel's Scriptures – became the controlling principle (i.e. the rule or canon of faith) for determining right from wrong written kerygmas of the gospel (thus, the NT canon).[46] Not only that, it was also understood to be the controlling principle for the right use of Scripture to formulate a right Christology. For example,

> Irenaeus explicitly blames the Ebionites for receiving Matthew alone, Marcion for receiving a mutilated Luke alone, the Docetics for receiving Mark alone and the Valentinians for making copious use of John. . . . Irenaeus' major problem with the heretics was not the circulation of their peculiar documents but the wrong use they made of the common written heritage.[47]

Such wrong use of Scripture failed to see that "the apostolic Rule of Faith – understood not as something apart from Scripture but as an authoritative interpretation of Scripture which can be demonstrated out of Scripture itself – is the fundamental 'argument' (*hypothesis*) that clarifies the Bible's meaning."[48]

This tradition of the rule of faith was inherited by the Christian users of Scripture in the third and fourth centuries as exemplified in the hermeneutical practices of both Alexandria and Antioch – the two major centers where

---

44. Young, *Biblical Exegesis*, 16. Emphasis added.
45. According to Irenaeus,
    anyone who reads the Scriptures attentively will find in them the word concerning Christ and the prefiguration of the new calling. For Christ is "the treasure hidden in a field" [Matt. 13:44], that is, in the Scriptures which are in the world, for "the field is the world" [Matt. 13:38]; he was hidden, for he was signified by types and parabolic expressions which on the human level could not be understood before the consummation of that which was prophesied had been reached, namely, the coming of Christ.

    Irenaeus, "Against Heresies (IV.26.1)," in Froehlich, *Biblical Interpretation*, 44.
46. See, Holmes, "From Books to Library," 119.
47. Kyrtatas, "Historical Aspects," 41.
48. Trigg, "Apostolic Fathers," 330.

Christianity flourished during this period. The former was dominant in the third century, particularly as represented in the works of Origen,[49] while the latter gained strength as a viable alternative in the fourth century. Although the Antiochenes shared with the Alexandrians a two-tiered approach to reading Scripture, the former insisted on a much tighter relation of the higher or spiritual sense (*theoria*) of the text supervening on the plain sense (*historia*).[50] So, while Origen saw Christ or hidden spiritual meaning behind or beyond the physical literal words everywhere in Scripture, Theodore only saw such meaning within the literal narrative words of the text. Nevertheless, both schools held that Scripture in its totality was God's word to the church for knowing Christ her Redeemer (from both the Old and the New Testaments).

It is in this sense that Augustine speaks of the Bible as "Sacred Scriptures" or "divine utterances" given to enable Christians to grow in their love of God and neighbor. He thinks that using Scripture rightly does not mean we must all arrive at the same meaning or understanding of a given text, as long as its telos is attained and what we see in a given text does not contradict the rule of faith or a clear teaching found elsewhere in the Scriptures. He writes quite poignantly:

> Sometimes not just one meaning but two or more meanings are perceived in the same words of Scripture. Even if the writer's meaning is obscure, there is no danger here, provided that it can be shown from other passages of the holy Scriptures that each of these interpretations is consistent with the truth. The person

---

49. Origen intentionally pursued a two-tiered reading of the biblical text by first attending (quite carefully) to the physical or literal form of the text putting to good use his massive philological knowledge and skills. However, he insisted that a Christian reader of Scripture (unlike a Jewish reader) must seek after the deeper sense of the text, and this can only be attained through a spiritual or allegorical appropriation of Scripture. He expressly indicates that those who err in their reading of Scripture do so because "the holy scripture is not understood by them in its spiritual sense, but according to the sound of the letter." Origen, "On First Principles" 2.1, in Yarchin, *History of Biblical Interpretation*, 45. Indeed, "Origen saw the 'wording' of Scripture as the 'veil' in which the Spirit clothed the divine intent (*skopos*). For Origen attention to the words was important precisely because they both revealed and concealed what they signified." Origen, "On First Principles 4.3.4," in Graves, *Biblical Interpretation in the Early Church*, 87.

50. Theodore of Mopsuetia, a leading Antiochene theologian, insisted that any references to Christ in the prophetic writings must be consistent with the prophet's message. For this reason, he was opposed to the tendency of seeing Christ everywhere in Israel's Scripture. Yarchin, 350.

examining the divine utterances must of course do his best to arrive at the intention of the writer through whom the Holy Spirit produced that part of Scripture. . . . Certainly the spirit [*sic*] of God who worked through the author foresaw without any doubt that it would present itself to a reader or listener, or rather planned that it should present itself, because it too is based on the truth. Could God have built into the divine eloquence a more generous or bountiful gift than the possibility of understanding the same words in several ways, all of them deriving confirmation from other no less divinely inspired passages?[51]

Such understanding of the nature of Scripture gave room for its spiritual (i.e. theological) use in the faith and life of the church without at the same time validating any and every appropriation of Scripture, even ones that render clearly erroneous teachings.

The patristic period faced the challenge of fully understanding the apparent scriptural judgment that the identity of Jesus of Nazareth is united with that of the One true God of Israel in such a way that the Christ is at once both God and man.[52] According to Khaled Anatolios, this judgment first emerged and was already accepted at the level of primary reflection (i.e. an understanding deeply and pervasively embedded in the worship and proclamation of the church) or what David Yeago calls the inner logic of the church's worship life.[53] Afterward, attempts at clearer conceptual definition and terminological consistency (secondary reflection) inevitably followed.[54]

---

51. Augustine, "On Christian Teaching 3.27.28," in Graves, *Biblical Interpretation in the Early Church*, 241–42.

52. For an excellent explication of this thesis, see Yeago, "New Testament and the Nicene Dogma," 87–102.

53. Anatolios, *Retrieving Nicaea*, 35. See also Yeago, "New Testament and the Nicene Dogma," 87.

54. However, given that these were early formative years in the life of the church, the patristics were concerned, not only with clearly defining their understanding of Christ according to the Scriptures, but also with understanding how they are "the spiritual heirs of the OT legacy, of its revelation in divine matters and its sacred teaching on the human condition." (Kannengiesser, *Handbook of Patristic Exegesis*, vol. 1, 208). As a result, the spiritual or allegorical use of Scripture (as both hermeneutical and rhetorical) served these ends, enabling the church to make spiritual (i.e. theological) sense of God's word. It is in this light that Henri de Lubac argues for the idea of "spiritual exegesis" as a better description of the interpretive approach of early Christianity than just allegory. Contending with the generally negative perception of patristic exegesis as an antique misadventure, he points out that it is actually

The Trinitarian/christological debates or controversies of the fourth and fifth centuries were the epitome of such secondary reflections.⁵⁵ The Council of Nicaea 325 (also Constantinople 318) focused on the unity of the Godhead having agreed that Christ is united with God and concluded that this unity is a unity of being or essence as opposed to a unity of the will.⁵⁶ Chalcedon 451 attended to the unity of divinity and humanity in Christ without confusion, mixture, separation, or division.⁵⁷

Differences notwithstanding, the patristics shared a "general agreement on the contents of the scriptural canon, its normativity as the prime source of divine revelation, and the attribution of its ultimate authorship to the Holy Spirit."⁵⁸ In addition, they also held in common the belief "that apostolic tradition is a normative interpreter of scriptural revelation."⁵⁹

The Four Senses of Scripture: Medieval Methods

The medieval era in Christian history was characterized by so many changes such that, in many ways, it looked quite different from the patristic world that preceded it.⁶⁰ The era was predominantly shaped by the monastic and scholastic movements, which were distinct but related institutions. While these institutions fine-tuned and even systematized certain practices for reading Scripture, these practices were nonetheless patristic at their very core. Charles Kannengiesser opines that Bede, for example, "presents a clear picture of the process by which the legacy of patristic hermeneutics would shift over into the

---

"a spiritual transposition . . . effected through a symbolic utilization" of the biblical text. De Lubac, "Spiritual Understanding," 9.

55. Anatolios, *Retrieving Nicaea*, 35.

56. According to Anatolios, the pro-Nicene group of Alexander, Athanasius, and the Cappadocians construed the unity of the Trinity as a unity of being, while the anti-Nicene tract of Arius, Asterius, and Eunomius thought of it as a unity of will. Anatolios, 21.

57. See also Beely, *Unity of Christ*.

58. Anatolios, *Retrieving Nicaea*, 36.

59. Anatolios, 36.

60. Kannengiesser notes that this state of affairs led to "new beginnings in the history of Christian hermeneutics." He gives an obvious, yet penetrating reason why these new beginnings in Christian hermeneutics were inevitable and necessary: "In the living organism of Christian traditions, the same challenge resurfaces each time when a new generation of believers finds itself alienated from its own religious past, or when Christians attempt to redefine themselves and to deliver their spiritual message in a new culture." Kannengiesser, *Handbook of Patristic Exegesis*, vol. 2, 1478.

monastic [and later, scholastic] culture of the Middle Ages."[61] Bede was a careful student of the biblical text and of the writings of the fathers such that he appropriated their use of Scripture historically, allegorically, and morally (or tropologically). "He concentrated, like his predecessors, on the exact grammatical meaning of the text, then on the doctrinal meaning of the passage about Christ, and then gave the moral, interior spiritual meaning of it for the hearer or reader."[62] What cannot be missed here from Bede's approach is this idea that Scripture has multiple meanings rather than a single meaning – an idea that was dominant throughout the Middle Ages and clearly informed the way interpreters of Scripture at this time viewed and used the biblical text.

Henri de Lubac shows that a fourth sense of Scripture (anagogy) came to be widely recognized, even though many, like Robert of Melun, construed anagogy as a subset of allegory, such that "after the other components, he would subdivide allegory 'into simple allegory and anagogy.'"[63] Others simply oscillated between three and four senses without much explanation; for example,

> the author of the *Mirror on the Mysteries of the Church*, a disciple of Hugh of Saint Victor, writes in chapter 3 about "the fourfold sense of the Scriptures . . . that is to say, the historical, allegorical, tropological, and anagogical senses" and then, in chapter 7, explains that "Sacred Scripture . . . has three senses, that is to say, the historical, allegorical, and moral."[64]

However, the fourfold sense of Scripture eventually became standard usage so much so that, it was not just the way that Scripture itself was viewed, but also the practice of biblical interpretation, method of medieval theology, monastic life, homily, and liberal education (the kind advanced by both Hugh and Alcuin) took on this fourfold structure.[65] Therefore, for medieval theology in general, Scripture is taken to inform not just the content of theology but its method as well, since theology at this time was basically the reading (*lectio*) and explication (*explicatio*) of Scripture aided by the writings of the fathers.

---

61. Kannengiesser, 1494.
62. Ward, "Bede the Theologian," 60.
63. De Lubac, *Medieval Exegesis*, 90.
64. De Lubac, 90.
65. De Lubac, 16–17.

However, as medieval culture shifted more toward the schools than the monasteries, noticeable differences began to emerge. "While monastic 'lectio' tended, and is always inclined to tend, toward meditation and prayer, 'scholastic lectio tends toward the question and the disputation.'"[66] At first, this disputation was understood with reference to "a special application in the writings of the Fathers when they turned to explaining the Word of God,"[67] but it eventually came to mean "scholastic disputation" – a dialectical discussion (oral or written) that deploys dialectic or logic to clarify issues on any topic.[68] The Augustinian slogan popularized by Anselm "*fides quaerens intellectum*" ("faith seeking understanding") was a definitive motto for scholasticism, thus the use of dialectics, which in late medieval times "denotes the entire field of logic and its applications."[69]

In practice, the method was generally characterized by four major components (again, mimicking the fourfold nature or sense of Scripture). First is *lectio*, *expositio*, or *catena* – the presentation or reading of particular passages or sentences (from the fathers and Scriptures) and their explanation or interpretation.[70] Next is *quaestio* or *disputatio* which involves raising questions about the sentences in the light of other authorities, pointing out seeming or possible contradictions and engaging in a systematic discussion of issues.[71] The final stage is the *summa* – "the grand attempts to give a comprehensive view of the whole of attainable truth" after all objections have been satisfied.[72]

---

66. De Lubac, 52.

67. De Lubac, 52.

68. De Lubac, 55. Josef Pieper also points out that while its roots as noted above can be traced back to Augustine, Boethius in the sixth century, and the Carolingian period, Scholasticism as a method of theological discourse is considered (and widely so) to have gained more concrete and explicit expression in the eleventh century through the life and works of Anselm of Canterbury, Peter Abelard, and reaching its celebrated height in Thomas Aquinas. Pieper, "Scholasticism." See also Spade, "Medieval Philosophy"; and Novikoff, "Anselm, Dialogue," 387–418.

69. Perreiah, "Humanistic Critiques," 3.

70. Here, one notices the collapsing of lectio and explicatio in order to make room for a systematizing task at the end of the process. A second shift is an increasing focus on the writings of the church fathers as the text of lectio and explicatio, perhaps pointing to the influence of Peter Abelard's *Sic et Non*, as claimed in Norman, "Abelard's Legacy," 1–10.

71. De Lubac notes that well into the twelfth century the questions were directed at the text of Scripture because "theology is not yet, from a methodological point of view, clearly separated from exegesis." De Lubac, *Medieval Exegesis*, 67.

72. Pieper, "Scholasticism." See also Rouwendal, "Method of the Schools," 56–71.

The *Summa Theologica* of Thomas Aquinas is a prime example of this comprehensive and systematic task, the content of which he identified as *sacra doctrina* (sacred doctrine). Aquinas thought of sacred doctrine as an "accurate presentation" (or re-presentation) of divine revelation so much so that "he sometimes uses *sacra scriptura* (sacred scripture) as equivalent to *sacra doctrina* (cf. Ia,I,2, ad.2)."[73] His Christology basically continues the patristic tradition of explicating, as a scriptural judgment, the ontology of the person of Christ in relation to his two natures. In articulating, for example, the idea that the divine logos assumed into his person a human nature, Aquinas writes,

> What unites and what assumes are not the same. For whatsoever Person assumes unites, and not conversely. For the Person of the Father united the human nature to the Son, but not to Himself; and hence He is said to unite and not to assume. So likewise, the united and the assumed are not identical, for the Divine Nature is said to be united, but not assumed.[74]

The implication of this for Aquinas is that, if it was the divine nature that was assumed then it would mean that a man became God rather than the other way around; but as it were, it was God who became man (John 1:14). Aquinas therefore construes assumption as addition or incorporation rather than inhabitation or occupation; thus, a second nature (human) was added into an already existing person (Christ) and united to his already existing or original divine nature.

This, and other such helpful christological clarifications, was commonplace in medieval theology. However, by the end of this period, a slight methodological shift became noticeable, one that De Lubac captures quite well:

> At Paris and at Bologna . . . the reader of the Bible is given a humble role at the feet of the reader of "Sentences." He is not given the right "to dispute." For his course of studies, he is obliged to beg for an hour that has been left free and unaccounted for, and the sacred text disappears in the face of magisterial "summas." In the middle of the thirteenth century, the leap is thus made. The break has taken place. "Dialectic" and its "questions"

---

73. Davies, *Thomas Aquinas's Summa Theologiae*, 18.
74. Thomas Aquinas, *Summa Theologica*, III, Q. 2, Art. 8, ad. 2.

have won the day, and the change in methodology is found to have been accelerated by the inroads of an entirely new set of contents, that of the philosophy of Aristotle. Teaching no longer has as its framework the triple or quadruple *explication of the biblical text*.[75]

Nevertheless, the medieval schoolmen continued to regard and read the Bible as sacred Christian Scripture. For them, "'sacred doctrine' remained … closely linked with 'the contents of the sacred page' or 'the contents of the theological page.' So, it remained, even after the advent of the Questions, even after the victory of the Summas."[76]

Reformation and Modern Uses of Scripture in Theology

Scripture as Supreme Authority: Reformation and Post-Reformation Period

The Protestant Reformation was basically a protestation against ecclesial beliefs and practices considered by the Reformers to be unbiblical or thought to have been derived from a misuse, even abuse of Scripture. This is why Scripture – its nature, interpretation, and use – was central to the Reformation, particularly with respect to how to go about the task of theology. Should they (the Reformers) continue with the late medieval scholastic method they inherited, or were they to make a complete switch to that of their immediate context, that is, the humanist approach of the Renaissance? The task was both delicate and urgent so as to conserve and disseminate the theological contentions and convictions of the Protestant Reformation. While Martin Luther primarily championed the movement, his protégée, Philip Melanchthon seemed to be more suited and better equipped for this task.[77]

---

75. De Lubac, *Medieval Exegesis*, 72–73. Emphasis added.

76. De Lubac, 73.

77. The Reformer himself agrees no less with this assertion when in speaking of himself he said:
> I am rough, boisterous, stormy and belligerent. I am born to fight against innumerable monsters and devils. I must remove stumps and stones, cut away thistles and thorns, and clear away wild forests. Master Melanchthon comes along softly and gently, sowing and watering with joy, according to the gifts which God has abundantly bestowed upon him.

Melanchthon, "Brief Biographical Sketch," 30.

Melanchthon combined the skills of both humanism and scholasticism. The humanists placed greater emphasis on well spoken and written language as opposed to the (allegedly) overly technical and unprofitably esoteric language of the scholastics, which the humanists caricatured as barbaric.[78] Language, they asserted, should be employed for persuasion rather than disputation, thus preferring rhetoric over dialectic.[79] Christian humanists and the Reformers, who were concerned not only with educational reforms but more importantly with the renewal of theology, were also very critical of scholasticism.[80] Quite often, this meant a constant castigation of the institutional church and an emphasis on the service and ministry of the laity. In general,

> Christian humanists advocated a synthesis of classical, biblical, and patristic learning as the basis for an ambitious renewal of theology, piety, and public morality . . . thereby rejecting the dialectical modes of late medieval Scholasticism as too technical for the primary functions of theology, which they usually took to be pastoral and devotional.[81]

Consequently, the Reformers "devoted their energies to producing biblical commentaries rather than works of systematic theology; their tools were those of philology and rhetoric rather than dialectic."[82]

---

78. Gerard Lister for example is reported to have launched a vitriolic criticism of the scholastics as follows:
> No one, I think, is so stupid as to set any value on [their] foolish trifles. Nevertheless, it is astonishing how they dispute about nothing else than second intentions, common natures, quiddities, relations, ecceities, and countless other questions even more trifling than these trifles. And because they dream of these monstrosities, they appear subtle in their own eyes and contemn with stern eyebrows persons who spurn these questions and penetrate the real things themselves.

Melanchthon, 4. Many other humanists like Francesco Petrarca, Lorenzo Valla, Rudolph Agricola, Desiderius Erasmus, Juan Luis Vives, etc, directed no less damaging attacks at scholasticism and the schoolmen.

79. Perreiah summarizes the contentions of the humanists against scholasticism as follows: (1) Scholastics are said to speak a peculiar dialect of Latin – one which is, for all intents and purposes "meaningless." (2) Scholastic dialectic includes a large number of doctrines, e.g. "signification," "supposition," "consequences," "syllogism," etc. And (3) The notorious readiness of Scholastics to argue with anyone on practically any issue and their willingness to dispute either side of an issue raise questions about their sincerity no less than their certainty. Perreiah, "Humanistic Critiques," 11.

80. See for example Luther, "Disputation against Scholastic Theology."

81. Weiss, "Humanism," 265.

82. Burnett, "Educational Roots," 300.

However, Erika Rummel notes that "scholasticism was seriously challenged for only a brief period in the early sixteenth century, when humanists and Reformers combined forces. The second generation of Reformers returned to scholasticism, however, or more precisely, modified the scholastic method for their own purposes."[83] Burnett agrees, "dialectic had re-emerged as an *essential tool for theologians*" by the last quarter of the sixteenth century.[84] Besides the polemical and systematizing needs of Protestant theology at this time, Burnett argues that "a transformation of the discipline itself" explains why it made a comeback, evolving into a humanist-dialectic. This evolution is traceable to the eclectic projects of Lorenzo Valla and (by far more importantly) Rudolf Agricola.[85] Melanchthon was greatly influenced by this Agricolan school of thought,[86] as evident in his approach to theology and the use of Scripture.

In his *Loci Communes*, first published in 1521, Melanchthon reordered theological methodology. A year earlier, he had published a textbook in dialectics,[87] a work Robert Preus argues "had an effect on his *Loci Communes*

---

83. Erika Rummel, *Humanist – Scholastic Debate*, 39–40.

84. Burnett, "Educational Roots," 300. Emphasis added.

85. Agricola privileged Latin eloquence over terminological precision as well as organization of arguments over demonstration of truth. He argued for the use of *topics* or standardized categories as the first part of an argument to be decided upon in any given discussion. "Unlike late medieval logic, Agricola's combination of rhetoric and dialectic proved to be eminently practical. Called, alternatively, 'place logic', 'topical dialectic' or 'rhetorical dialectic', this humanist reinterpretation of dialectic was enthusiastically endorsed by Erasmus and took northern Europe by storm." Burnett, 302.

86. During his student days in the University of Heidelberg, Melanchthon stayed at the house of and enjoyed the friendship of one of his teachers named Pallas Spangel whose eclecticism with regards to scholastic and humanist approaches seemed to have impacted Melanchthon. Spangel was "a bridge between medieval scholasticism and renaissance humanism. Wide interests in the liberal arts enabled him to stimulate many students at Heidelberg, but his new learning remained a tool for the promotion of established dogma." A similar influence on Melanchthon during this time was that of a former lecturer at Heidelberg, the late Rudolph Agricola. "Agricola represented a break with scholastic logic and dialectic. His vitriolic attacks on scholastic traditions made him a storm center at Heidelberg." Melanchthon thoroughly studied Agricola's *Dialectics* by memorizing "large portions, adopted the order of argument, and came to discover new depths in the classics." Manschreck, *Melanchthon*, 34–35.

87. "Philipp Melanchthon published his first textbook on dialectic, *Compendiaria dialectices ratio*, in 1520, and it went through seventeen further printings in the next eight years. Although this text continued to be printed, Melanchthon produced a revised and expanded text in 1528 that proved even more popular. The third and final version of Melanchthon's dialectic text, the *Erotemata Dialectices* of 1547, was the most successful of all, becoming the basis for dialectic instruction in Lutheran Germany throughout the second half of the sixteenth century." Burnett, "Educational Roots," 304.

of the following year—not on the doctrinal content but on the method and arrangements he employed in presenting Christian doctrine."[88] Melanchthon thought of the use of dialectics in theology as a distinct "activity or office" with four parts, that is, "to define, to distinguish (*dividere*), to connect the arguments properly, and finally to refute poorly and falsely connected arguments, and, by making the reason for such error plain, to lead the student away from error."[89] How was this methodological strategy put to work in the *Loci Communes*?

Perhaps, the most striking feature of the *Loci Communes* is its structure, that is, the types and order of doctrines covered in the book. Melanchthon first employed the concept of *loci* in the Erasmian sense of basic moral principles, but then redefined them to mean the basic themes that can be drawn from Scriptures.[90] He derived these basic themes of the Christian faith from the book of Romans alone, thus departing from Peter Lombard's *Sentences* and its reliance on the writings of the fathers. In the first edition of the *Loci Communes*, Melanchthon covered only twelve topics in which he excluded such major doctrines as that of God, the Trinity, and Christ.[91] He grounds this move in the fact that the mysteries of God are better adored than investigated, which meant that he first treated "the doctrine of humanity, human ability and will, and continues with an extended exposition of law and sin. For, he notes, only when one knows the power of sin, the law, and grace can one know Christ, and not when one speculates about His two natures or the incarnation."[92] One sees here a certain shift away from the theological/metaphysical preoccupation of patristic and medieval Christology to an anthropological/epistemological emphasis. In the final edition however, which appropriates the fathers and the creeds of the church and is less antagonizing of scholasticism as was the case in the first edition, Melanchthon increased

---

88. Quoted in Preus, *Theology of Post-Reformation Lutheranism*, 77.
89. Preus, 77–78.
90. Asselt, *Introduction to Reformed Scholasticism*, 88.
91. See table in Asselt which compares the doctrines covered in both editions. Asselt, *Reformed Scholasticism*, 90–91.
92. Asselt, 89.

the number of topics covered to twenty-four and started with the doctrine of God, under which he situates his Christology.[93]

Melanchthon's Christology has as its starting point the testimonies of Scripture (both OT and NT), particularly the baptismal formula (Matt 28:19) in which the Son is identified as belonging to the Godhead. The Son has two primary properties that distinguish him from the Father and the Holy Spirit, and these are his eternal generation in the Father (by virtue of which he belongs to the same substance with the Father) and his incarnation in Mary's womb thus becoming human. This means that "the Son is the Christ, that is, the promised Redeemer, one person with two natures miraculously united, namely, that eternal image of the Father or the Word and a human nature."[94] To spell out right from wrong or true from false ways of understanding this union, Melanchthon references the Creeds and fathers of the church as sources of authority. He says,

> Care behooves the pious, for the sake of harmony, to speak in line with the church. And it was not without good reasons that the ancient church approved some ways of speaking and rejected others. Let us then avoid zeal for caviling and retain the forms received with weighty and true authority.[95]

Melanchthon argues, along with the fathers, that it is theologically appropriate for us to say:

---

93. The 1521 edition was the first while the last was that of 1559, but in between were several revised editions showing substantive changes.

Scholars divide the editions of Melanchthon's *Loci* into three periods. The first is from its first publication ... to first major recession in 1535. The second period includes all the editions from the 1535 publication to its final major revision in 1543. This final version saw its last revision and edition in 1559, a year before Melanchthon's death. By the time Melanchthon had finished his revisions, the *Loci* were almost four times the size of the original *Loci Communes* of 1521. Moreover, the name of the work had changed. While the term *Loci* remained, the word *Communes* was dropped in favor of *Praecipui* (*Chief*), reflecting a departure from the rhetorical aim of the first edition and a movement toward the dialectical arrangement of Scholasticism.

Christian Preus, "Introduction," in Philip Melanchthon, *Commonplaces: Loci Communes 1521*. St. Louis: Concordia, 2014, 15.

94. Melanchthon, *Chief Theological Topic*, 18.

95. Melanchthon, 28.

> God is man; the Word is man, Christ is man, Christ is God, God is born of a virgin, He suffered, because this person, in which the divine nature has been united by the personal union with the human nature, was born and crucified. They call this form of speaking in the concrete "the communication of attributes," that is, a predication in which the properties of the natures are correctly attributed to the person, so that the Son of God is the Redeemer, not only that the human nature is the Redeemer.[96]

What becomes clear here is the fact that Melanchthon's Christology, and indeed the general contour of Reformation Christology, remained primarily metaphysical but one that was more intentionally immersed in Scripture displaying an abundance of biblical citations and allusions.

The impact of Melanchthon's approach to theological inquiry outlived him.[97] His ability to appropriate all relevant and available tools from his personal, intellectual, and theological backgrounds without letting any of these other "sources" trump the magisterial role of Scripture as his ultimate source of theological knowledge was significant.[98] However, the Reformation's insistence on *sola scriptura* raised concerns about theological epistemology and authority. This concern, as we have seen, was pervasive (often, implicitly) in Melanchthon's theological methodology,[99] but the battle for Scripture as the source of theological knowledge and authority would be fiercer in the Enlightenment/modern period.

---

96. Melanchthon, 28.

97. Robert Preus notes that Protestant theology in general and German theology in particular "recognized its debt to Melanchthon, followed his theology where possible, *particularly his method*" (Preus, *Theology of Post-Reformation Lutheranism*, 32, emphasis added). Melanchthon is thus considered the pioneer of a distinctly evangelical or Protestant systematic/biblical theology. Richard Muller points out that even John Calvin is said to have seen his *Institutes of the Christian Faith* as a kind of loci communes and orders it in a Melanchthonian method. Muller, "Ordo," 123–40.

98. Heinze Scheible says that Melanchthon
   avoided the twin dangers that either the fledgling reform movement would get sidetracked into an anti-intellectual spiritualism or, at the opposite extreme, philosophy would be imposed upon theology, knowledge upon faith, and reason upon revelation. Because [he] allowed both poles to retain their own characteristics, he was able to bring about a fruitful joining of the two.
   Scheible, "Melanchthon, Phillip," 45.

99. This is also the case, perhaps more explicitly, in the works of Theodore Beza. For a comprehensive treatment of this subject using Beza's entire corpus, see Mallinson, *Faith, Reason, and Revelation*, 5.

The Bible as a Collection of Ancient Documents: Modern Biblical Scholarship and Theology

According to Michael Legaspi,

> Scripture died a quiet death in Western Christendom some time in the sixteenth century. The death of scripture was attended by two ironies. First, those who brought the scriptural Bible to its death counted themselves among its defenders. Second, the power to revivify a moribund scriptural inheritance arose not from the churches but from the state. The first development was the Reformation, and the second was the rise, two hundred years later, of modern biblical scholarship.[100]

The premodern world operated with "a closed epistemological system"[101] in which human knowledge directly depended on divine knowledge and thereby acknowledging the limitation of human knowledge as a consequence of divine mystery.

> Aquinas had been willing to submit his reason to the truth of revelation when the two seemed to clash. This was no longer so for the thinkers of the Enlightenment. Once this epistemological shift was well under way, there was no stopping it, and for many, methods of biblical interpretation had to conform to the new standards for assessing truth.[102]

The major philosophical figures that facilitated this epistemological shift (from the predominantly metaphysical leaning of previous generations) were René Descartes and Benedict Spinoza, with the latter having a more direct influence on the modern perception and reading of Scripture. Descartes's rationalist epistemology proposed the process of methodological doubt as the only means to certain knowledge of the self and the external world. For example, "in the Second and Third Meditations Descartes argues from the indubitability of the *cogito* reasoning to the trustworthiness of intellectual perception to the existence of a perfect being (God)."[103]

---

100. Legaspi, *Death of Scripture*, 3.
101. Legaspi, vii.
102. Legaspi, viii.
103. Hatfield, "René Descartes."

Spinoza extended this approach to the use and interpretation of the Bible in his proposals for social and political reforms.[104] Having experienced firsthand the Wars of Religion, the Inquisitions, and the abusive use of power by religious authorities/communities on dogmatic grounds, Spinoza saw dogmatic religion as not only superstitious and false but also dangerous to social life. Hence, the Bible as the source of Christian dogma must be subjected to rational analyses in order to purge it of such religious or dogmatic interpretations (or misinterpretations) by theologians whom he accused of parading their own ideas as God's word.[105] "For Spinoza, the book of Nature was infinite and eternal. . . . [However] Stories from the Book of Scripture were conditional, contextual, and finite."[106] These were merely cultural stories or narratives appealing only to the imagination (as opposed to critical reason) for purposes of morality and should therefore be used as such. By doing this, "he delimited the role of revelation to theology and the role of reason to philosophy. He developed a method for better understanding the Bible by studying it in light of its own historical context, with special attention given to author, audience, and linguistic and textual analysis."[107]

Needless to say, Spinoza's proposals were vehemently attacked and rejected by many,[108] but others listened to him and began to put his ideas to work. John Toland showed himself to be one of those early followers of Spinoza when he reportedly said that people would only see that true religion is natural religion "if they read the sacred Writings with that Equity and Attention that is due to meer Humane works; Nor is there any different rule to be follow'd in the Interpretation of *Scripture* from what is common to all other

---

104. The fact that Spinoza was greatly influenced by Descartes is not in doubt. "In 1663 he [Spinoza] published the only essay in his lifetime under his name, *Descartes' Principles of Philosophy*, which established his reputation as a philosopher of note." Harrisville and Sundberg, *Bible in Modern Culture*, 36.

105. His method of interpreting Scripture therefore proposes three rules: (1) study of original languages; (2) rational explication of biblical claims; and (3) historical analyses of the text. Harrisville, and Sundberg, 38–39.

106. Frampton, "Spinoza and His Influence," 140.

107. Frampton, 141.

108. For example, Gottlieb Spitzel accused Spinoza of making the Bible so malleable that it is completely at the mercy of the interpreter; and Wilhelm van Blyenburg asserted that Spinoza's *Theological-Political Treatise* must "have been fetched from hell." Harrisville and Sundberg, *Bible in Modern Culture*, 46.

Books."[109] Herman Samuel Reimarus pioneered these efforts in Germany, especially through his *Apology*, thus introducing "historical criticism into the mainstream of Protestant theology."[110] In his desire to reconcile the Christian faith and reasonable religion, he engaged in a critical reading of the Gospels and concluded that Jesus never intended to establish new beliefs such as his divinity or the Trinity. However, his post-crucifixion heart-broken disciples found new hope by "employing fantasy to make of Jesus' followers a fellowship totally at their disposal."[111]

Friedrich Schleiermacher proposed a romanticist or subjectivist biblical criticism as a way to rehabilitate the respectability of the Bible in that rationalistically antagonizing climate.[112] Similarly, David F. Strauss would employ the notion of myth and Ferdinand Baur would seek to diffuse historical criticism with Hegelian idealism.[113] The discoveries and development of more sophisticated and technical tools of biblical analyses (e.g. source criticism, textual criticism, etc.) would eventually lead to an ever-increasing dismembering of the Bible into distinct and discrete minute parts or texts that cannot possibly hold together as a coherent whole. Standard practice required of the biblical scholar to first "reckon with a contested and disordered text."[114] Consequently, J. P. Gabler famously called for a clear distinction between biblical theology as a science and dogmatic theology as doctrinal formulations of the church. For him, the two cannot coexist since the latter has "a strong propensity for reading doctrines *into* the biblical text."[115] G. L. Bauer would appropriate this distinction in his treatment of the two testaments, thus becoming "one

---

109. Harrisville and Sundberg, 48.
110. Harrisville and Sundberg, 49.
111. Harrisville and Sundberg, 57. Quoting Reimarus from the *Apology*, Harrisville and Sundberg report his as saying:
> There is a clear contradiction between the disciples' constant hope for a temporal redemption, for an earthly empire, and such speeches of Jesus as indicate a spiritually suffering Redeemer . . . If he had wanted to rid ideas of temporal honor and power totally from their minds, why then does he promise them they should have such a share in his kingdom? . . . The shattered hope in an earthly kingdom which no longer found nourishment after the crucifixion birthed the new system of the apostles." Harrisville and Sundberg, 57.

112. Harrisville and Sundberg, 64–65.
113. Harrisville and Sundberg, 87.
114. Legaspi, *Death of Scripture*, 26.
115. Hauser and Watson, vol. 3, 18.

of the first to distinguish between the theology of the OT and the theology of the NT."[116]

Generally speaking, then, modern historical-critical interpreters of the Bible operated from the standpoint of methodological naturalism – an attitude of neutrality toward the biblical text devoid of any religious assumptions or commitments as a necessary first step to discovering the true (scientific) meaning of the text. A corollary of this posture is a view of the Bible as a collection of purely human ancient documents (as opposed to God's word), thus the deployment of historical-critical and modern philosophical analyses (both higher and lower criticisms)[117] to ascertain their veracity and relevance or usefulness for modern people.[118]

With respect to Christology, this historicist[119] view and use of the Bible yielded a certain distinction between the Jesus of history and the Christ of faith, thereby opening the door to an earnest quest for the historical Jesus, devoid of the allegedly fantastical embellishments of the church. In its rationalistic and idealistic mode, the quest rejected the dogmatic understanding of Christ (noted above in Reimarus and later Strauss), dismissing any accounts

---

116. Baird, "Overview of Historical Criticism," 102.

117. Higher criticism includes *form criticism* (study of the period between the occurrence of an event and the first written source of that event); *source criticism* (the analysis of written sources used by an author); and *redaction criticism* (the analysis of the distinctive ideas an author adds to or highlights from the sources used). *Lower criticism* (also, textual criticism) is employed to clarify textual confusion(s) over certain word(s) or phrase(s). With all these in place, an attempt to reconstruct the original event as it must have happened becomes possible rather than just relying on religiously colored account of the biblical author/redactor.

118. Given the emphasis on neutrality as a virtue, this has been the dominant approach to the Bible in departments of religious studies and many schools of divinity. In a sense, this can be a good thing as noted by John J. Collins. He argues that historical criticism
> has created an arena where people with different faith commitments can work together and have meaningful conversations. The historical focus has been a way of getting distance from a text, of respecting its otherness. The neutrality and objectivity at which the discipline has aimed has allowed Jews and Christians to work together and has allowed feminists to make their case in ways that initially unsympathetic scholars have found compelling.

Collins, *Bible after Babel*, 10.

119. We must point out here that historicism in the modern era did not have a fixed single meaning that everyone operated with. On the contrary, "the notion of historicism was used in manifold ways: for individual programmes, for the criticism of opponents and for the characterization of important tendencies." (Scholtz, "Notion of Historicism," 150). Scholtz goes on to identify five different senses in which historicism was construed and these are: (1) the universal historical view, (2) the metaphysics (and theology) of history, (3) historical romanticism and traditionalism, (4) historical objectivism and positivism, and (5) historical relativism. Scholtz, 151–52.

that cannot be explained by natural reason. Strauss, for example, after offering a critical analysis of the life of Jesus proposes that "the key to the whole of Christology" is to replace an individual (Jesus) with an idea (humanity) "as subject of the predicate which the church assigns to Christ."[120] He argues that the predication of two natures (divine and human) to one person is absurd and irreconcilably contradictory, but the contradiction dissolves when the idea of humanity is postulated. Therefore, we should not think of the dogmatic Christ as a real historical individual person, but an idea of an ideal humanity. It is humanity that has the two natures, died, resurrected, and ascended into heaven; and it is faith in humanity that brings justification. Any human being is capable of living this "life of Jesus;" simply "by the kindling within him of the idea of Humanity, the individual man participates in the divinely human life of the species."[121] The life of Jesus is simply a higher-level humanity, which is a divinely human life for all humans. Similarly, the romanticist phase of the quest was equally revisionist and reinterpreted Jesus merely "as a teacher of timeless morality, Jesus as a good example, Jesus as more the first Christian than the Christ—a flight from the Christ of dogma indeed!"[122]

However, these and other strands of Jesus research from Reimarus to the (relatively recently) Jesus Seminar all fail to see that "Jesus only becomes accessible to us not when we try and detach him from the witness of the early church . . . [as they have] endeavored to do."[123] It is noteworthy that these approaches were so dominant and pervasive that Ernst Troeltsch asserted, quite categorically, that "Christian dogma, as constructed by the early church, has finally disintegrated; there is no longer a unitary christian [sic] culture; and historical criticism of the Bible is now a reality."[124] It is interesting to note that those who invented historical biblical criticism did so with the intention "to

---

120. Strauss, *Life of Jesus*, 780.
121. Strauss, 780.
122. Dunn, "Quest for the Historical Jesus," 308.
123. Greene, *Christology in Cultural Perspective*, 14–15.
124. Troeltsch, "Significance of the Historical Existence," 184. This is not to say that there were no dissenting voices that rejected this way of using Scripture and understanding Christ; there were such groups as the "pietists, confessional Lutherans and some Reformed communities. [However] Their influence on public opinion was restricted." Reventlow, "Role of the Old Testament," 132.

nullify the arbitrary political power of those who *used the Bible to legitimate their authority*."[125] However, its side-effects were devastating:

> The doctrines of original sin and the Trinity, plus the Christology of traditional theology, were rejected with particular emphasis. These dogmas were attacked by the use of the historical method . . . which led to a separation between dogma itself and contemporary theology.
>
> Perhaps the most far-reaching change was that the same historical point of view was applied to the *Scriptures*. The Bible was inserted into the framework of human development. The Old Testament was separated from the New Testament as something belonging on a lower level. The content of the Bible was exposed to criticism on the basis of modern norms.[126]

On the other hand though, one cannot deny the fact that the broader field of biblical scholarship has greatly enlarged our factual and textual understanding of the Bible.[127] The trouble though, as Legaspi points out, is that "academic criticism in its contemporary form cannot offer a coherent, intellectually compelling account of what this information is actually *for*."[128] We therefore end up with this "ironic but unavoidable fact that while the church has been enriched by the knowledge that historical criticism provides, it nevertheless finds this preeminent scholarly discipline a hostile companion in the journey of faith."[129] Attempts to address this hostility would occupy and define the postmodern phase of Christian theological developments.

---

125. Harrisville and Sundberg, *Bible in Modern Culture*, 334. Emphasis added.

126. Bengt Hägglund, *History of Theology*, 346.

127. Michael Legaspi calls this the intellectual value of academic biblical criticism. He notes that this approach to reading the Bible "disciplined by academic standards [and] cultivated across a range of fields has produced, in a relatively short time, an astonishing amount of useful information." Legaspi, *Death of Scripture*, 169.

128. Legaspi, 169. Emphasis in original.

129. Harrisville and Sundberg, *Bible in Modern Culture*, 5.

The Bible as the Scriptures of Believing Communities: Postmodern Approaches

Modernism faced a crisis in the first half of the twentieth century, due largely to the two World Wars, and biblical scholarship was no exception.[130] Karl Barth was one of those who took this crisis seriously insisting that theology cannot be sustained for long if humanity, rather than God, is its foundation and end.[131] Barth therefore sought to break with the Protestant liberalism of his day and engaged "in what he referred to as 'theological exegesis.'"[132] In his pursuit of this goal, Barth did not dismiss historical criticism as an important component of biblical exegesis. Instead, "he wanted to press forward to the theological understanding of the biblical texts—a task which he saw had been brought to extinction by limiting exegesis to historical analysis."[133] For Barth, actual exegetical work had priority over hermeneutical principles and questions, thus allowing (or at least seeking to allow) the underlying theological nature and telos of the text to order its interpretation.[134]

---

130. The humanistic hubris of modernism was shockingly made explicit by the First World War (1914–1918); its aim and notion of human progress through scientific and rational means, devoid of religious sentiments and its attendant conflicts, was dethroned. "During the war, there began to emerge an altered religious sensibility, nothing less than the reassertion of Augustinian faith with its harsh view of the human condition, its austere spirituality, and its exultation in the strangeness and otherness of God." Harrisville and Sundberg, *Bible in Modern Culture*, 220.

131. Barth noted in the preface of his 1919 Romans commentary that the events of the First World War changed his view and use of the Bible. Precisely, "in October of 1914, he had experienced the greatest cataclysm of his life which brought to a head by his discovery that ninety-three German intellectuals had signed a manifesto supporting the war policy of the Kaiser and among the signatories were several of his teachers whom he had studied under in Germany." Burnett, *Karl Barth's Theological Exegesis*, 265.

132. Burnett, 4.

133. Quoted by Burnett, 8. Burnett argues that Barth's dedication to biblical exegesis is unrivaled in Modern theology. He points out that "no theologian since John Calvin has been more committed to biblical exegesis than Karl Barth. There are over fifteen thousand biblical references throughout the *Church Dogmatics* and more than two thousand examples of detailed exegesis of specific biblical passages." Burnett, 9. Burnett further says, "In fact, it has been shown that the later volumes of the *Church Dogmatics* contain even more exegesis than the earlier ones and that overall, there is almost twice as much exegesis in each volume produced after than before or during the war." Burnett, 31.

134. This was not only counter institutional practice of that time but counter-intuitive as well, which was no surprise that Barth's approach received a barrage of fierce criticisms and condemnations. Burnett, 14–31. This move by Barth is also regarded as nothing less than the recovery of theological interpretation of Scripture into the mainstream of discussion after its loss for about two centuries. See for example, Treier, *Introducing Theological Interpretation*, 11–36.

Rudolph Bultmann, however, differed from Barth in his demythologization project, thus birthing the new hermeneutic approach and triggering diverse energetic discussions on the interpretation and use of the Bible.[135] This increased polarization of interpretative approaches notwithstanding, it became clear at this time that it was no longer "business as usual" for the typical modernist biblical historicism. The contributions of Georg-Hans Gadamer and Paul Ricoeur also affected the understanding and appropriation of Scripture. Gadamer's claim that "the fundamental prejudice of the enlightenment is the prejudice of prejudice itself"[136] strikes at the heart of modernism's preoccupation with a rationalistic objective method and universal truth. His work shows that we can have confidence in tradition because, "through its history of reception, the tradition itself creates the conditions of its understanding. Thus, Gadamer is able to rehabilitate prejudgment. Prejudgments are the prior understanding of succeeding understanding. We may entrust ourselves to the traditions."[137] For Paul Ricoeur, the interplay of the reader and the text must be taken seriously in the process of understanding – an interplay that yields what Ricoeur calls the world of the text.

> Unlike the earlier Romantics, Ricoeur is unable to say that what is appropriated is the author's intention. But unlike modern structuralists, Ricoeur is unwilling to abandon his key idea that discourse is *about* something. The notion of the "world of the text" provides him with a solution to both problems.[138]

He speaks of the concept of hermeneutic conflict as a means to integrate both critical hermeneutics of suspicion and Gadamerian hermeneutics of confidence for the life of faith.[139]

---

135. Harrisville and Sundberg, *Bible in Modern Culture*, 231.
136. Gadamer, *Truth and Method*, 239–41.
137. Theissen, "Das Verschwinden des hermeneutischen," 268 (author's translation).
138. Vanhoozer, *Biblical Narrative*, 89.
139. According to Gerd Theissen, Ricoeur thinks that the understanding of the Bible must be through this hermeneutic conflict throughout. The two hermeneutics that are standing in conflict with each other shift the meaning of texts to a source beyond the subject: critical hermeneutic to unconscious factors in life and society – in the "economy" of fear, desire, and power or the unconscious power of timeless structures. Conservative hermeneutic, by contrast, shifts the central meaning of texts to holy things beyond our living world which breaks into the Bible as Kerygma in our living world. Critical hermeneutic pursues an archaeology of meaning and discovers its source in the unconscious depth of life, while the conservative seeks its reality

The implication of all these for theology was a definite departure from the critical liberalism of modernity with respect to the Bible and the church (or the Christian tradition generally speaking). The goal of deducing historically-based universal ideals for human existence, verifiable only through autonomous human reason, was no longer tenable; and so too was the idea of using the Bible as a source book or data pool for historically reliable reconstructed knowledge. Thus, many theologians and biblical scholars began to think and speak in terms of reading the Bible and doing theology in a postmodern age – a theological reading of Scripture that is postcritical, or postliberal, or post-metaphysical, or simply postmodern.[140] John Webster points out that these "Post-critical theological interpreters often counter the hermeneutical sufficiency of historical reconstruction by *appealing to the ecclesial community as the proper location of Scripture* and its interpretation, and to the cultivation of virtue as its chief end."[141] This attitude to the Bible and theology, according to Webster, is not merely a rejection of modernism and liberalism but an engagement with it.[142] The idea of a postmodern or postliberal theology therefore refers to a theology that engages with, rather than takes flight from modernity's liberalism in all its ramifications, and yet, surmounts liberalism's

---

in a teleology in which it follows the suggestions of symbols for it to further think critically. Theissen, "Das Verschwinden des hermeneutischen Konflikts," 266.

140. John Webster argues that, in spite of its inherent limitations, "postliberal" is the most suited term to be deployed in identifying and describing these varieties of approaches to theology because it *emphasizes* a change in attitude than method. He cautions against the negative deployment of the term "liberalism" noting that "At worst, the term becomes a weapon in the hands of theological terrorists of various faction, who use it (like its close cousins 'modernism' or 'fundamentalism') to dismiss or denounce what outrages them." Webster, "Theology after Liberalism," 52.

141. Webster, *Domain of the Word*, 108. Emphasis added.

142. Webster says,
If "theology after liberalism" is a way of recommending a theology which ignores or refuses to engage with those traditions which cluster theology around the term "liberal," then theology *after* liberalism is, in effect, simply theology *before* liberalism . . . Like "postmodernism," "postliberalism" is on shaky ground if it assumes too readily that it has neatly extricated itself from the entanglements of the past. Webster, 108.

George Lindbeck affirms the same position when he said that the shortcomings of the modern view of dogma "cannot be solved by, for example, abandoning modern developments and returning to some form of preliberal orthodoxy." Lindbeck, *Nature of Doctrine*, 7.

inherent flaws (e.g. prejudice against prejudice).[143] Three prominent exemplars here include Hans Frei, Brevard Childs, and George Lindbeck.

In *The Eclipse of Biblical Narrative*, Hans Frei argues that historical criticism was, among other things, a rebellion against what he calls traditional realistic interpretation of the Bible – an understanding of biblical narratives as having a "history-like (though not necessarily historical) element . . . that went into the making of Christian belief."[144] In this approach, both literal and figurative readings of biblical narratives function as allies rather than the strange bed fellows that historical criticism and biblical theology have turned them into. Frei contends that "the Gospels are neither straightforward histories nor myths. Unlike histories, the meaning of the Gospel narratives is not the historical reference outside the story; unlike myths, the meaning of the Gospel narratives is what the stories actually say rather than what they supposedly symbolize."[145] Therefore, rather than a historical reconstruction or a mythological reinterpretation of biblical narrative, the reader of Scripture simply works with the self-rendering and depiction of such narratives.[146] Frei applies this approach of reading biblical narratives to an understanding of the identity of Christ.[147]

Brevard Childs proposed the canonical criticism of the Bible as a way of doing theological exegesis – a theological exegesis that takes seriously the voice of the biblical text from a historical-critical point of view without at the same time jettisoning an understanding of the text in light of the rest of the canon of Scripture (e.g. the NT allusion to and appropriation of the OT). He

---

143. Some think of it as a *ressourcement* or a retrieval of precritical (i.e. dogmatic and/or theological) readings of the Bible. See Webster, "Theologies of Retrieval," 584.

144. Frei, *Eclipse of Biblical Narratives*, 10.

145. Vanhoozer, *Biblical Narrative*, 160.

146. Even though Frei's proposal fundamentally differed from that of Ricoeur (as demonstrated by Vanhoozer), they both shared the belief that "the fight for the 'rebirth' of narrative in the postmodern world is a specific Christian task." Vanhoozer, *Biblical Narrative*, 180. While Frei, as well as Ricoeur, fought to restore a narrative approach to reading Scripture for theology, Vanhoozer argues that neither of them was a narrative theologian. He describes Frei, for example, as
> an Anselmian theologian who is seeking to understand the Christian faith, particularly its central narrative expression, on its own terms . . . Narrative theologians, on the other hand, have in common a desire to make narratives central to the whole theological enterprise . . . On this view, becoming a Christian is more a matter of changing stories than doctrines or beliefs. Vanhoozer, 178.

147. See Frei, *Identity of Jesus Christ*.

perceived that the practice of separating the descriptive from the constructive elements of interpreting the Bible is problematic.[148] Therefore, he "constantly reached for a comprehensive goal for biblical studies."[149] Childs agrees with Barth "that one could not get *behind* the text, could not get at Scripture from a context other than the 'canonical,' since there was no neutral position from which to begin and from which to move from neutrality to commitment."[150] On this ground, the final form of the canon is taken for what it claims to be – a unified document that can only be understood as such. For Childs, "Only by beginning with the final form can the peculiar features of a passage's intertextuality be discerned which is blurred if one first feels contrained [sic] to force the text through a critical sieve."[151] Canonical criticism is indeed a thriving way of reading the Bible theologically, especially among biblical scholars who are keen to keep historical criticism and theological exegesis together.[152]

In *The Nature of Doctrine*, George Lindbeck advanced the cultural linguistic approach to theology as opposed to propositional-cognitivist and experiential-expressivist approaches.[153] The problem with contemporary evangelical theology, Lindbeck says, is the fact that

> Protestants of Reformation persuasion . . . want to maintain that the Bible is in some significant sense self-interpreting, that it corrects rather than simply serving church and tradition, and that it resists being taken captive by culture or philosophy (which remain now, as in the days of early Gnosticism, the main sources for the proliferation of interpretations).[154]

Lindbeck however "relocates authority in the church, that singular 'culture' within which, and only within which, the Bible is used to shape Christian

---

148. Childs doggedly pursued this hermeneutical vision in all his major works on the subject matter. See Childs, *Introduction to the Old Testament*); *New Testament as Canon*; and *Biblical Theology of the Old and New Testaments*.

149. Seitz and Greene-McCreight, "Work and Witness of Brevard S. Childs," 4.

150. Harrisville and Sundberg, *Bible in Modern Culture*, 318.

151. Childs, *New Testament as Canon*, 41.

152. See, for an example, the writings and biblical commentaries of Christopher Seitz, one of the most active adherents of this approach.

153. Lindbeck, *Nature of Doctrine*.

154. Lindbeck, "Postcritical Canonical Interpretation," 44–45.

identity."[155] He holds to a rule theory of doctrine in which doctrine is understood as second-order (not first-order) propositions that make intra-systematic (rather than ontological) truth claims.[156] On this view therefore, Nicaea and Chalcedon should only serve as paradigms that instantiate the rules for articulating Christology in new settings, but not as "formulas to be slavishly repeated."[157] We will return to this concern in chapter 4.

In the meantime, we will concern ourselves with construing a normative approach to the use of Scripture in theology, but not before summarizing the import of our historical sketch for the theological interpretation of Scripture as follows:

1. Attend to the NT use of the OT as exemplary for our own use of Scripture in doing theology.
2. Consider premodern ways of reading Scripture as faithful imitation of NT practice and seek to recover these.
3. Resist the modern transmutation of Scripture into the Bible and with it such critical reading of biblical texts that proceeds purely from methodological naturalism.
4. Relocate the reading and use of Scripture within the life of the church such that theology is carried out as an ecclesial (rather than a mere academic) activity.

With these considerations in mind, let us turn our attention to tracing a theological approach to using Scripture for Christian theology.

Construing and Using the Bible Theologically

We noted earlier in this chapter the conclusion of David Kelsey that there are a variety of ways in which Scripture is both construed to be authoritative and used to authorize theological proposals. Contra Kelsey however, the use of scripture to authorize theological proposals cannot be purely descriptive unless one takes Scripture itself to be merely descriptive. But if Scripture is taken to be normative (more on this shortly) then its use will also have to

---

155. Vanhoozer, *Drama of Doctrine*, 10.
156. Lindbeck, *Nature of Doctrine*, 80.
157. Lindbeck, 96.

be normative. If its use is not normative then there cannot be invalid uses of Scripture, which is a rather odd idea since this will mean that two people who use Scripture to make completely contradictory theological claims will both be right.[158] Therefore, affirming and articulating a normative use of Scripture in theology is inevitably necessary. This requires that a multiplicity of factors must be taken into account to have a properly nuanced position – a theological use of Scripture.[159]

Situating Scripture and Its User within the Divine Economy

John Webster argues that the idea and use of Scripture can be understood and approached from two different (not necessarily opposite) economies: the biblical economy and the divine economy. Interpretative approaches that focus exclusively on elements of the biblical text and are reluctant or unable "to trace those elements to their cause in the fullness of God's own life" fall under the first economy.[160] Webster believes that biblical criticism operates in this mode of detaching the text of Scripture from its life-giving principles, thereby resulting in the secularization of biblical science and the naturalization of Protestant theology. Robert Jenson also warns against this "concentration on texts detached from their interweaving with the church's personally embodied continuity."[161] The idea here is this: when Scripture is seen to be merely textual and naturally apprehended by autonomous human reason, thus subjected to methodical examination like any other text using one or more tools of textual analysis (historical, philological, literary, philosophical, canonical, etc.), it ends up being dislocated from its originating and sustaining habitat (the divine economy) thereby losing both its life and its life-giving capacity. Kevin Vanhoozer and Daniel Treier note that if *sola scriptura* would not be construed as *solo scriptura*, then we must treat "theological prolegomena,

---

158. On this point, Vanhoozer notes that "Kelsey seems unaware of the danger of conflating biblical authority with its ecclesial use. Some uses of Scripture may be inappropriate or incorrect." Vanhoozer, *Drama of Doctrine*, 12.

159. Although this study will appropriate John Webster's construal of the theological reading and use of Scripture, this is, to a large extent, the view also explicated in O'Collins and Kendall, *Bible for Theology*, 19.

160. Webster, *Domain of the Word*, viii.

161. Jenson, *Canon and Creed*, 6.

the biblical gospel and the church together by situating all three within the triune economy: the 'collected works' of the triune God."[162] Similarly, Webster argues that to interpret and appropriate Scripture correctly, we must begin with a theological ontology of both biblical writings and human reason as elements in the divine economy.

First, on the theological ontology of biblical writings, Webster believes that there are no metaphysically neutral attitudes to Scripture because "historical criticism is as much a metaphysical as an historical or literary enterprise."[163] Historical criticism is an instance of methodological naturalism – premised on the causal closure of the physical realm – so that it offers (necessarily so) only naturalistic accounts of Scripture. These accounts lack "a conception of the ways in which in the prophets and apostles divine speech takes creaturely form, and assuming that 'creaturely' is interchangeable with 'purely natural,' such accounts of the Bible *exclude from the beginning* the actual conditions under which God's revelation makes itself present."[164] While acknowledging that we cannot completely eradicate this tension (i.e. of the relation of divine word and human word in Scripture), Webster argues that within the divine economy, the human words of Scripture are signs that serve certain things – these things include not only "the historical and religious conditions of their [human words'] production" but also their "primary object of signification, namely, God himself ministering his Word to creatures."[165]

The implication of this for Webster is to read the Bible theologically, listening to it for the divine word that reveals the triune God in Christ Jesus. In other words, "The task of biblical interpretation is a function of the nature of Scripture; the nature of Scripture is a function of its appointment as herald of the self-communicative presence of the risen one."[166] This for Webster is what theological interpretation of Scripture is about; it is interpretation

> informed by a theological description of the nature of the biblical writings and their reception, setting them in the scope of the progress of the saving divine Word through time. Theological

---

162. Vanhoozer and Treier, *Theology and the Mirror*, 14.
163. Webster, *Domain of the Word*, 12.
164. Webster, 9. Emphasis added.
165. Webster, 10.
166. Webster, 32.

interpretation can take many forms, some commentarial, some in other genres; not all theological interpretation is immediately recognizable as such. Theological interpretation is not simply a matter of audience (church rather than scholars of the history and literature of biblical religion); nor is it a kind of topical or thematic interpretation, interspersing commonplaces into exegesis; nor is it necessarily a preference for ancient interpretative practices. It is more a way of reading which is informed by a theologically derived set of interpretative goals, which are governed by a conception of what the Bible is: Holy Scripture, God ministering his Word to human beings through human servants and so sharing with them the inestimable good of knowledge of himself.[167]

The second element crucial to understanding Scripture for Webster is the idea of theological reason. To characterize human reason theologically is simply to think of it as created, fallen, and redeemed and to spell out what that entails for rational fellowship with God – an instance of which is Christian theology. Because human reason is created, "To talk of reason, therefore, we have to talk of God (for example, by a doctrine of the divine image)."[168] In this sense, reason depends on God both for its nature and ends – that it is not self-originating and needs to be oriented by the divine word toward its goal of rational fellowship with God. The idea of human reason as fallen points to a general collapse and corruption in its very structure: "Embroiled in the creature's bid for freedom from the creator, reason loses its orientation to its proper end, and so compromises its goodness. It becomes 'pure' reason, reason on its own; and precisely this is its corruption."[169] Fallen reason is often in flight from fights against (rather than listen and be oriented by) the divine word, thus further descending into the abyss of its own depravity. This state of affairs necessitates redemption, which is the bringing about of a new creaturely nature enlivened by the risen Christ through the Holy Spirit, and this, according to Webster, "restores to reason its orientation to the divine

---

167. Webster, 30.
168. Webster, 124.
169. Webster, 125.

Word and enables it to perform its ministerial role."[170] What is noteworthy in this theological characterization of reason is the fact that, from creation to redemption there is never a point that human reason is not dependent on God for its being and purpose.

How does this impact on the use of Scripture in theology? This is where Webster offers an intriguing account of Christian theology. He asserts,

> Christian theology is biblical reasoning. It is an activity of the created intellect, judged, reconciled, redeemed and sanctified through the works of the Son and the Spirit. More closely, Christian theology is part of reason's answer to the divine Word which addresses creatures through the intelligible service of the prophets and apostles.[171]

In this sense therefore, biblical reasoning is an activity of theological reason, the outcome of which is Christian theology. This activity of biblical reasoning for Webster consists of two parts: exegetical reasoning and dogmatic reasoning.

Exegetical reasoning is the act of reading the Bible, the direct engagement with Scripture in the totality of its textuality in order to figure out what it says. Webster calls this "the intelligent (and therefore spiritual) act of following the words of the text."[172] The idea that exegetical reasoning is an intelligent-spiritual activity follows from Webster's concept of theological reason; when created-fallen-redeemed human reason or regenerate intelligence engages in reading Scripture, such reading is at once rational and spiritual, or rationally spiritual and critically submissive. In this sense, biblical commentary becomes a theological act that seeks to provide a contemplative paraphrase of the text – a cursive representation that "always points back to the text from which alone it draws its substance."[173] In a rather counterintuitive comment, Webster further claims that

> This is the theologically primary act; the principal task of theological reason is figuring out the literal sense, that is, what the

---

170. Webster, 127.
171. Webster, 115.
172. Webster, 130.
173. Webster, 130.

text says. This would be an absurdly naïve claim if the literal sense were thought of merely as information to be retrieved from an inert source in which it had been deposited.[174]

It is in this sense that historical-critical/grammatical reading of Scripture, or what Craig Blomberg calls "*chastened* forms of historical criticism,"[175] becomes a theological practice of seeking to hear the voice of God in and through the words of the human authors of the Bible. Here, one may be able to draw a distinction between hard historical-critical/grammatical method that proceeds from methodological naturalism and the soft historical-critical/grammatical approach of Blomberg (and other evangelical biblical scholars), which admits of both the divine and human authorship of Scripture. Soft historical-critical/grammatical approach therefore, one may say, is *theologically chastened*.

If exegetical reasoning produces a *cursive* representation of Scripture, a constant looking back at the text, then dogmatic reasoning produces "a *conceptual* representation of what reason has learned from its exegetical following of the scriptural text."[176] By conceptual representation Webster refers to the activity of piecing together into a coherent whole the exegetical product of individual texts, abstracting "from the textual surface by creating generalized or summary concepts and ordering them topically."[177] It is "seeing Scripture in its full scope as an unfolding of the one divine economy; seeing its interrelations and canonical unity; seeing its proportions," which in turn "inform exegetical reason as it goes about its work on particular parts of Scripture."[178] Rather than being suspended in a permanent state of seeing only parts, dogmatic reasoning both appropriates and determines the outcome of exegetical reasoning, and the two activities are inseparably joined together in this grand activity Webster calls biblical reasoning – regenerate reason's apprehension of God in response to his self-revelation.

---

174. Webster, 130.
175. Blomberg, "Historical-Critical/Grammatical View," 37. Emphasis added.
176. Webster, *Domain of the Word*, 130.
177. Webster, 131.
178. Webster, 131.

From Theological Interpretation to Theological Theology

If the interpretation of the Bible ought to be theological, how does this impact on the theological task in general? Webster transitions from theological interpretation to *theological theology*. The idea of a theological theology for him is a conception of theology based on the triune God as the operative ontological principle of theology (i.e. the divine economy). This comprehensive explication of the character of theology weaves together accounts of theology's object, its principles, its ends, and its practitioners. First, on theology's object, Webster points out that this is two-fold: the triune God and all things relative to God. Christian theology considers God both absolutely (God in himself) and relatively (God in his relation to creatures). This relativity of God is flipped to provide us with the second aspect of the object of theology, that is, a consideration of all things in relation to God. In this sense, Christian theology is resistant to talking about non-divine things in a non-divine way. Instead, "In talking of non-divine things, theology talks of the effects of God, and does so as an enlargement of its consideration of the outer work of God the origin and cause of all being."[179] However, as creatures who are finite and dependent on God for our knowledge of God both in himself and of his effects, God's knowledge has to be mediated to us.

Consequently, the cognitive principles of theology come next in Webster's account of a theological theology. As noted above, he defines Christian theology as biblical reasoning (call this "the Webster definition" of theology) and biblical reasoning is both exegetical and dogmatic. This process of reasoning for Webster involves a number of activities that must all be construed theologically in order to render theology theological. He writes:

> Theological work involves a range of intellectual acts—acts of reading and interpretation, of historical inquiry, of conceptual abstraction, of practical judgement. *All these different acts will count as theological insofar as they are undertaken in accordance with theology's cognitive principles*, which may be stated thus: the objective cognitive principle of Christian theology is God's infinite knowledge of himself and all things, a share of which

---

179. Webster, "What Makes Theology" 19.

God communicates to creatures; the subjective cognitive principle of Christian theology is regenerate human intelligence.[180]

In this sense, theology's cognitive principle is dependent on its primary matter or object – the triune God. Objectively, a portion of God's infinite knowledge of himself and of all things is shared with rational creatures (through the prophets and apostles) as an act of rational fellowship. Subjectively however, our created rational faculties are fallen and must be "reborn, ordered to right objects, liberated from self-reliance and so set free to begin to operate to their utmost extension."[181]

The corollary of this regeneration of created intelligence is the pursuit of theology toward its proper ends. Webster makes a distinction between the idea of ends (being something natural or intrinsic to a thing) and purpose (a human intention often conditioned by corrupt human desires). "In all domains of human existence and activity, therefore, we are required to exercise vigilance and conform purposes to ends."[182] The ends of Christian theology are scientific (related to information and facts), contemplative (an inner or spiritual attention to God), and practical (implications for and impact on human conduct). These ends of theology redirect the focus of the intellect away from the human self, placing "us in a situation and establish a vocation not of our own invention, to which we are required with divine assistance to conform ourselves, which we must learn to love and take into our intentions."[183] In this way, the ends of theology connect to the practitioners of theology.

On the practitioners of theology, Webster notes that they are obligated to exercise certain virtues; they are called to be studious rather than merely curious. While studiousness emanates from the deep desire of a regenerate intellect, curiosity is an outcome of "the disorder of the intellectual appetite. . . . Curiosity seeks to know created realities without reference to their creator—as phenomena, not as created things—and the process of coming-to-know takes places inordinately, indiscriminately, and pridefully."[184] For theology to be theological therefore, its practitioners must be moved by God – working

---

180. Webster, 20. Emphasis added.
181. Webster, 22.
182. Webster, 23.
183. Webster, 25.
184. Webster, 26.

under the workings of the Son and the Spirit (the missional operations of God), and moved toward God – knowing and acknowledging him.

Webster's theological theology self-consciously seeks to recover from "the cultural and religious history at whose latter end we find ourselves, in the course of which this understanding of the nature of Christian divinity has largely disappeared."[185] This recovery aims to undo the fragmentation and naturalization of Christian theology, and this cannot be accomplished through piecemeal approaches. Instead, "Something more comprehensive is asked of us: a recovery of *sacra doctrina* in its full sense and with its attendant notions of divine instruction, church, holiness, and the like."[186] Vanhoozer makes a similar claim for such comprehensiveness in executing the task of Christian theology. He says,

> We must not think about God—at least not for very long—apart from the authorized witness of Scripture. Similarly, we must not think about Scripture—again, at least not for very long—apart from its divine author and central subject matter. Nor must we think about hermeneutics—about interpreting Scripture—apart from Christian doctrine or biblical exegesis.[187]

Conclusion

The history of the interpretation of Scripture is quite instructive for discerning how well to read Scripture in contemporary theology. This chapter has shown that the use of Scripture in Christian theology has come full circle. The New Testament use of the Old Testament was inspired and informed by the identity of Christ as Israel's Messiah and God in human form. The Old Testament was appropriated to authorize and proclaim this mystery that was once hidden but made known through the apostles. This is nothing less than a theological use of the Old Testament. Patristic, medieval, and Reformation users of Scripture continued this practice while expanding the different senses

---

185. Webster, 27.
186. Webster, 28.
187. Vanhoozer, *First Theology*, 10.

of Scripture and deploying the intellectual furniture of their time ministerially for the theological task.

However, the Enlightenment/modern era accorded a magisterial role to human reason, especially the tools of historical criticism, and sought to free the Bible from its theological underpinnings. Many treated the Bible as nothing more than a collection of ancient texts that needed to be explicated critically. Those who still had use for it appropriated it rationally so as to accommodate its ancient strange content to the prevailing realities of human existence. The trouble however was the fact that attempts to appropriate the Bible in universalized and objectivized ways could not be sustained in a postmodern intellectual climate. The need for a theological appropriation of the Bible now became more obvious, reasonable, and possible as many, like Webster, have demonstrated.

In view of the foregoing, we are ready to explore in the next chapter the place and use of Scripture in contemporary analytic theology – chapter 4 will address the same issue with respect to contextual theology. In other words, we will be seeking to understand how Scripture is used in analytic theology and how it compares to Webster's proposal. In addition, is analytic theology theological as explicated above? The next chapter attends to these and other questions focusing primarily on how a theological view and use of Scripture might shape the nature and practice of analytic theology such that it is poised to benefit the task of global theology, with particular focus on Christology.

CHAPTER 3

Using Scripture in Analytic Theology

The previous chapter narrated (albeit roughly) a story of the interpretation and use of Scripture in theology and, borrowing from John Webster, concluded with an account of Scripture that situates it within the divine economy. This account construed Scripture's ontology and teleology as God's word by which he shares with humans part of his infinite knowledge – that of himself and of all things relative to him – so as to make rational human fellowship with him possible. From this, theology emerges as theological insofar as God is its primary object, his shared knowledge through the prophets and apostles its cognitive principle, its ends leading back to God, and that it is practiced through regenerate human intelligence. With this account of theology in mind, the present chapter explores the field of analytic theology as a theological discipline. What exactly is analytic theology? What are its aims and methods? What contributions can or does it make to Christian theology in general, and by extension for purposes of this project, what potential benefits does it provide for the task of global theology in particular? What might hinder or limit these benefits, and how might analytic theology be bolstered so as to remedy such hindrances?

This chapter attempts to answer these questions with the aim of demonstrating that analytic theology needs to be apprenticed under the theological use of Scripture both for it to be adequately theological and beneficial for the task of global theologizing. To do this, the story of analytic theology is first narrated quite briefly; then its nature and method, as widely held and exemplified by its proponents and practitioners, is explicated. Next, we explore the use of Scripture in Christian analytic philosophical theology in general, and then (more precisely) in some select Christology-related discourses of

73

Oliver Crisp and Thomas McCall. At the end of the chapter, I hope to show what exactly makes analytic theology deficient as a comprehensive approach to the theological task, and to also point out how it might be strengthened through an interaction with the theological use of Scripture so as to serve global theology and the global church.

Understanding Analytic Theology: Its Story

Nicholas Wolterstorff explains that contemporary analytic philosophical theology started budding when the branch of logical positivism began to die. Another reason was the emergence of what Wolterstorff calls meta-epistemology. These two factors resulted in the rise of the philosophy of religion and consequently the very possibility of analytic philosophical theology.[1]

Logical positivism – the view that a claim is only meaningful if, and only if, it is analytically true or false or empirically verifiable – dominated the philosophical landscape in the 1950s. For the logical positivist,

> only empirical statements refer to genuinely theoretical content and are about reality; metaphysical and theological statements, by contrast, may express "only" an existential attitude toward life. In this sense, they have meaning in the sense of being able to influence one's feelings, beliefs, or behavior but not in the sense of being true or false.[2]

This backdrop made philosophical theology impossible because the limits of what is sensibly assertible (even if thinkable) were delineated by these conditions and these conditions only; such that any form of metaphysical and theological claim or knowledge or discourse was considered merely conjectural or out-rightly nonsensical. However, "the positivists found it impossible to articulate, even to their own satisfaction, the concept of *empirical verifiability*; that inability proved to be their downfall. The death of the movement meant

---

1. Wolterstorff, "How Philosophical Theology Became Possible," 156. Wolterstorff points out that there are two major historical developments which made analytic theology possible; these are: the fact that analytic philosophers gave up on certain assumptions characteristic of modern philosophy; and two, the emergence of a new self-understanding of the task and role of philosophy.

2. Gasser, "Toward Analytic Theology," 25.

that a formidable obstacle to the development of philosophical theology had been removed from the scene."[3]

However, the demise of logical positivism was only a necessary condition for analytic philosophical theology to be possible, but it was not sufficient in and of itself. Another important factor was the rethinking of philosophy's task and role in culture identified by Wolterstorff as meta-epistemology, which emerged in the 1960s within the analytic tradition. Here is why this is important: while medieval philosophers held that we simply need reasons for our beliefs (e.g. about God) to be rational, modern philosophy, Wolterstorff notes, raised the stakes much higher by insisting that our reasons must be grounded in certitude; that only certain reason can allow a given belief to be held rationally and responsibly, making it difficult for metaphysical claims to qualify as true beliefs.[4] But meta-epistemologists faulted this preoccupation with certain evidence as an untenable theory of knowledge.[5] Its untenability for analytic philosophers was primarily attributed to the fact that it is self-referentially defeating – that is, it has to be false for it to be true or that it leads to an infinitum of foundational beliefs. Naming it classical foundationalism, meta-epistemologists began to show that it is just one out of a number of plausible epistemological theories, thus the emergence of epistemological pluralism – the belief that besides classical foundationalism, other epistemological theories (e.g. coherentism) or other forms of foundationalism might indeed be plausible. The implication for the philosophy of religion was that one could hold theistic beliefs responsibly (just like our everyday beliefs) without having to first (and necessarily) justify or ground such beliefs in certain evidence.[6]

Consequently, some Christian philosophers like Alvin Plantinga endeavored to demonstrate that theistic beliefs indeed can be considered as properly basic beliefs, in the same sense as our perceptions, such that they need not be justified before one can responsibly and rationally affirm them.[7] In this sense, if someone were to argue by appeal to a given epistemological theory

---

3. Wolterstorff, "How Philosophical Theology Became Possible," 157.
4. Wolterstorff, 159.
5. Wolterstorff, 160.
6. Wolterstorff, 160.
7. This seminal idea would form the crux of what came to be known as reformed epistemology. See Plantinga, *Warranted Christian Belief*.

that theistic beliefs of the everyday are irrational, "it will be at least rational for the believer to retain her conviction concerning the acceptability of her theistic belief and reject the theory, as to accept the theory and give up that conviction."[8] This development in the wider analytic philosophical tradition led to the emergence of the philosophy of religion in the 1970s.

From Analytic Philosophy of Religion to Analytic Philosophical Theology

To restate, the shift away from both empirical verificationism and classical foundationalism meant that philosophers could engage in philosophical reflections about religious claims/concepts without hindrance. This opportunity was vigorously seized and pursued by Christian analytic philosophers in the Anglo-American context more than anywhere else, and this is largely due to "the sociological fact that a good many American philosophers are theists, Christian and Jewish especially."[9] In particular, Christian philosophers working in this tradition began to engage in robust philosophical discussions on the concept of God, theodicy, and the possibility of miracles, thereby heralding a flood of philosophically sophisticated and theologically relevant writings.

Some of these philosophers went a step further and began exploring particular doctrines of Christian theology (e.g. the Trinity, Christology, etc.) with the tools of analytic philosophy – a practice akin to the one that thrived in medieval scholasticism.[10] At this initial point, analytic philosophical theology was the exclusive domain of Christian analytic philosophers of religion, such that there was neither any difference, nor the need to speak of it, between analytic philosophy of religion and analytic philosophical theology. In fact, Georg Gasser thinks that, as an outgrowth of analytic philosophy, analytic theology need not be distinguished from its ancestor since "there is no clear conceptual differentiation to hand, and it seems insignificant to demand one."[11]

---

8. Plantinga, 161.

9. Plantinga, 162.

10. While analytic theology is not identical to scholastic theology, the similarity between the two is unmistakable and has been acknowledged by some analytic theologians. See for example McCall, *Analytic Christian Theology*, 22. This similarity (and dissimilarity), in my opinion, needs to be further spelled out.

11. Gasser, "Toward Analytic Theology," 23.

However, the last decade has witnessed a growing number of trained theologians taking up this approach in earnest, thereby birthing a more theologically informed kind of analytic theology. Nevertheless, the dividing line between the two disciplines remains faint. Max Baker-Hytch has suggested that the most crucial difference-making element between analytic theology and analytic philosophy of religion is not that of intellectual tradition, since the "overlap between the practitioners of the two is very large at present and hence they can scarcely be said to constitute distinct intellectual traditions," neither will their difference be found "at the level of subject matter" since that is obviously not the case (with discussions on the concept of God, Christology, and atonement as examples).[12] He claims instead that the difference hinges on the additional appeal that analytic theology makes to Scripture and ecclesial tradition. The extent of such appeal determines the degree to which analytic theology differs from analytic philosophy of religion such that "several forms of analytic theology" can be exemplified, "each of which differ from one another with respect to the epistemological status that they accord to scripture and tradition."[13] This distinction is significant if it must be conceded that the analytic theologian is actually doing theology rather than just philosophy. But more importantly, it underscores the fact that the place and use of Scripture in analytic theology deserves close attention if we are to better understand and define its theological status (more on this later in the chapter). For now, we will examine the nature and method of analytic theology in order to better understand it.

Understanding Analytic Theology: Its Nature and Method

Thomas McCall describes analytic theology (AT hereafter) as "a growing and energetic field at the intersections of philosophy of religion and systematic theology."[14] William J. Abraham defines it as "systematic theology attuned to the deployment of the skills, resources, and virtues of analytic philosophy. It is the articulation of the central themes of Christian teaching *illuminated by the*

---

12. Baker-Hytch, "Analytic Theology," 349–50.
13. Baker-Hytch, 359.
14. McCall, *Analytic Christian Theology*, 16.

insights of analytic philosophy."[15] Also, Oliver Crisp thinks of it as "primarily a faith-seeking-understanding project, where 'metaphysical' analysis is the means by which theologians *make sense* of what they already believe."[16] AT, generally speaking then, may be considered as the noble efforts of Christian philosophers (and some theologians) to engage the doctrines of Christian theology using the analytic philosophical method. Michael Rea explicitly says that "analytic theology is just the activity of approaching theological topics with the ambitions of an analytic philosopher and in a style that conforms to the prescriptions that are distinctive of analytic philosophical discourse."[17]

AT therefore leans on the methodology of Anglo-American analytic philosophy, which is usually distinguished from continental philosophy (so-called). According to Thomas Flint and Michael Rea,

> The analytic tradition has, by and large, treated philosophy as an explanatory enterprise aimed at analyzing fundamental concepts ("person," "action," "law," etc), and at using this analytic method to clarify and extend the theoretical work being done in the natural sciences. The Continental tradition, on the other hand, has viewed philosophy as an autonomous discipline aimed, more or less, at exploring and promoting our understanding of the human condition in creative and decidedly non-scientific (and not even mostly explanatory-theoretical) ways.[18]

While the continental approach prevails in most of Europe, "philosophy in the English-speaking world is dominated by analytic approaches to its problems and projects."[19]

However, one may ask for more clarity: what precisely are the key features that clearly delineate the analytic tradition? In other words, what makes the analytic tradition analytic? Michael Rea identifies these key delineating features to be the ambitions and the style of the analytic approach. These ambitions are: "(i) to identify the scope and limits of our powers to obtain knowledge of the world, and (ii) to provide such true explanatory theories

---

15. Abraham, "Systematic Theology," 54. Emphasis added.
16. Crisp, "On Analytic Theology," 51. Emphasis added.
17. Rea, "Introduction," 7.
18. Flint and Rea, "Introduction," in *Oxford Handbook of Philosophical Theology*, 2.
19. Rea, "Introduction," 1.

as we can in areas of inquiry (metaphysics, morals, and the like) that fall outside the scope of the natural sciences."[20] Clearly the first of these ambitions is epistemological while the second is metaphysical/ethical. The epistemological ambition accepts the fact that classical foundationalism (source foundationalism) is untenable given its impossible search for indubitable and incorrigible knowledge; but this does not translate into a wholesale rejection of foundationalism simpliciter (doxastic foundationalism).[21] The metaphysical/ethical ambition explicates issues from both a "local" (particulars) and a "global" (universals) dimension, which means that analytic philosophy can be carried out in both the nominalist and the realist mode respectively. For Oliver Crisp, this metaphysical ambition is of greater importance to analytic theology than the epistemological one. He writes: "In short, the main task of analytic theology as it has been characterized thus far is primarily metaphysical. If it is a project that deals with epistemological matters, these are secondary to its primary goal."[22]

Turning to the rhetorical style of analytic philosophy, Rea advances five prescriptions that a standard analytic work generally exemplifies:

P1. Write as if philosophical positions and conclusions can be adequately formulated in sentences that can be formalized and logically manipulated.

P2. Prioritize precision, clarity, and logical coherence.

P3. Avoid substantive (non-decorative) use of metaphor and other tropes whose semantic content outstrips their propositional content.

P4. Work as much as possible with well-understood primitive concepts, and concepts that can be analyzed in terms of those.

---

20. Rea, 4.

21. Rea thinks that very few authors make this distinction when attacking foundationalism. While identifying source foundationalism as basically either rationalism or empiricism, he argued that: "Doxastic foundationalism is the (entirely commonsensical, even if not universally held) view that some of our beliefs are *properly basic*. Basic beliefs are those that are based on other beliefs. Properly basic beliefs are those that are rationally or justifiably held in the basic way." He mentions perceptual beliefs as an example of a properly basic belief because it is based on experience rather than on other beliefs. Rea, "Introduction," 12.

22. Crisp, "On Analytic Theology," 51.

P5. Treat conceptual analysis (insofar as it is possible) as a source of evidence.[23]

Rea is however cautious and thus posits a disclaimer to the effect that these prescriptions in no way make "claim to either completeness or universality."[24] Again, while this style may have some aesthetic appeal, it is primarily tailored toward getting at the truth of the matter as close as possible, and to explicate it as clearly as possible. In this sense therefore, the style of analytic philosophy serves its ambitions.

This is the sense in which AT is analytic (i.e. it employs the analytic style and seeks to realize these stated analytic ambitions – secondarily for Crisp). At this point, the natural question to ask is, what makes AT theology or theological? Granted that the purpose of AT as noted above is to help clarify certain conceptual conundrums inherent in particular Christian doctrines, which the analytic theologian already believes. However, the question is whether this is sufficient (or even necessary) for AT to be theological. In other words, is AT (or any theology for that matter) theological merely by virtue of the content or substance of its discourse?

Non-Substantive and Substantive Analytic Theology

One may wish to note that AT (like any other academic enterprise) is not necessarily homogenous. Different practitioners of AT have different ways of viewing and characterizing it; that is, what exactly it is and what precisely they see themselves to be doing varies. There are those who construe AT as carrying no substantive commitments. Michael Rea's characterization of AT is an excellent representation of such an account. On this construal, AT is an approach that can be employed in doing any kind of theology (Jewish, Muslim, Buddhist, etc.) and not just Christian theology. As such, it does not come to the theological task with any underlying Christian assumptions (or some other religious or non-religious assumptions for that matter), but seeks to explicate these with certain tools and the same degree of rigor.[25] While it is true that AT seeks to do that, this view of AT seems to assume that method is a theology free zone, which is not the case as already seen in chapter 2.

---

23. Rea, "Introduction," 5.
24. Rea, 5.
25. See for example Flint and Rea, *Oxford Handbook of Philosophical Theology*.

There are others however who pursue AT as a procedural task with substantive commitments. Oliver Crisp, for example, thinks of the procedural aspect of AT as the instrumental use of reason, drawing from both the ambitions and the style of the analytic tradition, while its substantive component is basically the content of orthodox Christian beliefs. He states as follows:

> On this way of thinking, reason is a tool for establishing the logical connections between different propositions, for distinguishing what I am talking about from what I am not, and whether what I am saying makes sense, or is coherent. Such reasoning also enables me to consider the validity of a particular argument that is put forward, and whether or not it is subject to less obvious defects of reasoning, like question-begging or affirming the consequent, and so on.[26]

In addition, he argues that such instrumental use of reason does not only tease out a given doctrine's internal logic but carries with it substantive implications. He says,

> If I argue that the internal logic of a particular construal of Chalcedonian Christology is internally consistent, that will have implications for other doctrines, such as the Trinity. It will also have implications for wider issues, such as realism and anti-realism, or scepticism about metaphysical truth. Thus, even this modest use of reason raises issues beyond that of the coherence of particular doctrines, including within its scope matters that are properly apologetic, or prolegomenal.[27]

Crisp is explicit about the fact that AT subscribes to a descriptive metaphysics with regards to Christian doctrine rather than a revisionist commitment. One may therefore say that Crisp's construal of AT is intentional about upholding and clarifying Christian doctrine and tradition. He argues in another place that AT can be carried out as systematic theology (ST) insofar as it meets the threshold of the shared task of systematic theology, which he defines as:

---

26. Crisp, "On Analytic Theology," 41.
27. Crisp, 42.

> Commitment to an intellectual undertaking that involves (though it may not comprise) explicating the conceptual content of the Christian tradition (with the expectation that this is normally done from a position within that tradition, as an adherent of that tradition), using particular religious texts that are part of the Christian tradition, including sacred scripture, as well as human reason, reflection, and praxis (particularly religious practices), as sources for theological judgments.[28]

It is in this sense that Crisp articulates an aspiration: "AT as ST *is a way of doing ST that utilizes the tools and methods of contemporary analytic philosophy for the purposes of constructive Christian theology, paying attention to the Christian tradition and development of doctrine.* That sounds like a properly 'theological theology' to me."[29] The idea here is that AT qualifies as theological to the extent that it explicates the Christian tradition internally using the tradition's sources of theological knowledge.

This construal of AT seems to cohere quite well with Webster's vision of a theological theology, clearly noting the need to use Scripture in doing AT. The question however, is whether analytic theologians do indeed use Scripture in their actual practice of AT. Do the ambitions and style of AT allow for the use of Scripture in this mode of doing theology? What might such use of Scripture look like, and is it adequate for doing theology theologically?

The Use of Scripture in Analytic Theology: Revelational Control

Thomas V. Morris has articulated a method for perfect being theology that yields "a *philosophically adequate*, as well as a *biblically responsible*, concept of God."[30] Following Anselm's idea of God as that than which none greater can be conceived, perfect being theology posits that "God is to be thought of as *the greatest possible being*, an individual exhibiting *maximal perfection*."[31] The attractiveness of this approach for Morris is that it is generic such that

---

28. Crisp, "Analytic Theology as Systematic," 160.
29. Crisp, 165. Emphasis in original.
30. Morris, *Our Idea of God*, 45. Emphasis added.
31. Morris, 35. Emphasis in original.

it provides us with a non-arbitrary starting point. Therefore, "it is more like the main element in a recipe for cooking up our idea of God in detail."[32] With this main element in place we can then proceed with the details of predicating great-making properties on God. Morris defines a great-making property as "any property, or attribute, or characteristic, or quality which it is intrinsically good to have, any property which endows its bearer with some measure of value, or greatness, or metaphysical stature, regardless of external circumstances."[33] The distinction of the intrinsic nature of these great-making properties as opposed to an extrinsic-type property is critical to how the greatest possible being is great – that is, that he is not great in virtue of something outside of himself because that thing will then have to be greater.

Having established that fact, the next step in this process of "cooking up our idea of God in detail" employs the use of our value intuitions about what basic properties are great-making properties. Here, intuition is taken to mean natural judgment, and indeed, one of "our most basic judgments about the world around us."[34] The process takes off in an ascending order by proposing the least controversial great-making property, and then stacks up the deck with an array of great-making properties until we have a fuller and better concept of what a maximally perfect or great God ought to look like. So, for example, we can think of God as:

1. conscious (a minded being capable of and engaged in states of thought and awareness),
2. a conscious free agent (a being capable of free action),
3. a thoroughly benevolent, conscious agent,
4. a thoroughly benevolent conscious agent with significant knowledge,
5. a thoroughly benevolent conscious agent with significant knowledge and power,
6. a thoroughly benevolent conscious agent with unlimited knowledge and power, who is the creative source of all else,

---

32. Morris, 35.
33. Morris, 35.
34. Morris, 39.

7. a thoroughly benevolent conscious agent with unlimited knowledge and power who is the necessarily existent, ontologically independent creative source of all else.[35]

At this point, one may object that our value intuitions cannot possibly capture all of the great-making properties that are necessary for a maximally great God to have. Morris is not oblivious of this problem and therefore asserts: "It is quite plausible to think that if there were any such divine attributes that would be important for us to know of, and yet which are such as to slip through the net of our intuitions and of our explanatory needs, *God would reveal them to us*."[36] Not only that we are open to missing out on some great-making properties, but also that "it is possible for our value intuitions to be skewed or distorted by a dominant or powerful philosophical tradition."[37] Given this possibility of completely missing or somehow distorting one or more great-making properties, Morris proposes what he calls a revelational control in his method of perfect being theology. By revelational control, he simply means that a "well-attested data from revelation should be allowed to overturn or correct, contrary value intuitions."[38] The overarching motivation for assigning this function to Scripture is as follows:

> The challenge for the Christian philosopher or theologian should not be that of confining what he says about God to what the Bible has already said, but rather it should be that of constructing a philosophical theology which is thoroughly consonant with the biblical portrayal of God. What should be sought are not just philosophical ideas which happen to be logically consistent, or minimally compatible, with the biblical materials, but rather ideas which are deeply attuned to the biblical revelation, and thus consonant with the whole tenor of the Bible.[39]

This, perhaps, is the most robust and straightforward articulation of Scripture's role in philosophical theology advanced by any Christian analytic philosopher or theologian. It is a very attractive proposal given its clear

---

35. Morris, 40.
36. Morris, 42. Emphasis added.
37. Morris, 43.
38. Morris, 43.
39. Morris, 31.

insistence on ideas that are "deeply attuned" to, and in "consonant with the whole tenor" of Scripture. One cannot miss the clear, indeed commendable, deference to Scripture firmly embedded in Morris's approach to Scripture's role in analytic philosophical theology. It is not surprising therefore that many Christian analytic theologians continue to work with or are sympathetic toward it. Thomas McCall, for example, commends this approach in saying, "Analytic theology—whether occurring as 'natural analytic theology,' 'perfect being analytic theology,' 'Barthian analytic theology' or as some eclectic combination—*needs 'revelational control' if it is to be genuine Christian theology.*"[40]

However, it seems one would not be wrong to suggest that Morris's use of Scripture is rather thin or minimalist. This is because our concept of God on this approach is not necessarily authorized by Scripture but only needs to be complemented by Scripture. This point is underscored by Kevin J. Vanhoozer when he said, "Modern philosophical theism takes its marching orders not from the canon but from the concept of a being of infinite perfection."[41] The problem is further highlighted by the challenge of divine hiddenness as Pseudo-Dionysius suggests:

> Mind beyond mind, word beyond speech, it is gathered up by no discourse, *by no intuition*, by no name. It is and it is as no other being is. Cause of all existence, and therefore itself transcending existence, *it alone could give an authoritative account of what it really is.*[42]

The point is that given divine transcendence and human finitude, the intrinsic nature of God is not possibly accessible to human ken and intuition, thus the necessity of divine self-revelation as our first recourse rather than our final resort (e.g. after we have missed or distorted some great-making property) in doing theology.

This is not saying that we cannot predicate anything of God, but that, *pace* Morris, just using our value intuitions to assemble a list of great-making properties that we can then predicate of God is inadequate for authorizing our God-claims. Yes, since God has designed us to have these intuitions, we

---

40. McCall, *Analytic Christian Theology*, 55. Emphasis added.
41. Vanhoozer, *Remythologizing*, 94.
42. Pseudo-Dionysius, *Complete Works*, 50. Emphasis added.

need not treat them with suspicion only, but "be grateful for them and treat them as evidence."[43] Nevertheless, it is difficult to see how such an approach can be sustained in the face of what Vanhoozer calls the Feuerbachian projection – the claim, originally by Ludwig Feuerbach, that all predications of God stem from the religious impulse to divinize our human qualities. It turns out on this view that "God is thus humanity writ large."[44] On a purely naturalistic view of Scripture as a wholly culturally-conditioned human document, even predications of God from Scripture cannot escape this charge. But if one takes Scripture to be God's revelation (as Morris clearly holds), then assigning it a merely controlling function seems minimalistic. Instead of speaking of just revelational control then, what if we think more in terms of revelational authorization?[45] David Kelsey quite rightly asserts that, "In the making of theological proposals, Scripture is to be used in such a way that it helps somehow to authorize the proposals."[46] This, perhaps, is the primal or most visible test of a theology that is Christian.

Authorization, as I am thinking of it, requires that our concept of God is authored, that is originates (and shown to originate) from Scripture. While revelational control begins with a rather generic concept of God and uses Scripture to check it for error, revelational authorization – in keeping with Webster's account of theology as theological – begins with what God says of himself and all things relative to him, before (where necessary) using metaphysical analysis to parse it out. Vanhoozer makes the same claim as follows, "A distinctly Christian concept of God must derive its content 'not simply from general metaphysical intuitions, however, but from unique, contingent things that God has done in history and, in particular, in Jesus Christ.'"[47] Therefore, the idea of revelational authorization recommended here for doing analytic theology as Christian theology is one that takes seriously the

---

43. McCall, *Analytic Christian Theology*, 48.

44. Vanhoozer, *Remythologizing*, 19.

45. Thomas McCall does not draw any distinction between these two notions and thus seems to imply (even if subtly) that revelational control is the same as biblical authorization. See his discussion in McCall, *Analytic Christian Theology*, 55. However, I do think that a distinction can be drawn between the two on the basis of the starting point of each.

46. Kelsey, *Proving Doctrine*, 109.

47. Vanhoozer, *Remythologizing*, 95.

theological use of Scripture for the theological task.[48] But is this what analytic theologians actually do? To find out, we will now consider the works of some analytic theologians qua theologians. We will attend primarily to some of their discussions on Christology with the aim of seeing if and how Scripture is used to authorize (or control?) their understanding of the person of Christ.

Explicating the Person of Christ in Analytic Theological Discourse

Oliver Crisp on the Anhypostasia and Enhypostasia Distinction

The Council of Chalcedon 451 held that Christ is one person or hypostasis, who is both fully God and fully human – thus the hypostatic union. For Thomas F. Torrance, since Christ was already God before he became man, it simply means that "The crucial factor here is the meaning of the 'human nature' of Christ."[49] Yet, it is impossible to discuss his human nature in and of itself without reference to the divine nature.[50] It seems then that, if we must understand the person of Christ, the status of the human nature of Christ vis-à-vis his divine nature must be fully articulated. Generally speaking, therefore, what is a human nature and how does it relate to the idea of a human person? In what sense can we speak of Christ as having a complete human nature and also being a complete human person that is at once a divine person?

---

48. The difference of revelational control and revelational authorization might also underscore the different attitudes that Christian analytic philosophers bring to theological discourse from those of their peers who are originally trained as theologians. See for example the very different outlook of Thomas V. Morris' *The Logic of God Incarnate* and Oliver Crisp's *God Incarnate* even though both are projects in analytic Christology.

49. Torrance, *Incarnation*, 201.

50. As Richard Norris points out,
    Orthodoxy consists in the acknowledgment that Jesus is one subject, who is properly spoken of both as God – the divine Logos – and as a human being. To give an account of Jesus, then, one must talk in two ways simultaneously. One must account for all that he is and does by reference to the Logos of God, that is, one must identify him as God acting in our midst. At the same time, however, one must account for him as a human being in the ordinary sense of that term. Both accounts are necessary. One cannot understand Jesus correctly by taking either account independently, even while recognizing that they really are different accounts.
Norris, *Christological Controversy*, 31.

This is where the anhypostasia and enhypostasia distinction proves to be a highly effective conceptual framework for our understanding of the hypostatic union. It focuses on the human nature of Christ as the "crucial factor" in the discussion while fully referencing the divine nature whether implicitly or explicitly. Crisp expresses the formula thus, "the human nature assumed by the second person of the Trinity, though never a person as such (independent of the Word), exists 'in' the *hypostasis* or person of the Word and is thereby 'personalized' (that is, *hypostatized*) by the Word."[51] Anhypostasia underscores the claim that the human nature of Christ has no independent existence or subsistence, which means that it is not an individual hypostasis. Rather, the human nature of Christ is (is thought of as) first of all impersonal or anhypostatos. But this claim unarguably seems counterintuitive even apparently untrue; especially so when we take into account the fact that, for Jesus to be a complete human person he had to possess both a human body and a rational soul.[52] It seems then that, either his human nature is an independent human person or the body-soul composite is not sufficient for grounding human personhood.

Crisp therefore suggests that there are two levels at which we might proceed with an explication of the human nature of Christ. The first focuses on how we should understand nature. Here, we can make a distinction between two views of nature: a concrete-nature view (nature as a concrete particular) and an abstract-nature view (nature as a property). "The important difference between concrete- and abstract-nature views of Christ's humanity on this matter is that the advocate of a concrete-nature view thinks that the human nature of Christ is a concrete particular assumed by the Word, not just a

---

51. Crisp, *Divinity and Humanity*, 72–73. Torrance thinks that this distinction "actually goes back to Cyril of Alexandria, *Contra Theodoretum*." However, it is widely thought to have been well articulated by Leontius of Byzantium who used it to rebut "the idea held by extreme Antiochenes that the human nature of Christ had an independent *hypostasis*." Then in the early seventeenth century, Robert Boyd further developed it. Torrance, *Incarnation*, 84. In recent theology, Karl Barth is credited with both recovering and appropriating it. Shults, "Dubious Christological Formula," 431.

52. On this, Cyril of Alexandria said, "We must admit, of course, that the body which he united to himself was endowed with a rational soul, for the Word, who is God, would hardly neglect our finer part, the soul, and have regard only for the earthly body. Quite clearly in all wisdom he provided for both the soul and the body." St. Cyril of Alexandria, *On the Unity of Christ*, 64.

property possessed by the Word."[53] The second level issue is on the parts or components (not nature) that Christ is made up of. Here again there are two positions. The first asserts a two-part Christology – that Christ is composed of the Word and a human body only; in which case, the Word becomes (and not just plays the role of) a human soul. The second holds to a three-part Christology and claims that Christ is the union of the Word and a human body-plus-soul composite. The interaction of these issues will provide clarity for anhypostasia and, by extension, on the human nature of Christ.

According to Crisp, the abstract-nature view has two versions and he thinks that both of them are problematic. The first is the Alvinized Version (named after Alvin Plantinga) and it holds that "In addition to having a divine nature, the Word becomes a human soul by assuming the property of human nature."[54] This version obviously adopts a two-parts Christology with the Word becoming a human soul in virtue of its exemplification of the property of human nature. The Reaified Version (named after Michael Rea) claims that "The Word stands in a certain relation to the body of Christ assumed at the Incarnation, which makes the Word the soul of the body of Christ."[55] This claim clearly construes Jesus's soul in a functionalist way and presupposes a two-parts Christology, since there is no additional substance involved in the interaction.

Consequently, a major problem for the abstract-nature view is that there is no substantial distinction between the Word and the human soul of Jesus since the Word becomes the soul of Christ's body in virtue of either instantiating the property of human nature (Alvinized) or standing in a soul-functioning relation to Christ's human body (Reaified). Crisp is careful to note however that these versions of the abstract-nature view as explicated are not identical to Apollinarianism. This is because the latter claims that there is no need for a distinctly human soul in Christ, thus the Word replaces it; while the former (both Alvinized and Reaified views) affirm the need for a human soul in Christ but argue that the Word becomes or functions as the human soul of Christ. Even so, the abstract-nature view on both versions turns out to be monothelitic because it is not possible to have more than one will in

---

53. Crisp, *Divinity and Humanity*, 46.
54. Crisp, 46.
55. Crisp, 58.

Christ when it is the Word that acts as Jesus's human soul. Given that monothelitism was condemned by the Council of Constantinople in AD 680–1, Crisp concludes that the abstract-nature view, though not Apollinarian still lacks a thoroughly orthodox outlook.

The concrete-nature view of the human nature of Christ can also be articulated in two possible ways. The first way is to say that: when composed of body plus soul, a human zygote exemplifies the property of being an individual human person "unless assumed by a divine person."[56] The second way to construe it is to claim that "if a human body-soul composite usually comprises an individual person, in the case of the Incarnation, the body and soul of Christ are conjoined with the soul of the Word to form a 'larger' person."[57] Since to have properties is not identical with being a property (e.g. on Alvinized abstract-nature view), it follows that though the human nature of Christ still has properties (e.g. of being the human nature of Christ) it is a concrete particular rather than a property.

The key idea in both ways of articulating the concrete-nature view is that, while in the case of all human beings the body-soul composite results into a human person, such a state of affairs failed to obtain in the incarnation of the Word and this is due to the fact that a preexisting divine person was assuming the particular human nature (i.e. the body-soul composite) that came into existence at that point in time. It is by virtue of assumption therefore that the particular body-soul composite failed to become an independent human person from the person of the Word. In this sense therefore, the Word becomes a human being (John 1:14). Crisp thinks that both ways are consistent with dyothelitism – the view that Christ had two wills, as affirmed at Constantinople 680–81. He therefore supports as orthodox a concrete-nature view of the human nature of Christ on a three-parts Christology.

On any version of abstract-nature view it is difficult to see how the human nature of Christ is distinctly anhypostatic or impersonal if there exists independently of human beings the property "human nature." If human nature is a universal, thus something impersonal that all human beings instantiate or personalize, then,

---

56. Crisp, 64.
57. Crisp, 64.

> The human nature assumed by Christ is impersonal (the way the *anhypostatos* is often construed in the literature), because all human natures are impersonal.... (So this is not something peculiar about the human nature of Christ and seems a rather unimportant point to make such theological mileage out of.)[58]

On this account, there is not much sense in saying that the human nature of Christ was hypostatized, which then makes the hypostatic union trivial. Crisp takes this to an oversimplification of the matter from a theological point of view. Matters do not get any better when we factor in two-part Christology, because the Word's "ensoulment" (so to speak) of Jesus's body turns out to just be identical with hypostatization.

On the other hand, the concrete-nature view on a three-part Christology seems to provide a more theologically satisfying as well as a philosophically adequate way of speaking about the human nature of Christ as anhypostatos. It begins from the claim that human nature does not exist independently of human beings, and then affirms what is evident in Scripture – that Christ has both a human and a divine nature on account of the incarnation. Consequently, "The concrete particular that is the human nature of Christ *does not* [rather than cannot] exist independently of the person of Christ."[59] This particular human nature was not a human person prior to the incarnation, because if the human nature of Christ was personal then a unity of two persons rather than two natures would have occurred. But on what account then is Christ a perfectly human person given the impersonal (anhypostatos) nature of his human nature? Here lies the need for enhypostasia.

Enhypostasia is the claim that the impersonal human nature of Christ is personalized (enhypostatized) by the person of the divine Logos who unites it with his divine nature in his one hypostasis. "It becomes a human person on its *assumption* by the Word."[60] Assumption here is in the sense of addition or incorporation rather than inhabitation or occupation – that is, a second nature (human) is added into an already existing person (the Word) and united to his already existing or original nature (divine). Unless there is such an assumption (thus enhypostasia), it seems the hypostatic union

---

58. Crisp, 77.
59. Crisp, 80. Emphasis added.
60. Crisp, 61. Emphasis added.

would have been unnecessary and the incarnation unrealized. The hypostatic union becomes unnecessary just in case it is not a pre-existing divine person that is "incarnationally" conceived by the Holy Spirit in the womb of Mary as Crisp argues:

1. Possibly, the Holy Spirit specially creates a human body-soul composite (i.e. human nature), via parthenogenesis in the womb of Mary, *that is not assumed* by the Word.
2. This human nature constitutes "part" of Christ only if it is hypostatically united with the person of the Word.
3. So, the human person generated by this process is not "part" of [Christ] the God-man.[61]

We end up with a different person who might have been born in Bethlehem by Mary and named Jesus of Nazareth but who would still not be the Christ as it were.

What follows then is the fact that the Logos remained what and who he has always been pre-incarnation – a divine person on account of his divine nature. But by virtue of the assumption – personalizing an impersonal human nature into his person – he becomes a perfectly human person as well. He already had personhood, so that he did not need to add another one, but only needed to add what he did not have (a human nature), thus becoming a divine and a human person at once. Enhypostatization therefore is accomplished by an act of assuming or adding of the impersonal human nature into union with the original divine nature of the Logos in his one person. Crisp captures it well:

> It is the Word who exists in some sense "prior" to the first moment of the Incarnation and it is the Word who assumes human nature at the Incarnation. In so doing, the Word takes to himself the human nature of Christ and becomes a human being in addition to being a divine being. But prior to this event in time, no human called Christ existed, although the divine person who is Christ existed.[62]

Crisp concludes that this way of telling the christological story (i.e. the anhypostasia and enhypostasia distinction) is consistent with a concrete-nature

---

61. Crisp, 86–87. Emphasis added.
62. Crisp, *God Incarnate*, 56.

view on a three-part Christology; in addition, it is consistently orthodox. What the an-enhypostasia distinction shows is how the christological description of Chalcedon is possible, so that this distinction provides us with the conceptual framework to construe and clarify Chalcedon.

Crisp's Use of Scripture

In the process of making explicit his christological method, Crisp made obvious the fact that he subscribes to a high view of Scripture without further qualifications. He holds to the tradition of viewing Scripture as *norma normans*, "the norm which stands behind and informs all the subordinate 'norms' of catholic creeds, or the confessional documents of particular ecclesial traditions."[63] Scripture for him is God's revelation, which means it has (or must be seen to have) ultimate authority for doctrinal formulations. The catholic creeds and confessions of the church are both *norma normata* with the understanding that their authority is derivative from Scripture. Crisp opines that these traditions are so important that "those who claim their own views comport with Scripture but not these *norma normata* should be treated with a healthy dose of scepticism by the theological community."[64] Finally, the works of Christian theologians, past and present, are *theologoumena* (theological opinion) that can be appropriated in given contexts. The implication of the foregoing for Crisp's Christology is not in doubt:

> In my view Christology should begin with divine revelation and the catholic creeds. This should yield a "high" Christology. It should also yield an orthodox Christology—attention to the tradition will certainly help in this regard. An *analytic* Christology may take this direction, using the tools of analytical philosophy to make sense of doctrinal claims about Christ in the light of Scripture and the tradition.[65]

But how, one may ask, does Crisp put this stated commitment to work? *Prima facie*, as the discussion above reveals, his discourse has very little direct reference to and engagement with the text of Scripture. It must be quickly

---

63. Crisp, 9.
64. Crisp, 18.
65. Crisp, 33. Emphasis in original.

noted though that this alone does not make his discussions unbiblical since he is careful to keep his conclusions within the confines of orthodoxy, which comports with his high regard for tradition as *norma normata*. He takes the doctrinal formulations of the church, especially in the creeds as givens that only need clarification via the analytic method. However, his direct use of Scripture to authorize theological proposals is quite negligible. In fact, what we see actually doing the job of authorizing theological proposals in his approach is metaphysical analysis or argumentation. For example, in a discussion on monothelite versus dyothelite Christologies, Crisp settled for dyothelitism based on support, supposedly from Scripture, tradition, and metaphysics. He argues as follows:

> It seems to me that there is a strong case for retaining dyothelitism. There is biblical support for the doctrine (e.g. "not my will, but your will be done" Luke 22:42); it is . . . affirmed by one of the (later) ecumenical councils of the Church and by almost all orthodox theologians; and (I would argue) it is difficult to see how Christ could be said to be fully human without having a human will that is distinct from the divine will.[66]

This, actually, is the only instance that Crisp cites Scripture as part of an argument. Outside of the quote above, Crisp does not mention the text again, let alone explain exegetically how it entails dyothelitism. Instead, he goes on to extensively elaborate on the other two supports he gives for his proposal. Therefore, his use of Scripture here might pass for nothing more than proof-texting – maybe not in principle, but clearly in practice.

In addition, Crisp's use of Scripture appears to be mainly propositionalist. For example, if we ask what aspects of Scripture are taken to be authoritative, one begins to see that Crisp takes the propositional content of Scripture to be authoritative. In drawing the conclusion that Jesus's statement in Luke 22:42 "not my will, but your will be done" supports dyothelitism, Crisp is basically focusing on the underlying propositional content of the text. If we then ask, what is it about this aspect of scripture that makes it authoritative? We see that for Crisp, it is the claims or truth that it affirms and the doctrine that it teaches. Consequently, the kind of logical force ascribed to the Scripture to

---

66. Crisp, *Divinity and Humanity*, 49.

which appeal is made is that of asserting and such assertion is then shown to be the case by the use of analytic tools. It seems then that this approach to the use of Scripture belongs in Vanhoozer's propositionalist quadrant discussed in the previous chapter, which also seems to fit quite well with the nature and method of analytic theology outlined above, unless it is an approach unique to Crisp alone. Let us then consider a second analytic theologian to see what might emerge.

Thomas McCall on the Relation of Christ in the Trinity

In *Forsaken: The Trinity and the Cross, and Why It Matters*,[67] Thomas McCall explores the question of whether or not the Trinity was broken on the cross when Christ agonizingly blared out his famous cry of dereliction "My God, my God, why have you forsaken me?" McCall presents the thoughts of several modern theologians who have concluded that this cry highlights nothing less than a rupture in the Trinity, and that this rupture is not problematic but is, in fact, a very good thing. One of the key proponents of this claim, McCall notes, is Jürgen Moltmann, whose "view of the cry of dereliction has exerted massive influence in contemporary theology."[68] This broken-Trinity view insists on "the utter, total, complete separation between Jesus and his Father. For 'when God becomes man in Jesus of Nazareth, he not only enters into the finitude of man, but in his death on the cross also enters into the situation of man's godforsakenness.'"[69] It is this forsakenness of the Son by the Father that, for Moltmann, makes the gospel *good news* and makes God, *God*.[70] McCall goes on to survey several contemporary theologians and biblical scholars who affirm the broken-Trinity view along with Moltmann (even if in varying degrees).

However, McCall finds this view to be gravely problematic given its lack of catholic continuity, conceptual coherence, and canonical consistency – even though McCall does not use these descriptors, it is quite clear these factors are his referents. First, McCall traces how the cry of dereliction has been interpreted in the Christian tradition (patristic, medieval, and Protestant)

---

67. McCall, *Forsaken*.
68. McCall, 15.
69. McCall, 18.
70. McCall, 18. emphasis in original.

and notices a clear consensus position – precisely, that "the Father forsook the Son to *this death*, and he did so for us and our salvation. But even so, the communion of Father and Son is unbroken. And this too, the tradition tells us, is good news."[71] Although Christ as man identifies with us in our godforsakenness, as God, his unbroken and unbreakable union with the Father remained, even on the cross. Therefore, Jesus's cry of dereliction in premodern theology is not seen to signify the seeming assumption so pervasive in contemporary theology that the Trinity was broken for our sake. It is in this sense that the broken-Trinity view is said to lack catholic continuity.

On conceptual coherence, McCall analyzes the very concept of the Trinity on both the Latin and social Trinitarian views and finds the broken-Trinity view to be incompatible with either. Latin Trinitarianism identifies a unity of essence among the divine persons and a distinction based on their individual relations to one another (e.g. the Father generating the Son and the Son being generated of the Father). In this sense, "the divine persons are *numerically* one in an important sense (rather than merely generically of the same nature, as social theorists hold)."[72] Yet, the divine persons are distinct by virtue of their unique triune relations (e.g. the Father as generating the Son, the Son as generated of the Father, etc.). On the Social Trinitarian view, emphasis is placed on the individuality of each divine person as a distinct center of consciousness. They are however united on the basis of their perichoretic relationality – "that the unbreakable bond of loving communion (or *perichoresis*) that the divine persons share is strong enough to satisfy the (relevant) criteria for monotheism."[73] Without having to side with any of these Trinitarian views, McCall proceeds to show that on both sides of the discussion, the Trinity is the Trinity in communion such that the Trinity fails to obtain on a broken-Trinity reading of the cry of dereliction.

He writes:

> if what makes the Trinity one God rather than three gods is their relatedness (as on social trinitarianism), and if this relationality is lost or destroyed, then we lose all claims to monotheism. And if this intratrinitarian communion of self-giving and receiving

---

71. McCall, 29.
72. McCall, 33.
73. McCall, 33.

of holy love is essential to the very being of the Christian God, then without such relationship there simply is no Christian God. To make the point a different way, for Latin trinitarianism there is no *Trinity* without the relations between the persons, while for social trinitarianism there is no *monotheism* without the relations between the persons. Either way, then, the triune God of the Christian faith does not exist apart from the relations between the divine persons.[74]

By seriously taking into account the metaphysics of the Trinity, McCall is able to conclude that since the Trinity cannot be broken without the Christian God ceasing to exist, Jesus's cry of dereliction cannot possibly entail a broken-Trinity.

Finally, McCall reads the relevant texts of Matthew 27:46 and Mark 15:34 canonically, attempting to explain what he takes the texts to be saying and not saying. His main concerns are:

> Does a proper interpretation of this cry demand the conclusion "the Father rejected the Son?" Does the text of either Matthew or Mark actually *say* that the Father turned his face away from the Son? Does a responsible interpretation of this text demand that we believe "God cursed Jesus with utter damnation?" Is there anything here that says—or even implies—that the eternal communion between the Father and the Son was ruptured? Does the text actually say that the Trinity was broken?[75]

His canonical reading goes in two directions. First, he reads the accounts of Matthew and Mark along with those of Luke and John, particularly in the light of all the other utterances of Jesus on the cross. What comes out of this exercise is the fact that the cry of dereliction as proof for the broken-Trinity view becomes increasingly less plausible. For example, the last cry of Jesus committing his spirit into the Father's hands renders the idea of forsakenness or rupture in the Trinity inconsistent. McCall therefore concludes that we cannot answer in the affirmative any of the questions he raised above with respect to the texts of both Matthew and Mark. The second canonical direction

---

74. McCall, 36–37.
75. McCall, 30.

McCall takes is reading the texts in the light of Psalm 22 where this cry of dereliction was originally voiced. He argues against those who think that the whole Psalm should not be used to understand Jesus's cry of dereliction since Jesus only quoted the opening part of the Psalm and no more. McCall thinks otherwise based on the fact that the Psalm also refers to insults and mockery directed at the "crier" (vv. 6–8) as well as the gambling and dividing of his clothes (vv. 17–18). Therefore, the other portions of the Psalm (cf. vv. 3–5; 24–31) that convey complete trust in the Lord and deny the idea of forsakenness and abandonment must be taken into account for our understanding of Jesus's cry of dereliction. This move leads McCall to conclude as follows: "Understood in the light of Psalm 22, Jesus' cry of dereliction does not support the broken-Trinity view. It does, however, cohere remarkably well with the more traditional approach. The Father forsook the Son to this death, at the hands of these sinful people, for us and our salvation."[76]

McCall's Use of Scripture

McCall clearly uses Scripture in an expansive manner, paying attention to the text in its canonical shape as well as reading it with catholic sensitivity and logical consistency. His use of Scripture in actual practice to authorize theological claims is more robust than that of Oliver Crisp. He discusses the biblical text in some detail and in conversation with other commentators (past and present) in order to show how he reaches his conclusions. However, what he shares with Crisp is the privileging of Scripture's propositional content, the doctrinal truth it teaches, and its attendant logical force of asserting. Granted that the purpose of McCall's project was to show how a particular claim (that the Trinity was broken on the cross of Christ) is false, which may explain the need to focus on the propositional content of the texts he used. Yet, it seems that a more fundamental reason why that had to be the case is simply because analytic reasoning, generally speaking, is propositional and sentential – this much is evident in Rea's P1 and P2 above.

Therefore, when it comes to Scripture's use in theology, it seems the analytic theologian understandably cannot but privilege the propositional content of the text over other aspects. McCall, for example, seems to argue for the primacy of the propositional aspect of Scripture when he points out

---

76. McCall, 42.

that other forms of Scripture (e.g. narrative) in some way necessarily make propositional claims. In a rebuttal of Daniel Harlow's appeal to narrative theology as an adequate approach to his (Harlow's) revisionist account of original sin, McCall says:

> Theology is not only or merely about making propositional claims. But if narrative theology really is theology, then it is making some propositional claims about God (regardless of how it communicates these claims). So when Harlow says that this is narrative theology and *not* propositional revelation, we can dismiss the red herring about "propositions."[77]

McCall is right to note that theology generally speaking makes some propositional claims about God even if it is not purely propositional. However, he seems to be silent about the fact that AT is generally inattentive to other forms of Scripture or transforms them to propositional forms before it is able to attend to them. This goes to show that either the practitioners of AT think that the original diverse forms of Scripture are without an intended purpose or that AT lacks the tools to analyze these other forms in their own right. Perhaps further investigation might sound a different tone that will make us reconsider the present outlook that is clearly emerging about the use of Scripture in AT.

Between Analytic Theology and Theological Theology

Certain problems (as will soon be clear) notwithstanding, it should be noted first of all that the analytic mode of doing theology, particularly Christology, has many benefits for the practice of Christian theology in general. Thomas McCall has elaborated on this well in his monograph[78] and there is no point rehashing his very positive presentation of the discipline here. However, two key benefits are worthy of mention in view of their significance to the overall aim of this project.

---

77. McCall, *Analytic Christian Theology*, 142.
78. McCall, *Analytic Christian Theology*.

The first and (for purposes of this project), perhaps, the most crucial benefit of AT is the explication of important, but often quite difficult theological concepts from the Christian tradition. This kind of important work is exquisitely demonstrated by Oliver Crisp as seen above. What makes such careful explication important work is the fact that it helps us make the same theological and christological judgments today that the early church made in the past. While we may use different concepts from those they employed, understanding the judgments that are contained in and conveyed by their concepts will help ensure that we are articulating the same gospel of the one historical Christian faith. Perhaps, the most widely emphasized feature of the theological interpretation of Scripture is the recovery of patristic exegesis as a legitimate, even superior way of reading Scripture.[79] Quite often, this feature is pursued with regards to the interpretation of biblical texts in a spiritual and ecclesial mode as opposed to the naturalism of modernity's biblical historicism. In this sense, the doctrinal concepts of patristic and medieval interpreters are often affirmed and appropriated for contemporary theologizing. Therefore, adequate analysis of these concepts is critical to the theological understanding of Scripture in order to show that we are actually saying the same things the fathers meant when they used those terms and concepts as *homoousios, perichoresis, hypostasis, phusis, persona,* anhypostasia, enhypostasia, etc.[80] The adequacy of such analysis will require sure-footedness in both conceptual analysis and theological knowledge. Here, analytic theology makes a critical contribution to the general task of doing theology in a way that is unrivaled and unmatched by any other theological discipline.

The second major benefit of AT to the theological task for purposes of this project is the articulation of the logical coherence of issues arising from

---

79. See Steinmetz, "Superiority of Pre-Critical Exegesis," 27–38, and Yeago, "New Testament and the Nicene Dogma," 87–100.

80. Richard Swinburne, quite helpfully, makes this same point as follows:
Some doctrines of the Creed (e.g. the doctrines that Jesus "was crucified . . . buried . . . and rose up on the third day") simply repeat Scripture, which – it was agreed – must be understood literally unless there is reason to deny the literal sense. But the doctrines of the Trinity and the Incarnation as stated in the Creed and as defined by the Ecumenical Councils of the fourth and fifth centuries clearly do not repeat Scripture. Nor can they be deduced from Scripture without the aid of some definitions of the philosophical terms that occur in the Creed, such as *ousia* (substance), *hupostasis* (individual), *phusis* (nature), and so on.
Swinburne, "Authority of Scripture," 17.

the biblical text. This is quite similar but not identical to the first benefit just discussed. While the first is focused on the explication of theological concepts from early Christian tradition, the second is concerned with discussions at the level of the biblical text itself. Thomas McCall, out of the two analytic theologians considered above, is perhaps the best at this particular task. His treatment of Jesus's cry of dereliction clearly demonstrates why this kind of careful analytic work with Scripture is important: that certain concepts thought of by biblical scholars to be present in a particular biblical text may not necessarily be the case on further and more careful analytic examination. This is often the case because, as McCall points out, discussions of "issues that are attentive to exegetical concerns and grounded in biblical theology . . . proceed without sufficient carefulness."[81] The analytic theologian is therefore needed to offer help in this respect: for "while the biblical theologian can help us with the 'narrative coherence,' the analytic theologian can assist with logical coherence."[82] The analytic theologian is able to show us, beyond just the extra-biblical history of a given concept, whether or not it is the logically identical concept that is being affirmed in contemporary biblical scholarship or theologizing.

What is not totally clear from the foregoing though is whether or not McCall is recommending a division of labor approach to discussing Scripture in theology. He had asserted earlier on, in relation to issues bordering both biblical studies and AT, that "any genuine progress in these discussions will need expertise in both fields."[83] But later on, he says, "The study required for genuine expertise in biblical studies is vast, and the requisite skills and background knowledge . . . take a veritable lifetime to master. To suggest

---

81. McCall, *Analytic Christian Theology*, 80. To show how this is the case, McCall (in a similar exercise to his treatment of Jesus's cry of dereliction) interacts with Don Carson's explication of, and argument for compatibilism from a biblical theological point of view. As McCall reports, Carson thinks of compatibilism as affirming both the utter sovereignty of God and the moral responsibility of human beings and then presents a number of biblical texts to argue that it is the normative view of biblical theology and Christian orthodoxy. McCall however points out that "Compatibilism is generally taken to be the view that *determinism* and freedom—not *divine sovereignty* and freedom—are compatible" (McCall, 61). McCall also engages with some of the events of biblical texts used by Carson as support (e.g. selling Joseph and the crucifixion of Jesus) and shows that nothing in them necessarily entails metaphysical compatibilism. He therefore concludes that "what Carson calls 'compatibilism' really isn't compatibilism." McCall, 80.

82. McCall, 80.

83. McCall, 79.

that the analytic theologian must have genuine expertise in all these fields is unrealistic and likely pretentious."[84] On this ground then, he concedes that "analytic theology might best be done within a community of scholars where there is appropriate division of labor, cross-fertilization, mutual beneficial correction and feedback."[85] This is, undoubtedly, a very positive picture of theological communion and corporation; even if it is not quite clear how this is still, strictly speaking, analytic theology. In addition, and more importantly, a division of labor approach with respect to doing theology is quite problematic as will be seen shortly. It is appropriate therefore on this note of ambiguity (even irony) that we transition into considering some problems that need addressing if AT is to interact well with theological interpretation of Scripture and also benefit the task of global theology.

Analytic Style and Scriptural Form

Perhaps, the most obvious feature of the use of Scripture noted above in both analytic theologians under consideration is their emphasis on the propositional aspect of Scripture. As mentioned earlier, the very nature of analytic thought is that it focuses on statements and the various ways of verifying the validity and soundness of these statements. This is why the analytic process functions best when one writes, quoting Rea's P1 above, "as if philosophical positions and conclusions can be adequately formulated in *sentences that can be formalized and logically manipulated*."[86] (emphasis added). In spite of the important work that this way of reasoning and writing does for Christian theology, Kevin Vanhoozer calls attention to "Webster's exhortation not to let systematic theology drift away from the idioms of Scripture so that its mode of argument is exclusively logical analysis."[87]

Webster's exhortation is informed by what he saw as the danger of the division of labor approach to the dual tasks of biblical studies and systematic theology, whereby the former simply supplies the raw materials needed

---

84. McCall, 174.
85. McCall, 175.
86. Rea, "Introduction," 5.
87. Vanhoozer, "Analytics, Poetics," 39.

for serious theological work to be carried out by the latter.[88] In this sense, Scripture is (wittingly or unwittingly) relegated to a subordinate role or rendered invisible in the process of doing theology. For Webster, this problem can be avoided only through "the substantial presence of exegesis, showing that Scripture is doing real work, not simply furnishing topics to be handled in a non-Scriptural idiom or proofs for arguments constructed on other grounds."[89] While it is true, as McCall points out, that "every treatise in analytic theology should [not] be reduced to an exercise in biblical exegesis, or even that all work in analytic theology should begin with biblical exegesis,"[90] Webster's prescription of "the substantial presence of exegesis" is critical if the use of Scripture in AT will go beyond just the propositional aspect of the text. In this sense, the analytic theologian will do well not to leave Scripture's "canonical form to be studied by another discipline."[91]

However, it is important to note Vanhoozer's caution that we must not confuse propositional content – used "to identity, classify, and individuate our mental states and speech acts"[92] – with propositional form (i.e. the formulation of a philosophical position into a sentence "that can be formalized and logically manipulated"[93]). In this sense, propositional form is constant while propositional content changes based on a subject's mental states and speech acts. This distinction is important for progress to be made because some narrative theologians, for example, want to completely distance theology from propositional revelation. But this distinction helps us to see that this is impossible as McCall also points out: "Theology is not only or merely about making propositional claims. But if narrative theology really is theology,

---

88. Daniel Treier and Uche Anizor argue that such division of labor should not translate to a separation of practice. They write:
> The pragmatically necessary division of labor between biblical studies and theology must not ossify into a fundamental separation of the two. In earlier eras theologians freely exegeted Scripture as an integral part of their dogmatic enterprise. At then, "biblical scholars" and "theologians" as discretely specialized disciplines did not exist. Today, a theologian making exegetical claims in the present academic climate frequently incurs the ridicule or even ire of biblical scholars.

Treier and Anizor, "Theological Interpretation," 8.
89. Webster, *Domain of the Word*, 148.
90. McCall, *Analytic Christian Theology*, 174.
91. Vanhoozer, "Analytics, Poetics," 10.
92. Hanks, *Propositional Content*, 1.
93. Rea, "Introduction," 5.

then it is making some propositional claims about God (regardless of how it communicates these claims)."[94]

The problem for AT on this matter though is that it intentionally isolates and abstracts propositional content from communicative forms that are non-propositional and reformulates it in propositional form for purposes of attaining precision, clarity, and parsimony of thought. With regards to the use of Scripture, this may suggest that the non-propositional forms of Scripture are dispensable or that they are not doing important work. But Vanhoozer raises some critical questions for us: "Is biblical authority—Scripture's *rightful say-so*— solely a matter of *what* rather than *how* it is said, a question of content rather than form? Would theologians be right in thinking that the only normative element in a biblical text is its propositional pearl of great price?"[95] He went on to show how this cannot be the case because the forms of the biblical texts are tailored to address us with respect to "not only *knowing-that* but *seeing-as,* even *feeling-as.*"[96] Therefore, AT cannot afford to ignore the various forms of Scripture and the important work that they do if it must engage more fully the totality of the biblical text. The question though is whether AT will still be analytic if it were to engage with Scripture in this way.

Philosophical Versus Theological Reason

Another issue to consider is the idea of philosophical reason vis-à-vis Webster's conception of theological reason. Theological reason according to Webster, as noted in chapter 2, holds that human reason is created, fallen, redeemed, and sanctified. In this sense, created and fallen intelligence is incapable on its own of fully understanding the truth about God – an understanding that should lead to faith and worship. Instead, it must be redeemed and sanctified by the Holy Spirit for it to truly understand and rightly respond to the divine address delivered through the prophets and the apostles. Webster therefore notes that Christian theology as a kind of reasoning should be understood as biblical reasoning (exegetical and dogmatic) such that our theological claims and knowledge are shown to be the deliverances of the divine triune economy.

---

94. McCall, *Analytic Christian Theology*, 142.
95. Vanhoozer, "Love's Wisdom," 248. Emphasis in original.
96. Vanhoozer, 253.

On the other hand, philosophical reasoning by default proceeds from the human faculties of (borrowing from John Locke) sense, perception, and reason. Locke, for an example, states: "To show . . . that we are capable of knowing, i.e., being certain that there is a God, and how we may come by this certainty, I think we need go no further than ourselves, and that undoubted knowledge we have of our own existence."[97] The goal for Locke is to find a way for certain speech about God without reference to what God has said of himself as this will be philosophically inadequate. Reference to revelation in God-talk is philosophically inadequate because, while reason seeks by rigorous logical deductions to *arrive* at certain truth, faith simply *assents* to revealed truth, which may or may not be ascertained. This is similar to what Thomas V. Morris said about those who think, like J. L. Tomkinson, that Anselm – through his ontological argument for God's existence – has "given the world a purely rational way of thinking about God, a way of doing theology completely free of the vagaries and uncertainties of claims to revelation."[98]

Morris however, wants us to think of Anselm's – and by extension, a broadly Anselmian – approach to philosophical theological reasoning quite differently, in which case, biblical revelation is accepted and used as a source of theological reflection.[99] AT is indeed Anselmian in this sense as evident in our discussion so far, and seems to take seriously both philosophical and theological reason. The main question for us however is whether or not this approach is capable of not only enabling us to arrive at the truth, but also assent to the truth, and adore or worship the Truth (the One about whom the truth refers to). William Wood points out that certain practices of the analytic style can actually serve a spiritual purpose in the life of the person reading and, especially, doing AT. He identifies four such virtues as

---

97. John Locke, *An Essay Concerning Human Understanding*, Book IV, Chapter X: 1 (1690).

98. In this respect, Morris says of Anselm,
> He was a *Christian* theologian. One of the sources of, and controls on, his thinking about God was the general conception of God as a greatest conceivable being. But it was not the only source of and control on his theology. As a Christian theologian, Anselm accepted the documents of the Bible and the traditions of the church as providing vitally important and inviolable standards for theological reflection.

Morris, *Anselmian Explorations*, 3. Emphasis in original.

99. Morris, 3. Emphasis in original.

cultivating attention, argumentative transparency, imaginative identification with opponents, and passively waiting for insight. All four are ordinary philosophical practices, but they can also have the effect of fostering the virtue of humility and of cultivating a desire for truth, which in the Christian tradition may be understood as a desire for God.[100]

McCall, in agreement with William Wood, answers in the affirmative as well saying that "we should not neglect to notice those shining examples of theologians for whom analytic theology indeed is closely related to worship and spiritual nurture."[101] These shining examples for McCall include many patristic and scholastic theologians. The argument simply is that AT can and indeed has been spiritually edifying for some people who do theology as both theoretical and practical.

However, Vanhoozer is not convinced because, unlike the idea of theological reason (biblical and dogmatic), he suggests that analytic philosophical reason strictly speaking does not take us far enough, thus his scathing assertion, "Even the demons can do analytic theology."[102] For Vanhoozer, even Webster's account of theological reason falls short here because of its inattention to the non-analytic aspect of biblical and dogmatic reasoning. If we are to do justice to biblical discourse as a whole, he says, "we require both analytic skills and poetic sensibilities: the ability *conceptually to elaborate* what is said and the ability *imaginatively to feel* the particular force with which it is said."[103] In this way, one might be able to say that while the idea of spiritual edification is intentional in Vanhoozer's dogmatic construal of theological reason, it is only incidental, as outlined by Wood and McCall, in analytic philosophical reason.

It seems though that a defender of the analytic approach might be able to say that being intentional about spiritual formation is not a problem of AT itself but is dependent on the attitude of a given practitioner (or reader) of AT. To tow this line however will be to suggest that the intentions of a given practitioner of AT might actually undermine its stated ambitions. Take P3 for

---

100. Wood, "Analytic Theology," 55.
101. McCall, *Analytic Christian Theology*, 34.
102. Vanhoozer, "Analytics, Poetics," 15.
103. Vanhoozer, 15.

an example: here, the non-decorative use of metaphor (whereby its semantic content outstrips its propositional content) is proscribed. While this prescription will definitely enhance clarity of thought and parsimony of expression, it is sure to fall short when it comes to arousing our imagination to facilitate worship. It suffices then, at this point, to say that analytic reasoning is insufficient in and of itself for doing theology qua theology. This much we must concede even as both Wood and McCall agree.[104] Now, we turn to one more concern for consideration.

Accessibility of Content and Attention to Context

The very possibility that AT might (or should) be accessible to non-analytic theologians as well as be applicable in non-Western contexts deserves attention, particularly as we hope to explore the potential of a global analytic theology. Analytic theologians would be the first to admit that their work may not be comprehensible to non-initiates of the analytic tradition. According to Wood, analytic philosophy, and by extension AT, is a historical and living intellectual tradition (in the sense construed by Alasdair MacIntyre) into which one must be socialized in order to fully comprehend its discourses.

> To be socialized into the tradition of analytic philosophy, one must learn how to read and what to read, how to argue and what to argue about. One learns to be an analytic philosopher when one learns a particular intellectual vocabulary; one also learns to see specific issues and not others as fruitful intellectual problems, and one learns specific techniques by which those problems should be addressed.[105]

Since AT belongs to this intellectual tradition, it is carried out with the vocabulary, devices, virtues, even (many times) the concerns of this intellectual tradition, such that non-initiates of the tradition, while intellectuals themselves, are unable to understand its theological discourses. While the converse

---

104. According to Wood, "There are some kinds of theological work for which analytic tools are especially well-suited, and some kinds for which they are not." See Wood, "Trajectories, Traditions, and Tools," 259. McCall also says that "it would be mistaken and probably dangerous for analytic theologians to think that their tools and skills are the only ones necessary, or even the most important" in doing theology. McCall, *Analytic Christian Theology*, 159.

105. Wood, "Trajectories, Traditions, and Tools," 262.

of this is also true, we will not delay ourselves considering it. The question to consider at this point is: should analytic theologians write in such a way that non-analytic theologians will find accessible?

One might say that this is not even possible given the fact that the analytic theologian, like other theologians, writes for their peers in the analytic tradition, thus employs a style and a set of vocabulary that their intellectual tradition takes to be erudite and standard. Other theological specialists do the same thing (necessarily so, it seems) from their given theological disciplines; thus, the inevitable fragmentation of the theological enterprise. However, to answer this question in the affirmative is to say that it is important that Christian theology is carried out in community such that other theologians who do not share our particular specialization are able to engage with our work. To prioritize these specializations and intellectual traditions over and above the needed ecclesiological orientation of theology is to hinder the broader community of faith from engaging our work. Therefore, Christian AT qua Christian needs to be carried out in a way that other Christian theologians who do not have any training in analytic philosophy are able to comprehend and engage with its discourse. This simply means that analytic theologians should give priority to the fact that, "Theology constitutes an inquiry into the specific language peculiar to, in fact constitutive of, the specific semiotic community called the Christian Church or churches."[106]

Similarly, to do analytic theology in a global context will require, not only such sensitivity to the accessibility of theological discourse, but also a keen attention to the lived realities of people in such contexts as opposed to mere preoccupation with conceptual abstraction and analysis. This, perhaps, is why in his proposal for a global analytic theology McCall states that "we need more Western theologians who have the humility and patience to learn from their global colleagues *and* more theologians from Africa, Asia and Oceania who are able to employ analytic skills and tools in a helpful way."[107] The statement does imply (and rightly so) the possibility of analytic skills and tools to be employed in an unhelpful way, particularly for purposes of engaging the global theological enterprise. This terrain is full of historical and cultural mines that the analytic approach may find quite daunting to navigate

---

106. Frei, *Types of Christian Theology*, 78.
107. McCall, *Analytic Christian Theology*, 158. Emphasis in original.

safely let alone produce any fruitful work. The next chapter will attend to this concern in some detail.

CHAPTER 4

Christ in Global Theological Perspectives

"From the Copernican revolution that substituted the sun for the earth as the center of the universe, through the discoveries in modern physics and astronomy, we know now—cosmologically, philosophically, and culturally—that *there is no center*."[1] This momentous shift is known, all too well, to have impacted intellectual life in general and the practice of Christian theology in particular. We saw earlier in chapter 2 that in the first half of the twentieth century, the practice of theology took a major turn away from the variety of critical attitudes toward the Bible that were dominant from the seventeenth to the nineteenth centuries. This major turn brought forth certain theologies that are widely thought to be postcritical, or postliberal, and postmodern. What we left unsaid at that point is the fact that the second half of the twentieth century witnessed deliberate efforts to also drive theology in a direction that is post-Western and postcolonial.

This second shift was informed primarily by a number of factors: (1) the general disenchantment with Western Enlightenment/modernity; (2) the struggle by colonized peoples for independence from European imperial control that culminated in the official end to colonialism; and (3) the exponential growth of the Christian faith in the Majority World as noted in chapter 1. The combination of these factors resulted in a decreasing involvement and influence of Western missionaries in the evolving Christianity of these nations, and an equally increasing local participation and indigenous

---

1. Paul Lakeland, "Preface," in Tanner, *Theories of Culture*, vii.

(re)orientation of the faith. If it is true that Christianity was first Judaic or Hebraic before it was Hellenized and then Europeanized – meaning that these cultural blocks respectively dominated the faith when it thrived in those settings more than anywhere else – then it is only natural to expect that the faith will be (or at least attempted to be) Africanized, Asianized, and Latinized; or better still, decentralized and globalized in the present climate of what has been called world Christianity.[2] As noted in chapter 1, the most attractive and most treated doctrine in global theology[3] presently is Christology. This is clearly due to the centrality of the person and works of Christ to the Christian faith; perhaps, also due to the narrative form of the Christ event in Scripture, since stories travel well globally. But even more importantly, it is because of the many implications that can be drawn from Christology for the diverse and often oppressive and dehumanizing contexts of people in the Majority World. In considering global theology therefore, focusing primarily on the understanding of Christ seems quite appropriate, even strategic.

This chapter first gives a brief overview of the basic character of global approaches to Christology, particularly with respect to its critical concerns and its general methodological approach. We then narrow down to the African context, providing a synopsis of the more prominent approaches to doing theology in Africa, and noting how these have shaped the various christological constructions that have emerged from the continent. For more specificity, we then consider two concrete christological constructions from Nigeria, the Guest Christology of Enyi Ben Udoh and the Revealer Christology of

---

2. Lamin Sanneh's idea of world Christianity looms large at this point. While the concept is contestable, it is nonetheless insightful and widely used. Sanneh takes the idea of "global Christianity" to be synonymous with Christendom (i.e. medieval imperial Christianity), which identifies the Christian faith with "Christian" Europe. In contrast,

> "World Christianity" is the movement of Christianity as it takes form and shape in societies that previously were not Christian, societies that had no bureaucratic tradition with which to domesticate the gospel. In these societies Christianity was received and expressed through the cultures, customs, and traditions of the people affected. World Christianity is not one thing, but a variety of indigenous responses through more or less effective local idioms, but in any case, without necessarily the European Enlightenment frame.

Sanneh, *Whose Religion Is Christianity?*, 22.

3. Global theology as a nomenclature seems to have a wider acceptability among practitioners even though there are other ways that this way of doing theology is being called: for example, intercultural theology, contextual theology, local theology, etc. See for example: Wrogemann, *Intercultural Theology*, vol. 1; Sedmark, *Doing Local Theology*; and Schreiter, *Constructing Local Theologies*.

Victor Ezigbo. The aim here is to understand, assess, and interact with these contextual christological formulations. What should become clear at the end of the chapter, it is hoped, is the need for a global analytic theological Christology – taking into account fidelity to the canon of Scripture, commitment to theological catholicity, carefulness for conceptual clarity, and without losing attention to contextual realities. At this point, we will begin with the basic character of global theology/Christology.

From Context to Text: Method in Global Christology

Although somewhat simplistic, it is widely acknowledged that while theological works in Western contexts tend to begin with theorization and conceptual abstractions/systematization, theologians in non-Western (also, Western minority) contexts often begin with attention to the concrete particulars or lived realities of their specific communities.[4] With respect to the use of Scriptures, it is often the case that Western theologians first focus on interpreting the text, drawing universally-applicable truths or principles before applying such to their (or any) context. On the other hand, non-Western theologians tend to reverse this order as they move from critically analyzing their all-too-familiar contexts to figuring out what Scripture has to say to that specific situation. While theology in the West, so to speak, emphasizes orthodoxy, non-Western theologies, it is said, put the accent on orthopraxis. It must be noted however that the distinguishing line has been growing much thinner as many theologians in the West today continue to be critical of "high" modernity and its tendency for the hierarchical stratification of peoples in society (majorly based on race and gender) and the worth of their intellectual works. As a result, many Western theological endeavors today consciously proceed from the contexts of various interest groups, either ethnic or gender-based.

Nevertheless, non-Western theologians have often noted Western theology and Christianity's witting or unwitting disregard for right actions (both social and personal) over merely right beliefs, which has led to quite devastating

---

4. Even though convenient, these broad and widely used distinctions betray a certain mistaken assumption: that while all non-Western theologies are contextual, Western theology is universal and/or contextually-neutral.

consequences in Majority World societies. It is pointed out that this mindset had made Western missionaries to be (knowingly or unknowingly) either silent about or complicit in the mistreatment of colonized peoples by European colonial authorities. This is evidenced by the fact that their teachings and theologies, for the most part, failed to venture into the social (i.e. incorporating cultural, political, economic, etc.) arena. Therefore, theologians in these formerly colonized contexts have been making efforts to reshape Christian theology in ways that will address this major deficiency.

Doing Christology from this perspective therefore entails a critique and rejection or rehabilitation (either in whole or in part) of the Christology received from Western missionaries against the backdrop of European imperialism and colonization – we may call this the postimperial or postcolonial (thus postmodern) or post-missionary component of non-Western Christologies. It is a necessary component because the received Christology of the West was inattentive to the people's cultural ways of understanding and making meaning of the world, as well as to their sufferings owing to the social injustices meted out by their colonizers. It is often pointed out that the missionaries presented only a divine Christ who is the personal savior of the human soul for eternal life in heaven, but failed to show us the human Jesus who brings deliverance to the dehumanized and restores their full humanity for a flourishing life here on earth.[5] For this reason, Christology in non-Western contexts generally begins from the humanity of Christ as one who lives among us – the impoverished, the oppressed, the marginalized, the violated, the disrespected, the dehumanized, and in the words of Frantz Fanon, "the wretched of the earth."[6] This methodological starting point highlights the fact that Christ is just like us, which means he knows our pains all too well and is in full solidarity with us. He is the answer to all the ills (spiritual, economic, social, political, cultural, etc.) that trouble us. Due to the fact that received Western missionary Christology was inattentive to these realities and concerns it was rendered irrelevant, at best, and, at worst, served in aiding the colonization process by making the people of these colonized regions docile. M. A. C. Warren notes quite poignantly:

---

5. See for example Boff, *Jesus Christ Liberator* and Sobrino, *Christology at the Crossroads*.
6. Frantz Fanon, *The Wretched of the Earth*.

For more than four centuries the expansion of the Christian Church has *coincided* with the economic, political and cultural expansion of Western Europe. Viewed from the standpoint of the peoples of Asia, and to a growing extent from that of the peoples of Africa, this expansion has been an aggressive attack on their own way of life. Quite inevitably the Christian Faith has for many in these lands been inextricably bound up with this Western aggression. But it has also to be admitted quite frankly that during these centuries the missionaries of the Christian Church have commonly assumed that Western civilization and Christianity were two aspects of the same gift which they were commissioned to offer to the rest of mankind.[7]

Therefore, this mistaken assumption held by the missionaries would have affected their presentation of the gospel and teachings about Christ to the people. To see how these dynamics all interact in a specific context, I have elected to look closely at two constructive Christologies by Nigerian theologians. Before then however, it is important to situate the Nigerian conversations within the broader christological discourse in African theology.[8] This is crucial for a number of reasons. (1) the authors we interact with self-identify their efforts as exercises in African theologizing; (2) we cannot fully understand their discussions without the larger continent-wide conversation; and (3) it helps us note the similarities and differences of the issues raised by a country or culture-specific Christology in comparison to those addressed generally at the continent-wide level. This enables us to see that, generalities or similarities notwithstanding, it is impossible and unwise to construe African Christology as a monolith. So, what are the approaches to theology in general and Christology in particular on the continent of Africa? What are the origins, major concerns, and key methodological moves?

---

7. M. A. C. Warren, general introduction to *The Primal Vision: Christian Presence Amid African Religion*, by John V. Taylor (Philadelphia: Fortress, 1963), 5–6.

8. The idea of some theology being called "African" is highly debatable. While some insist on differentiating between African traditional theology (i.e. the theology of African indigenous religions) and African Christian theology (i.e. Christian theology from an African perspective), others think of it as an all-embracing descriptor that includes both categories. See Knighton, "Issues of African Theology," 147–61. In this study, African theology will be used as shorthand for the practice of African Christian theology unless otherwise stated or qualified.

The Quest for an African Christology: An Overview

In less than five decades of serious reflections and conversations, Christology has advanced quite remarkably in Africa.[9] Clifton Clark helpfully points out, as an evidence of this remarkable progress, John Mbiti's claim in 1972 that there are no christological conceptions in Africa, only for Charles Nyamiti to posit in 1991 (and without exaggeration) that Christology is the most developed doctrine in African theologizing.[10] What informed this fast development in less than three decades, and what are the indicators of this growth? We will briefly trace the major developments here and seek to understand the dominant christological models that emerged. From the late 1950s, the anti-colonial and anti-imperial agitations of African nationalists started blooming as African countries began to gain independence from colonial rule with its inherently dehumanizing venom. According to J. Shola Omotola,

> The colonial state was essentially an extractive and exploitative state, which necessitated the unbridled use of force to suppress local resistance, and it was also racist and gender-insensitive. These preoccupations of colonialism provoked Africans throughout the region, particularly the educated elites, who eventually became disgruntled with the racism and exploitation inherent in the colonial administration system and demanded self-rule.[11]

Expectedly then, there was celebration and rising optimism (albeit short-lived) across the continent as one nation after another assumed its right to govern itself, while the Western powers that previously held sway presumably left the stage. However, gaining apparent political independence was not enough because, according to Leonard Barnes, this independence, even "with the best will in the world, would have to remain pretty nominal for some time to come."[12] Thus, the death of colonialism was the birth of neo-colonialism, what Kwame Nkrumah describes as "imperialism in its final and

---

9. This project does not pretend to speak for Africa as it is obvious (and will be seen to be the case in this work) that no individual or group is able to do that given the complexity of Africa as a whole. However, it is possible for one to identify and trace the major issues and discussants in the christological conversations in the continent of Africa.

10. Clarke, *African Christology*, 1.

11. Omotola, "Independence Movements," 1.

12. Barnes, *African Renaissance*, 9.

perhaps its most dangerous stage."[13] Africa's educated elite would continue to contend against prevailing oppressive treatments of Africans, the derogatory characterization of African culture and religions by Western intellectuals, colonial personnel, and missionaries alike, and the neo-colonialist economic manipulations of Western superpowers to the detriment of African nations and their people.

Therefore, some African theologians began to reflect upon the African situation with the aim of speaking theologically for the emancipation of the African from every form of mistreatment, whether political, economic, social, or cultural. This was further necessitated by the fact that Christian teaching (as noted above) was used as a tool – even weaponized – for Western domination. Therefore, efforts in African Christian theological reflection generally focused on the motifs of liberation and inculturation. Kwame Bediako, quoting Archbishop Desmond Tutu, notes that "African theologians have set about demonstrating that the African religious experience and heritage were not illusory and that they should have formed the *vehicle for conveying the Gospel verities to Africa*."[14] The fundamental aims of theological reflection therefore were made very clear: there was the need to contend for the emancipation of Africans from all forms of domination and oppression, as well as to affirm Africa's cultural and traditional religious heritage as inherently good in opposition to the negative narratives of the West. However, these efforts were not homogeneous: "while in independent Africa the *Negritude movement* in francophone Africa and *African personality* in anglophone Africa contributed significantly to the emergence of African theology of indigenization (or inculturation), in apartheid South Africa, the *Black consciousness movement* contributed immensely to the emergence of Black theology of liberation."[15]

---

13. Nkrumah, *Neo-Colonialism*, ix. Nkrumah further notes what he means by neo-colonialism as follows: "The essence of neo-colonialism is that the State which is subject to it is, in theory, independent and has all the outward trappings of international sovereignty. In reality its economic system and thus its political policy is directed from outside." Nkrumah, ix.

14. Bediako, *Theology and Identity*, 2. Emphasis added.

15. Martey, *African Theology*, 1. See also: Ezeh, *Jesus Christ the Ancestor*, 304–5; and Ezigbo, *Re-imagining African Christologies*, 2–3.

Missionary Christology as Deficient

With respect to reflections on Christ, the often-cited statement of the English missionary John V. Taylor is generally considered as the first consciously christological proposal in the English literature on African theology. He writes:

> Christ has been presented as the answer to the questions a white man would ask, the solution to the needs that Western man would feel, the Saviour of the world of the European world-view, the object of the adoration and prayer of historic Christendom. But if Christ were to appear as the answer to the questions that Africans are asking, what would he look like? If he came into the world of African cosmology to redeem Man as Africans understand him, would he be recognizable to the rest of the Church Universal? And if Africa offered him the praises and petitions of her total, uninhibited humanity, would they be acceptable?[16]

Even though Taylor's probing questions seem to suggest that Christology only needs to focus on who Christ is *for us* without any reference to what or who he is *in himself*, the questions remain critical to Christology in Africa. Just before citing Taylor, Judith Bahemuka points out that "When the Gospel was brought to Africa, it came as a foreign religion; Christ was, as it were, obstructed by European culture. The presentation was faulty."[17] Naturally, one would ask, what was faulty about the presentation of Christ in Africa by the missionaries? On top of the list is the imperialistic character of their Christology so that it necessarily served as an oppressive rather than liberating message to Africans. Next is the fact that this Christology was intellectualistic, too abstract, dismissive of African cultures and life concerns, and lacking the necessary framework to be relevant or meaningful to the African.

By the late 1970s and early 1980s therefore, a number of theologians set out to redress this alleged faulty presentation of Christ in Africa. The christological constructions that emerged claimed to be (or at least aimed at being) both truly Christian and authentically African.[18] Whether or not they were

---

16. Taylor, *Primal Vision*, 24.
17. Bahemuka, "Hidden Christ," 6.
18. It has been widely claimed, as noted by Clarke that before this time, there existed a crisis of Christology in African theology. He argues that Christology was already being done at the local level by ordinary Christians in the context of worship, prayers, songs, etc. As such, he

successful is a different question, and closely related to that is the idea of what it really means to be authentically African in one's Christology. In view of the issues highlighted, these early efforts in African Christology focused primarily on either liberation or inculturation. Later developments on the world stage would inform the emergence of a third category that focuses primarily on the idea of reconstruction of African societies. A cursory account of each of these theological and christological approaches is what follows.

Christologies of Liberation: Jesus "for" Africa

Liberation Christology in the African context shares an affinity with the more widely known Latin American version, but it is certainly different in its own right. It expresses the general emphasis on the humanity of Christ and his unwavering solidarity with the poor, downcast, marginalized, and oppressed of society as the necessary first step to their emancipation from these ills. However, according to Diane Stinton, theology (and by extension Christology) of liberation in Africa "is not confined to modern socioeconomic and political levels but includes emancipation from other forms of oppression such as disease, poverty, hunger, ignorance, and the subjugation of women."[19] This form of theologizing was more pervasive in South Africa where the struggle against apartheid continued long after the independence movement had ended in other African countries. Thus, Emmanuel Martey notes that the main concern of this form of Christology is the sociopolitical realities of Africans in general, but particularly black South Africans.[20] Takatso Mofokeng's *The Crucified among the Crossbearers*[21] is a powerful example of this approach to Christology in Africa. "Mofokeng advocates an epistemological break in a new praxis of liberation and a new theological language."[22] He

---

construes the so-called crisis as "nothing more than a crisis amongst the theological elite, many of whom have been educated in the west." Clarke, *African Christology*, 1. Kwame Bediako also makes a similar point by presenting the prayers of Madam Afua Kuma, whom he described as illiterate but possessing a rich contextual Christology. Bediako gives an extended analysis of her Christology, which he categorizes as "spontaneous or grassroots" theology. He then notes that "academic or written theology cannot replace this spontaneous or grassroots theology, because the two are complementary aspects of one reality, and the 'spontaneous' is the foundation of the 'academic.'" Bediako, *Jesus and the Gospel in Africa*, 17.

19. Stinton, *Jesus of Africa*, 49.
20. Martey, *African Theology*, 1–3.
21. Mofokeng, *Crucified among the Crossbearers*.
22. Stinton, *Jesus of Africa*, 13.

attempts to accomplish this through his Black Christology in which "*Black* goes beyond color to signify the commitment of the poor and marginalized who seek to realize their humanity through humble dependence on Jesus Christ and obedience to his radical demands for establishing true humanity."[23]

African women theologians also employ the liberationist model for their christological discourse. Mercy Oduyoye's Christology echoes this theme of liberation, particularly for African women who contend daily against diverse mistreatments ensuing from some African traditional practices. Martey says, "Because of the inherent oppressive elements in African culture, most African women set Christ in opposition to all cultural systems that dehumanize and oppress them."[24] In most traditional African societies,

> a woman should not talk when men are having a conversation. Women are not taken seriously, and at times they are belittled by men as to their intelligence. They are customarily looked upon solely as child-bearers and servers and often cruelly oppressed when they have failed in child-bearing or when their child dies.[25]

Thus, the understanding of Christ as liberator speaks to African women. It is in this sense that Oduyoye says that Christ "liberates women from the burden of disease and ostracism of a society ridden with blood-taboos of inauspiciousness arising out of women's blood."[26]

However, with respect to all people of Africa (both men and women), Christ as liberator appeals to the general yearning of the people for wholeness of life.[27] This yearning for wholeness of life is informed by the African worldview or spiritualized cosmology, which sees interconnectedness between the

---

23. Stinton, 13.
24. Martey, *African Theology*, 83.
25. Nasimiyu-Wasike, "Christology and an African Woman's Experience," 124.
26. Oduyoye, "Women and Christology," 4.
27. Randee Ijatuyi-Morphé has noted in his well-researched work that
    Africa's quest is essentially a quest for life *and* wholeness . . . [The] study reunites religion and society and designates a common quest in relation to both entities. The social and religious quest extends then to achieving both life and wholeness for individual/group and society alike; the one necessarily entails the other. Individual/group life or existence is enhanced to the same degree that the whole of society, with its "institutions," is achieved at any given period . . . Africa's quest, like the Jewish quest . . . strives for holism.
    Ijatuyi-Morphé, *Africa's Social and Religious Quest*, 4.

physical and spiritual realms. It is in this sense that Christ is understood as liberator and healer from all forms of and forces that hinder wholeness of life (spiritual, social, physical, economic, psychological, political, etc.). Without this understanding of Christ, Oduyoye and many other African theologians think that African Christians may be (and are) forced to seek wholeness of life elsewhere given their lived-reality of contending with these forces. Oduyoye writes:

> It is therefore not strange that if relief from evil influences, from the spiritual oppressors, is not felt by members of Christian churches, they move from church to church as well as to-and-fro between church and *Odunsini*, the traditional healer of body and soul. Nevertheless, Jesus, "the Great Physician," is the anchor of their faith, for he is preached as the healer par excellence.[28]

Christologies of Inculturation: Jesus "of" Africa

The idea of inculturation in doing theology in Africa "entails theological exploration of African indigenous cultures in an attempt to integrate the African pre-Christian religious heritage with the Christian faith."[29] If it is true that the Christ presented by Western missionaries was foreign or un-African, not relatable, and irrelevant to Africans, then the attempt to fashion an authentically African understanding of Christ is legitimate and necessary. This way of theologizing seeks to undo the negative estimation of African traditional religions and cultures, which has brought about an erroneous but justified view of Christianity in Africa as a foreign religion – that to be Christian is to jettison one's Africanness and take up (more or less) a Western identity. Bediako argues that the question of identity is (and should be) at the heart of understanding the concerns of Christian theology in Africa.[30] Only when Christ is dressed in African attires and conveyed in African conceptual categories will he be relatable and meaningful to African Christians. Martey notes that the inculturationist approach is preoccupied with the religio-cultural component of being African. "In this model, it is the traditional African

---

28. Oduyoye, *Hearing and Knowing*, 44. Quoted in Stinton, *Jesus of Africa*, 73.
29. Stinton, *Jesus of Africa*, 49.
30. Bediako, *Theology and Identity*, 1–3.

epistemology that serves as a point of departure. Jesus' presence in Africa today, the proponents of this model argue, cannot be acknowledged without Africa's past religious knowledge and experience."[31]

Charles Nyamiti, Jean-Marc Ela, Bénézet Bujo, and Kwame Bediako (among others) have thus advanced and popularized the use of the African idea of ancestor for doing Christology.[32] Nyamiti, for an example, begins by saying, "There are enough similarities between Christ's brother-relationship to men and that of the African brother-ancestor to show us that the two types of relationship have the same fundamental structure."[33] Belief in the brother-ancestor and its attendant practices is found in many African traditional religions, thus making it even more effective for Christology. "A brother-ancestor is a relative of a person with whom he has a common parent, and of whom he is mediator to God, archetype of behaviour and with whom—thanks to his supernatural status acquired through death—he is entitled to have regular sacred communication."[34] For the Christian who no longer believes in or carries out any duties to the ancestors, Christ is understood as the one who fittingly assumes this role. Nyamiti presents seven points of correlation (while noting dissimilarities too) between this African concept of brother-ancestorship and Christ's relationship to humans as we know from Scripture and the Christian tradition.[35]

This is perhaps the most popular constructive Christology from Africa and it is appreciated by many and criticized by others. Those who appreciate it point to the fact that it not only draws from a concept and practice pervasive in many African ethnic groups, but it also connects the ancestorship of Christ with the teaching of Scripture and the Christian tradition. Timothy Tennent for example argues that "the term *ancestor* can be fully utilized in a way consistent with the earlier [christological] formulations as long as the term is accompanied by careful explanation, qualification, and supplementation such that the true identity of Jesus is manifested."[36] More

---

31. Martey, *African Theology*, 80.

32. See Nyamiti, *Christ as Our Ancestor*; Ela, *My Faith as an African*; Bujo, *African Theology in Its Social Context*; and Bediako, *Jesus and the Gospel in Africa*.

33. Nyamiti, *Christ as Our Ancestor*, 23.

34. Nyamiti, 23.

35. Nyamiti, 19–20.

36. Tennent, *Theology in the Context*, 128.

precisely, Tennent points out that the idea of Christ's mediatory role as our brother-ancestor makes this christological model consistent with the biblical witness and Christian tradition besides making Christ less strange to Africa. For him, Christ as ancestor is "one who is 'fleshed out' in terms Africans can understand."[37] Uchenna Ezeh's work attempts to validate this christological model by showing that it is consistent with Christian theology in general and with the christological formulations of Nicaea (325) and Chalcedon (451) in particular. He concludes as follows:

> We maintain that the African cult of the ancestors epitomizes the African quest for salvation (soteriology), goodness in the community (ethics), union with God (spirituality), and it is the end of the human person (eschatology and anthropology). Through his incarnation, these African values are perfectly fulfilled in Christ as perfect God and perfect man. Hence Jesus is the Ancestor par excellence, who as God-man perfectly mediates salvation to the people. . . . In this way he becomes the perfect fulfillment of all the African aspirations or quest integrated in the cult of the ancestors. This Christological model is truly Christian and African.[38]

The trouble however is that today, not too many "Africans can understand" this way of speaking about Christ, which seriously undermines any African theology or Christology that employs concepts and categories from Africa's so-called primal religions as its starting point. This does not quite resonate with many people in present day Africa. Studies carried out independently by Timothy Palmer[39] and Diane Stinton[40] in separate parts of Africa both reveal that most African Christians will prefer not using the word ancestor for Jesus because they find it to be either inappropriate or unhelpful or both.

Martey however thinks that both liberation and inculturation approaches are limited by the fact that each is often carried out to the exclusion of the other. So, he advocates for the dialectical encounter of both approaches whereby the main concern is not just recovering Africa's religio-cultural past

---

37. Tennent, 130.
38. Ezeh, *Jesus Christ the Ancestor*, 316.
39. Palmer, "Jesus Christ," 4–17.
40. Stinton, *Jesus of Africa*, 130–35.

or just apparent emancipation from colonialism, apartheid, and other forms of oppression, but the full humanity of the African in a new society. He writes, "Evidently, in its inculturation praxis, the African church and its theology have an important role to play in giving rise to a new society which will evolve out of a new harmony forged between traditional Africa and modernity."[41] Many like J. N. K. Mugambi agree with Martey that a new theological approach was necessary for the holistic advancement of Africans and African societies rather than piecemeal approaches that focus on piecemeal problems. However, Mugambi would not embrace Martey's dialectical encounter of both liberation and inculturation approaches as the solution. Instead, he calls for and heralded a complete paradigm shift from both liberation and inculturation models to a reconstruction model. He takes reconstruction to be the most appropriate or relevant metaphor for doing theology in contemporary Africa, and many who share his conviction have adopted this approach for christological discourse.

Christologies of Reconstruction: Jesus "in" Africa

The main idea that this category advances is that Christianity and Christian theology should help to build (more accurately, rebuild or reconstruct) African societies, enhance human flourishing, and chart a new future for Africa as a continent. Mugambi acknowledges that "In Africa, Christianity has been used for too long to destroy the cultural and religious foundations of African peoples."[42] This necessitates inculturation. But then he concedes that "Marc-Ela [sic] rightly emphasizes that inculturation is not possible in Africa as long as Africans are not in control of their own lives and destinies, both outside and within the Church."[43] This underscores the priority of liberation. However, while the inculturation model is limited given the priority of liberation, Mugambi thinks that the liberation model is contrived because of the superficial and mistaken "transposition of the liberation theme from the Old Testament to the African experience."[44] For Mugambi, the mistake lies in the fact that while the Exodus of Israel portrays a movement over time and

---

41. Martey, *African Theology*, 142.
42. Mugambi, *From Liberation to Reconstruction*, xiv.
43. Mugambi, 10.
44. Mugambi, 14.

space, Africans occupy the same geographical space over time. "The theme of *reconstruction* is made attractive by the fact that it highlights the necessity of creating a new society within the same geographical space, but across different historical moments."[45] In light of the historical moment in which Mugambi was writing, that is, "After the cold war, Africa needs theologians committed to the process of reconstruction as a multi-disciplinary endeavour."[46] Such reconstruction will be tripartite, consisting of personal reconstruction, cultural reconstruction, and ecclesial reconstruction.

Kä Mana similarly speaks of "the prospect of a new christology as foundational in building a new African society."[47] Mana notes that the present reality of African societies is characterized by three negatives. First is a sense of powerlessness, that is, "the inability of contemporary African societies to resolve the fundamental problems confronting them."[48] This powerlessness is a result of, among other things, "a serious underestimation of our own capabilities and of our historical ingenuities, 'the negative image' we have of ourselves."[49] The second problem is that of the inconsistency of our actions that do not adequately match and address the prevailing ills of the continent. The third problem is similar to the first but quite distinct in its own right; it is the problem of destroying our own self-worth through "the loss of meaning for our lives as peoples, cultures and civilisations. We have belittled, devalued and 'demonetised' ourselves, so to speak, by ceasing to believe in our own inner strengths and creative capabilities for building the future."[50]

In order to change these realities, Mana proposes what he calls a new way of thinking that will help "promote an 'Africa' which is responsible for its own destiny."[51] This proposal is primarily hinged on the person of Christ and its appropriation toward this project of reconstruction. He is convinced that a "dialogue with Jesus Christ offers to Africa new possibilities for the struggle against the powerlessness of our being, the inconsistency of our action and

---

45. Mugambi, 15.
46. Mugambi, 17.
47. Mana, *Christians and Churches of Africa*, 4.
48. Mana, 8.
49. Mana, 10.
50. Mana, 17.
51. Mana, 21.

the devaluation of our presence in the world of today."[52] In this dialogue, what kind of Christology would serve as the catalyst for fashioning a new future for Africa from its present non-being, non-sense, and non-life? Mana adapts Essoh Ngome's interpretation of the ancient Egyptian myth of Isis and Osiris as symbolic of Africa and extends it to understand the person of Christ for Africa's reconstruction. To this end, Mana claims that it is "necessary to think of Christ from a mythological perspective where he represents a revitalising power of our divided and dislocated Africa."[53] In this sense, Christ becomes for Africans the new force that empowers from non-being, inspires creativity rather than non-thinking, and repairs the bad self-image of the African before the rest of the world. This new vital energy that Christ embodies must be appropriated by the church in Africa for social reconstruction all over the continent.

These three approaches as overviewed are not necessarily exhaustive, but are presently the dominant models of theological/christological reflections in most of Africa – West, East, Central, and Southern Africa. What is conspicuously missing in the discussions therefore is any reference to North Africa and the current christological conversations in that region and this is the general state of affairs in the most popular literature on Christology in Africa. We will attempt this discussion quite briefly mainly because it important to also know the contemporary understandings of Christ in that part of the Christian world, but also because it helps to further demonstrate the complexity of identifying a given Christology (or any concept for that matter) as being African or un-African.

Other Christologies in Africa

According to Elias Kifon Bongmba:

> Africans have articulated two perspectives about Christianity that have historical groundings. The first view is that Christianity is an African religion because Christianity was established in North Africa before it went to Europe and other parts of the world. The second view is that Christianity is a colonial project

---

52. Mana, 27.
53. Mana, 32.

because modern Christianity came to Africa through extensive and intensive contacts between Africa and Europe.[54]

The first view is generally the case even today in North Africa and Ethiopia, particularly with respect to the Coptic Church of Egypt and the Ethiopian Orthodox Church, two surviving ancient churches in the continent. Christianity in the rest of Africa however is mostly understood from the second point of view. It is common knowledge in church history that Christianity in North Africa emerged from the earliest days of the faith and thrived into the seventh century. During that time, the region made remarkable and lasting contributions to the formation of the Christian tradition. This is evident in the contributions of such individual giants of the Christian faith from North Africa like Origen, Cyprian, Tertullian of Carthage, Didymus the Blind, Athanasius of Alexandria, Augustine of Hippo, and Cyril of Alexandria, just to name a few.[55]

This rich history notwithstanding, there is a visible absence of North Africa and Ethiopia in the literature on African theological discourse, which is due largely to the Islamic invasion of the region since the seventh following. Today, there is only a minority Christian presence in North Africa and most of the Christian traditions that have survived there are not continuous with the general characteristic of Christianity in the rest of Africa. However, this state of affairs may be changing in some small measure, as Anthony O'Mahony seems to suggest. He points out that the Coptic Church is experiencing a revival both in its monastic and ecclesial life, and also making inroads to the rest of Africa where the search continues for an authentic (non-Western) African Christianity. Therefore,

> as an ancient church of Africa it [the Coptic Church] is attempting to be part of the continent's future beyond the influence of Islam, not only in its most recent sphere of ecclesial influence in Ethiopia and now Eritrea, but also as a dynamic and evangelising church across east, west and southern Africa.[56]

---

54. Bongmba, "Christianity in North Africa," 25.

55. Bongmba, 29–34.

56. O'Mahony, "Coptic Christianity in Modern Egypt," 510. For an excellent treatment of Africa's impact on classical Christianity, see Oden, *How Africa Shaped the Christian Mind*.

With respect to Christology, these North African Christian traditions are generally non-Chalcedonian, and this is the case for both the Coptic Church of Egypt and the Ethiopian Orthodox Church. Since the former has historical ties with the latter, it is unsurprising that their Christologies are the same or similar. Donald Crummey says that the Ethiopian church continued to view itself as orthodox and, "Their sense of Orthodoxy came in their commitment to christological doctrine as they had received it from Alexandria."[57] They understand this received Alexandrian Christology "as *täwahedo*, or union, emphasising the union of the divine and human natures of Christ, whom they view as one person with one nature, which is uniquely divine *and* human. The common western designation of this position as 'Monophysite' sits uneasily with some of its adherents."[58] Similarly, in his comparative study of the Christology of the Ethiopian Orthodox Church (EOC) and Chalcedonian Christology, Stephen Strauss concludes that

> The EOC rejects Chalcedonian theology because it seems to imply that the deity and humanity of Christ were not perfectly united. Chalcedonian churches must ask themselves if a theology that teaches that Christ did anything—including die—in only one of his natures can ultimately preserve the perfect union of his deity and humanity."[59]

For Strauss however, this does not mean irreconcilable differences because, "Both the Chalcedonian ('two natures') and Ethiopian Orthodox ('one nature') verbal forms are used to express the idea that Christ is truly God and truly man."[60] In this sense therefore, both Christologies can be seen to affirm the union of full divinity and full humanity in Christ as one indivisible person. The difference is that Ethiopian Orthodox Christology emphasizes quite strongly the perfection of the union such that a *tertium quid* obtains (thus the charge of monophysitism), whereas Chalcedon seeks to maintain both the distinction of divinity and humanity as well as their union in Christ.

What stands out from this discussion is the fact that discourse about Christ in ancient and contemporary North African Christianity, unlike the

---

57. Crummey, "Church and Nation," 459.
58. Crummey, 459.
59. Strauss, "Perspectives on the Nature of Christ," 227–28.
60. Strauss, 226.

conversations in the rest of the continent as seen above, continues to necessitate engagement with creedal Christology. This discussion also shows that it is rather simplistic to construe some Christology as "African" when some part of the continent is ignored in the conversation. Another notable matter is the fact that this Christology does not appear to relate the person and work of Christ to the lived realities of the people (e.g. by engaging in or reflecting christologically on social and cultural issues). While tracing the christological conversations in North Africa in greater detail is beyond the scope of this project, it is hoped that the proposal to be advanced in chapter 5 might serve this context too, given its engagement with Islam and creedal Christology. In the meantime, the general overview presented above about the christological conversations in Africa suffices for present purposes. With this "big picture" account in our view, it is time to consider more specifically two christological formulations from Nigeria. These constructive Christologies may or may not appropriate the approaches just outlined. But as will be seen shortly, these broad approaches help in understanding particular Christologies in Africa like the ones we will now consider.

Some Constructive Christologies in Nigeria

There are about four Nigerian theologians (to the best of my knowledge) that have attempted creatively to construct a contextual Christology that is as African as it is Christian. These include Enyi Ben Udoh's Guest Christology, Ukachukwu Chris Magnus's King Christology, Victor Ezigbo's Revealer Christology, and Ikechukwu Anthony Kanu's Igbo-African Christology.[61] In this section, we will consider two out of these four christological formulations (those of Udoh and Ezigbo).[62]

---

61. See Udo, *Guest Christology*; Magnus, *Christ the African King*; Ezigbo, *Re-imagining African Christologies*; and Kanu, *Towards an Igbo-African Christology*.

62. The main reason for leaving out Magnus's Christology is a practical one, particularly with respect to space. In order to adequately present and robustly engage each christological formulation, a decent amount of space is required and which, for purposes of this project, is not quite feasible. But since Udoh's and Magnus's Christologies share a certain affinity, it seems reasonable that one rather than both of them should be treated. Since Udoh's is the earlier of the two and echoes both liberation and inculturation motifs, it seems fitting to explore this Christology. Anthony's Igbo African Christology is a more recent work (2017) than Ezigbo's (2011), but the choice of Ezigbo's Christology is informed by the fact that it attempts to

While Udoh wrote at a time when African Christology was blossoming, Ezigbo has emerged on the contemporary stage at a time when the theological enterprise in Africa is gaining global reckoning. Their combination therefore provides us with sample cases of intentional efforts in Christologizing from both the past and the present Nigerian context.

The Guest Christology of Enyi Ben Udoh

Enyi Ben Udoh, an ordained minister of the Presbyterian Church of Nigeria, first advanced the Guest Christology model in his doctoral dissertation at Princeton Theological Seminary in 1983, which was later published as *Guest Christology: An Interpretative View of the Christological Problem in Africa*. His main concern in this work is that "the image of Christ, the traditional way in which Christ was introduced in Africa, was largely responsible for the prevailing faith schizophrenia among African Christians."[63] By faith schizophrenia, a concept he borrows from Bishop Desmond Tutu, Udoh means the conflict of allegiance among African Christians between the Christian faith on the one hand and their indigenous religious beliefs and practices on the other. The solution is "that Christ must be encountered afresh within our historical and cultural context in order to make sense."[64] To help his reader better understand the problem, Udoh begins with a description of the rather disturbing scenario that forms the context of his christological reflection, and that is the missionary encounter in his hometown of Calabar, Nigeria – a scenario that passes for a case of forced entry. This situation is a clear instance of a wider problem, which he notes thus:

> The history of the Christian faith consists of a set of paradoxes in Africa. It is at once a story of triumph and hazard. On the one hand, it conveys a sense of relief and hope, and points to a whole new world of possibilities brought about by the Christian ethos. On the other hand, it speaks candidly of the continuing

---

integrate a number of approaches as opposed to Anthony's which focuses exclusively on the inculturation approach.

63. Udoh, *Guest Christology*, i–ii.
64. Udoh, ii

oppression, alienation and despair in which Christianity has conspired.⁶⁵

Udoh finds this bewildering and sets out to critically examine the story of Jesus Christ as communicated through the efforts of white missionaries in Africa as a whole, and particularly the Scottish mission in Calabar. His aim is to understand this story, not as it is understood and told by the missionaries, but "primarily from the standpoint of the audience."⁶⁶ He argues that the activities of white missionaries in Calabar point to the fact that Christianity has been equated with Western culture thus making it a mere tool of colonial imperialism. The person of Christ and the Christian gospel were introduced in Calabar (and to Africa) in a way that the people's cultural identity, sense of selfhood, religious life, communal structures, and economic status were all violated and vandalized. Udoh captures this sorry state of affairs as follows:

> Church and State in Calabar were dual only in theory. The distinction was practically non-existent. The Church took over the traditional authority system, stripped the rulers of their hereditary power, abrogated their laws and imposed new ones in their place, including the notorious Sabbath law of 1850. A system of government which was run by the Council of Ekpe (constricted social club)—the law enforcement agency—was cast aside in order to introduce the Ten Commandments and the Scottish Book of Discipleship. Calabar now has more laws than before the missionaries came. Education further undermined the traditional structure. Treaties were a viable strategy of acculturation, putting the indigenous party at a terrible disadvantage with their colonial counterparts. Behind all this was the force of arms, imposition of a hut tax and free labor. In short, a theocratic system was instituted.⁶⁷

For Udoh therefore, the entrance or introduction of Christ in Africa as Lord was technically an imposition – not only of the lordship of Christ but also of the Western colonial lords. It was a clear case of displacement and

---

65. Udoh, 1.
66. Udoh, 3.
67. Udoh, 72.

replacement backed by the force of arms, since the missionaries enjoyed the protection of the British colonial authorities. This allowed them to carry out their activities through fiat rather than through negotiation ensuing from mutual respect. In fact, those who dared to oppose the missionaries incurred the wrath of colonial might.[68] That the mission house served as a place of refuge for those who could no longer live in their communities for some misdemeanor is testimony to the protection the missionaries enjoyed. In addition, education was used as a tool for the "civilizing" work of the mission since every element of the native culture was considered depraved and barbaric. Schools "were used as an inducement to lure Africans into the missionary orbit for initiation into 'Christian' civilization. Africans attended mission schools with well-defined political, social and economic goals."[69] This became the only means to progress in life owing to the missionary condemnation and colonial disruption of every facet of the indigenous structures of society. As a result of all these things, Udoh scathingly concludes that "Christ entered the African scene as a forceful, impatient and unfriendly tyrant. He was presented as invalidating the history and institutions of a people in order to impose his rule upon them."[70] This has led to a commonly held view of Christ among Africans "as the most visible and publicized symbol of foreign domination ever."[71] Christianity in general, but more so, Christ in particular is considered a *stranger* among Africans, raising doubts as to "the validity and relevance of the Scripture for the African, and over the credibility of the Christian God in our part of the world."[72]

Consequently, Christianity has not been whole-heartedly embraced by Africans, and the most telltale sign of this is a schizophrenic faith – a case of divided allegiance or "the dilemma of combining the Christian principles with African traditional religion without being fully African or completely Christian."[73] This problem for Udoh is primarily christological because, while

---

68. Udoh notes that these punishments on the natives include the "imposition of fines on the Efik [an ethnic group] for 'insulting' missionaries, destruction of Old Town by the Royal Navy in 1855, and the formation of the Young Calabar—a watchdog organization of which the Consul, John Beecroft, made himself a member." Udoh, 60.

69. Udoh, 63.
70. Udoh, 64.
71. Udoh, 75.
72. Udoh, 6.
73. Udoh, 10–11.

the concept of God is inherent in Africa's religious consciousness, that of Christ is completely foreign or strange. He says quite poignantly that "While the average member conceives of Christ as a stranger, the church unequivocally keeps celebrating his Lordship. Creeds, sermons and liturgies are addressed in a lordship garb."[74] Udoh however insists that Africans find it difficult to accept a man who is also at the same time God, because in African thinking man is not God and God cannot be human – or as Udoh puts it in "Pidgin"[75] English, "*God no bi mann; man no bi god.*"[76] This makes it necessary for Jesus to be presented to the African in a way that is acceptable so that Christ not only enters Africa, but becomes fully African and is wholeheartedly accepted by Africans. But the question now is, how? Udoh considers three christological proposals preceding his that aim at addressing this faith pathology in Africa, categorizing them under the themes of healing, liberation, and kinship. While he commends them for sounding the alarm bell, he finds them to be inadequate in the sense that they all portray (and rightly so) "this underlying configuration of Jesus Christ as a stranger among us. But none is explicit enough in spelling out what that means for Christ in Africa."[77]

Therefore, Udoh employs, as a christological paradigm, the social framework that is widespread in African cultures "by which guests are received, resettled and initiated into the mainstream of society."[78] It is the process by which a stranger goes through in order to become part and parcel of a new community they move into. What does this process of naturalization look like and how does it inform Udoh's Christology? When a stranger or guest comes to an African community, they would present themself to a host who welcomes them and guides them on how to live in the new community. They are socialized into the life of the community over time and helped to understand the values and norms of the community. If the guest shows good behavior and contributes to the community's growth, they will be fully assimilated into and even honored in the community; but if they show bad behavior (e.g. stealing or murder), they risk expulsion from the community.

---

74. Udoh, 216.

75. The word refers to the non-formal English widely spoken by people in Nigeria. It is similar to but not the same with the Creole language.

76. Udoh, *Guest Christology*, 81.

77. Udoh, 167.

78. Udoh, 13.

In summary, the process entails submission to the host community's structures and authority, deferment to and depending on the host community for guidance about its ways, and serving the community so as to make positive contributions for its well-being.

Similarly, Christ should be construed as a guest rather than a (or the) Lord because the idea of Christ as Lord carries with it oppressive tendencies in the African context. Here, Udoh echoes the need for the liberation of Africans from such oppression by rejecting the priority of the lordship of Christ. However, this does not mean that Christ can never be Lord in Africa. It simply means that he cannot and must not be introduced as such from the onset. The only way that Christ can legitimately become Lord in Africa is for him to go through the naturalization process in African societies, and it is in this effort to naturalize Christ in Africa that we see Udoh's pursuit of inculturation. Christ needs to come, or be (re)introduced, to African communities not as Lord or a divine person but as a human being on equal footing with us. This move for Udoh entails the priority of Christology from below. He must first be received as a human guest who must defer to his host community. After a long time, and given good behavior, he may then be accepted as a member of the community. If he shows himself to be of great benefit to the people, he may become their ruler or Lord. To this end, Udoh categorically states that as Africans "we reject the Lordship of Christ as a proper starting point of African Christology."[79] Instead, a truly African Christology must be from below and not from above so that as a full human being Christ can be accepted into African society. Africans have to play the host and initiate Christ as a kin through the traditional process of naturalization and inclusion into the community's participatory life. It is only when this has happened that we can take Jesus not only as "a legitimate guest" but also make him "a kin whose presence we can celebrate, whose voice we can heed and in whom we can reaffirm our kinship with one another."[80] It is at this point that he can unfold his power and perhaps expand his mission and lordship in a new culture and among a new people. For Udoh, if Christ is to be fully embraced or accepted among Africans, thereby engendering an authentically African Christology,

---

79. Udoh, 167.
80. Udoh, 246.

he must be seen to have legitimately naturalized or else he will be rejected or at best half-heartedly accepted.

In response to Udoh's Guest Christology, one must first commend his genuine attempt at providing not only a diagnosis, but also a treatment for Africa's faith pathology or religious schizophrenia via a christological prescription. This commendation is not merely a matter of courtesy or intellectual charity, but an acknowledgment of the fact that the problem is indeed real in Africa, more than two decades after Udoh's submission. More so, his solution (a christological one) is most appropriate given the centrality of Christ to the Christian faith. Similarly, the need to address Africa's socioeconomic problems, which is rightly (though not solely) traceable to the activities of colonial authorities, is inescapable for Christianity and Christian theology. One cannot but agree with Udoh that in many instances, missionaries were regrettably complicit in these oppressive operations.

Tite Tiénou also points out that this christological model is more helpful than others on offer because of its appropriation of the idea of hospitality, which is an important element in all (not just African) cultures. This is something that the Western missionaries took for granted so that they were oblivious of the necessary humility of a guest if the much-needed hospitality of a host is to be enjoyed. Udoh himself makes this same point thus:

> If the missionaries had remained open and receptive, they might have avoided a mass condemnation of the society and might have discerned God's act and purposes therein. But having failed to work out clearly in their minds, the implications of their monotheistic doctrine in a different culture, they concluded that Africa had no knowledge of God and therefore could not be associated with the Father of Jesus Christ.[81]

It is not difficult to see that if Western Christian missionaries had entered Africa with this mindset, there would have been more circumspection on their part in executing the missionary project. Therefore, Tiénou says that "To understand Jesus as Guest is the most appropriate Christological approach in contemporary Africa. Furthermore, this approach has the potential of

---

81. Udoh, 69.

enriching global theological conversations."⁸² The intellectual humility necessary to genuinely and attentively listen to the theological and cultural "other" and to submit oneself to the other's intellectual hospitality is the point that is crucial here. This is the main strength of Udoh's Guest christological model.

However, Udoh's proposal suffers from a number of serious theological and conceptual problems. First, while it is true that Western missionaries were either silent about or complicit in the oppressive activities of colonial authorities, this does not necessarily warrant either a rejection of their Christology or a validation of the Guest christological paradigm. This will only be the case if it can be shown that there was something intrinsic to the Christology of Western missionaries that demeans and thereby grounds the dehumanization of African peoples. It is one thing to note the missionary understanding of Christ and another thing to show the appropriation (or rather misappropriation) of this understanding toward undermining African beliefs, values, and practices. This is where Udoh first stumbles. He identifies the Christology of missionaries with their misappropriation of the doctrine, and therefore calls for a wholesale rejection of that Christology, particularly the priority of the lordship of Christ. But the mere fact that the lordship of Christ was either projected by the missionaries or perceived by Africans (or both) as entrenching and legitimizing the lordship of colonial authorities does not in itself mean that there is an intrinsic problem with a Christology from above. Since it is a problem with its appropriation, the solution it seems, is not its rejection as a legitimate starting point for African christological reflection, but actually its re-appropriation in an African context (more on this in the next chapter).

Second, Udoh is sympathetic – even if he does not fully subscribe – to a critical reading of Scripture. This is why he demands that a properly African Christology must take into account the historicity of Jesus as recorded in the Bible. It must be noted that Udoh distinguishes his idea of the historicity of Jesus from that of the historical Jesus of historical-critical methods. The historicity of Jesus is not concerned about what might be known or not known about Jesus's historical life, but rather "seeks to see Jesus in a concrete human mold which can affect and be affected by African experience."⁸³ This recognition of the historicity of Jesus is, on the surface, unproblematic until one

---

82. Tiénou, "Jesus as Guest," 1.
83. Tiénou, 223.

considers Udoh's stated intention or purpose for this recognition. He claims that acknowledging the full humanity of Jesus and thus his initiation into African societies "puts him on equal footing with us, not only as completely human but also as one with whom we share a common history and destiny."[84] This claim may also appear unproblematic prima facie, but Udoh wants to use this as a premise to validate his rejection of Christ's divinity. He claims that African "traditional theism considers it an anathema for any historical being to claim for himself or for any other individual, living or living-dead, the divine prerogatives."[85] It seems therefore that Udoh's treatment of Jesus is simply a case of mistaken identity as seen above. He says that "Jesus is *far from knowing all* the social turns and experiential road signs of the African. Like any other guest, *his understanding of the new environment is limited*. A host has the responsibility of taking him on a tour of his world."[86] This by implication is a denial of omniscience, one of the divine prerogatives, and by extension, a denial of the divinity of Christ whose knowledge Scripture narrates includes knowing the thoughts of people (cf. Luke 5:22). While making every effort to preserve the full humanity of Christ, denying or de-emphasizing his full divinity in the process solves the problem by creating another one. Because Udoh's Guest Christology treats the human Jesus more like a nineteenth-century white missionary to Africa and, in doing so, buys into the same error he accuses the missionaries of doing (i.e. equating their lordship with the lordship of Christ), he seems to end up with "another Christ." We may grant that perhaps, because the missionaries themselves made the same move, Udoh simply follows suit in order to subvert this move, such that his rejection of their lordship inevitably means the rejection of the lordship of Christ as an unintended consequence. The problem however is that in stating this rejection of the lordship and divinity of Christ *ab initio*, Udoh's Guest Christology turns out to be nothing short of border-line Arianism.

Another problem with the idea of framing Jesus's picture using a guest paradigm is the fact that it would not be able to account for instances in Scripture where Jesus, as human, played the host. Two examples in this regard stand out and these are the story of the Last Supper in Luke 22:7–13 and that

---

84. Tiénou, 243.
85. Tiénou, 210.
86. Tiénou, 227.

of the encounter of the Emmaus road disciples in Luke 24:13–31. In the first story, we see Jesus giving instructions to Peter and John about making preparations for their Passover celebration. He directed them to a house where they asked the owner for the guest room in which he (the teacher) would eat the Passover with his disciples. Here, Udoh might be able to say that Jesus had to ask the owner for permission rather than taking over the house by force, and that he also asked to use the guest room rather than the main room of the house. This reciprocity of guest humility with host hospitality has been noted and affirmed above. However, the Jesus in this passage who knew that at the very time that Peter and John would enter the city, a man will be returning home with a jar of water, and knew the house the man would be going to, and knew that the house had a furnished guest room, cannot be the same Jesus of Udoh's Guest Christology who does not and cannot know his way around in an African culture and society without the guidance of his host. In the Last Supper event proper (Luke 22:14–20) just as in the Emmaus road story, we see Jesus playing the host by breaking bread, giving thanks, and giving it to those present with him – a rather Lordly act. What this entails for present purposes is that Udoh needed to account for Christ as both guest (human) and host (divine) at once.

Finally, and on a more practical note, this christological approach, if fully embraced as the Christology of some church in Africa, has the potential of traditionalizing an incomplete, thus erroneous understanding of Christ. Assuming Jesus is understood and received as a human guest but not as Lord, and that this understanding is passed on in the church from one generation to the next, will it be possible to reverse that belief? Would that understanding of Christ not crystallize and become difficult if not impossible to change at a later time? In addition, how many years or generations will it take for Christ to become fully naturalized in Africa? In following this approach, would we not run into the danger of having two Christs: one a guest the other naturalized? This is a real and present danger because of the sharp line that Udoh draws between the human Jesus and the divine Christ, which means that a Nestorian shadow also lurks in the corner somewhere in this Christology.[87] Therefore, we will consider another christological proposal,

---

87. While it is possible to pursue a rehabilitation of Udoh's Guest Christology as might become evident later in this chapter, it is beyond the reach of this project to attempt

one that is more contemporary to see if it offers a better understanding of Christ for the Nigerian Christian than Udoh's.

The Revealer Christology of Victor Ezigbo

Victor Ezigbo presents what is arguably one of the most significant recent contributions to the christological conversations in Africa. In *Re-Imagining African Christologies: Conversing with the Interpretations and Appropriations of Jesus in Contemporary African Christianity*, Ezigbo proposes a christological model he calls Revealer Christology – an understanding of Christ as one who reveals both true divinity and true humanity to us. He says, "Central to the concept of Jesus as a revealer of divinity and humanity is the claim that he functions as a figure through whom the Christians can have access to a true knowledge and relationship with God and their fellow human beings."[88] He further states that this christological model defends "the proposition that the Christ-Event interprets and mediates divinity and humanity for the purpose of enacting, sustaining, judging and rebuilding the relationship between God and humanity, and between human beings and the spirit being that many African Christians construe as malevolent."[89]

Ezigbo first considers some of the major constructive Christologies of contemporary African Christianity, which he grouped into three – missionary/neo-missionary Christologies, culture-oriented Christologies, and liberation-oriented Christologies. He sees and treats Byang Kato as advocating a neo-missionary Christology (as he calls it); Enyi Ben Udoh's Guest Christology, the Ancestor Christology of Charles Nyamiti, and others like Kwame Bediako as advancing a culture-oriented Christology; and Mercy Oduyoye's Feminist Christology, among others, as an instance of liberation-oriented. At the end of his analysis of these African Christologies, Ezigbo draws the conclusion that all these christological proposals fall short of a desirable and adequate Christology for the African context for two main reasons. The first is that these Christologies "have not allowed the person and work of Jesus Christ to critique their contextual approaches and agendas."[90] The point is a very

---

this rehabilitation.
    88. Ezigbo, *Re-imagining African Christologies*, 174.
    89. Ezigbo, 174.
    90. Ezigbo, 102.

important one because contextual categories should never be appropriated uncritically, which is the accusation that Ezigbo seems to be making against the christological proposals he considered, thus their inadequacy.

The second reason for such inadequacy, according to Ezigbo is that "while these christological models claim to be contextual, they seem not to engage seriously with the christological concerns of many Christians who do not have any formal theological training."[91] This can only mean one thing: an avoidable disconnect between the church in Africa and African theological practitioners, such that works produced by the latter turn out to be of no use whatsoever to the former. For this reason, Ezigbo ventures into an examination of these local Christologies also known as Grassroots Christologies of African Christians so as to avoid this disconnect. He concludes from his treatment that "many Christians, irrespective of their church denominations, perceive and relate to Jesus Christ merely as a problem-solver."[92] They are merely concerned about "the existential significance of Jesus for the issues of poverty, fear of evil spirits, the danger of insecurity, and quest to achieve wellbeing."[93] While these are legitimate concerns, Ezigbo thinks that the picture of Christ that emerges from these Christologies is also problematic. This therefore means that both the Christologies of African theologians and those of African Christians from the grassroots are equally deficient. While the former lacks a self-critical mechanism and a genuine interaction with the grassroots, the latter is purely consumerist and solution-oriented.

This is where Ezigbo's Revealer Christology comes in as a remedy to the inherent problems of both the Christologies of Africa's theological elite and those of grassroots Christians. This Christology not only seeks to know what Christ would look like if he is understood based on the questions and yearnings of Africans, but also what both Christ and African Christians would look like if he is construed "as the questioner who critiques and reshapes their perceptions of their existential problems and the solutions to such problems."[94] Ezigbo believes that articulating the issue in this way redirects the focus on the Christ and his significance not necessarily from our point of view but from his

---

91. Ezigbo, 102.
92. Ezigbo, 138.
93. Ezigbo, 102.
94. Ezigbo, 144.

point of view. It is in this sense that Ezigbo construes Christ primarily as God's definitive and complete revelation, who communicates and interprets divinity and humanity to us in order to make possible human relating with God. He rejects the classification of revelation as general and special because it betrays the unity of God's revelation. Instead, following Karl Barth, Ezigbo equates revelation with Christ himself as God-man, who is the revealer of, not only God, but also humanity. This concept of "revealer" is the key component that distinguishes Ezigbo's proposal from other christological models in Africa

> in that it construes Jesus is a revealer of divinity (God, lesser spirit beings, and the spirit world) and humanity (human beings and the human world). To say that Jesus is the revealer of divinity and humanity . . . means that he communicates and interprets divinity and humanity for the purpose of enacting a relationship between God and humanity.[95]

Christology, in this sense, is not just ontological but also relational, which implies that both "from above" and "from below" approaches to Christology are mistaken based on the fact that the focus in these approaches is purely on the metaphysics of the incarnation. In addition, and perhaps more importantly for Ezigbo, "the major christological problem with constructing a Christology either from below or from above is that such Christology will run the risk of introducing a destructive gulf and dichotomy between the divinity and humanity of Jesus Christ."[96] This simply means that one of the two natures is often prioritized and the other construed in light of the one given priority, a situation that Udoh exemplified above with respect to Jesus's humanity and one that is taken to its extreme end by the quest for the historical Jesus, just as Logos Christology is charged with doing the same with respect to Jesus's divinity. Ezigbo wants to avoid both extremes, so he proposes a dialectic-holistic approach to doing Christology. "The dialectic-holistic approach is grounded in the claim that in the Christ-Event we encounter *a figure*, Jesus the Christ, who embodies divinity and humanity."[97]

---

95. Ezigbo, 153.
96. Ezigbo, 158.
97. Ezigbo, 159.

Ezigbo posits four presuppositions that undergird this claim. (1) Christ must be understood as God's single complete and definitive revelation of both true divinity and true humanity. This understanding means that we will refrain from seeing Christ as the revelation of God alone but also of what it means to be human. (2) The Jesus question is not merely ontological but fundamentally relational with respect to God and humans and humans among themselves. Therefore, we must avoid the tendency to subsume the identity of Christ to just the relationship between his divine nature and his human nature. (3) God, by revealing himself in Christ, makes himself accessible to humans; thus Christ "is a divine *manifestational act*."[98] (4) Christ is also a hermeneutical act by which divinity and humanity are interpreted such that he is the basis for criticizing and judging our prior understandings of both divinity and humanity. With these presuppositions in place, Ezigbo proceeds to show how Christ reveals and critiques both divinity and humanity in the African contexts.

Christ, as the revealer of true divinity, becomes the reference point by which the idea of divinity in African indigenous religions as well as in contemporary African Christianity must be reexamined. Ezigbo construes "divinity in a way that includes spirit beings, such as ancestors, angelic beings, Satan, evil forces or spirits, and God."[99] The reason for this, he says, is the fact that Jesus is seen in Scripture to have contended with the spirit world, and that this broad definition intersects with the lived realities of Christians in Africa. First on the idea of God in both African Christianity and African indigenous religions, Ezigbo argues that God is viewed as absolutely powerful and utterly remote or transcendent. However, in the Christ event we are introduced to "a radical and a paradoxical picture of God—God is not only transcendent but ontologically immanent; God is not only sovereign and powerful, God is also powerless and vulnerable; and God is not only the *other* and unique in God's self, God is also self-giving."[100] Second, after an extended discussion on the idea of the malevolent spirits (ancestors, demons, and Satan), which is so pervasive in the spiritualized cosmology and experience of Africans, Ezigbo concludes that these are a distortion of divinity and the divine plan.

---

98. Ezigbo, 154. Emphasis in original.
99. Ezigbo, 176.
100. Ezigbo, 213.

Therefore, as is often the case in African indigenous religious practices, rather than attempting to make these malevolent powers act benevolently toward us either by ritualistic appeasement or exorcisms, they are to be resisted and restrained through the person and the power of Christ. "Like Jesus and the apostles, Christians have the authority to restrain demonic activities against God's rule on earth by following Jesus and the apostles in rebuking demons from people and combating demonic activities in their communities and societies."[101]

Finally, the Christ event also reveals to us true humanity, portraying to us humanity as dependent on God and thus standing in relation to him such that God, not humans, is the center of existence. This understanding disqualifies the solution-oriented Christologies so pervasive in Africa, which are generally anthropocentric. However, while humanity itself is not the center of human existence, humanity is shown by the Christ event to be precious before God who not only created us but also restores our broken relationship with him via Christ assuming our humanity. The implication of this for Ezigbo is that "The Christ-Event upsets, critiques, and condemns any understanding of humanity which is inherently oppressive."[102] Therefore, all forms of personal and social evils that hinder any persons from experiencing full humanity ought to be addressed by the church in and through Christ. This concludes our review of Victor Ezigbo's Revealer Christology, which must now be assessed based on its merits and demerits.

Ezigbo's is a highly commendable christological construction for many reasons. Of great significance is the fact that he grounds his christological model on the foundations of Nicaea (325) and Chalcedon (451). He points out that although creedal Christology does not necessarily solve the christological problem, it does provide the necessary parameter for any Christologizing. It is based on this "necessary parameter" of Nicene-Chalcedonian Christology that Ezigbo identifies both divinity and humanity as the two aspects of Jesus's revelation. This is important because many African Christologies either completely disregard this important tradition of the faith or treat it marginally as a mere appendage to their christological construction. Some even take it to be irrelevant to the African situation as will be seen in the next chapter. However,

---

101. Ezigbo, 242.
102. Ezigbo, 269.

if christological discourse in Africa desires to pick out the same Christ as the historical Christian church, then the appropriation of and engagement with creedal claims about Christ is needful as exemplified by Ezigbo.

Ezigbo's treatment of Grassroots Christology is also highly commendable. He not only presents the individual and corporate perceptions of Christ among local Christians in Nigeria, he also engages such perceptions in a way that both informs and is corrected by his constructive Christology. This differs quite remarkably from another work that pursued a similar project but on a wider scale, which seems to present these views about Christ on the streets of Africa as completely valid in their own rights.[103] Such an approach is not only relativistic but also seems to suggest that the lay Christian does not need the trained theologian in the formation of their understanding of the person of Christ. What Ezigbo's work demonstrates is the need for the trained theologian to be attentive to the christological reflections of the lay Christian for purposes of both information and correction. This comports with the idea of doing theology as providing direction to the church in its performance of the divine drama.[104]

Another attractive aspect of Ezigbo's Christology is the fact that it treats African cultural and pre-Christian religious heritage as neither inherently good (as some African theologians do), nor as completely evil and thus not useful for Christian theological reflection (as some Western missionaries have done). Instead, he engages with this heritage in his christological reflection in a way that is both charitable and critical – sometimes using them to clarify the Christ event and other times using the Christ event to critique these indigenous beliefs and practices. Ezigbo's holistic-dialectic approach makes it possible for him to sustain this balance. It is a balance that must be maintained in order to construct a Christology that attempts to be, at once, both African and Christian, a goal that Ezigbo (and many other theologians in Africa) seem interested in accomplishing.

Having noted these commendable features of Ezigbo's Revealer Christology, we may also note that the use of Scripture in this christological model could be better. Besides a few proof-texts, Ezigbo did not think it necessary to show how Scripture authorizes his theological claims. The only

---

103. See Stinton, *Jesus of Africa*.
104. See Vanhoozer, *Drama of Doctrine*.

place that Ezigbo provides a sustained treatment of a biblical text in order to ground a theological proposal is in a discussion about the incarnation serving to reveal God as self-giving and self-dispossessing rather than self-serving.[105] On this note, one may say that the use of Scripture in Revealer Christology is generally thin. But a greater, albeit related concern is that Ezigbo's view of Scripture is somewhat ambiguous. One may deduce this from his critique of Kato's so-called Neo-Missionary Christology given the fact that Kato insists on the idea of biblical Christianity in Africa. Reacting to this idea with respect to Christology, Ezigbo says, "The images of Jesus Christ that some theologians have developed for African Christianity need not be exactly the same as the one contained in the Bible. This is not to suggest a denial or a weak idea of the authority of the Bible."[106] Even though Ezigbo does not explain (beyond merely asserting) how this claim is not suggestive of a weak authority of Scripture, it seems quite agreeable that Christology (in Africa or anywhere else for that matter) should not just repeat what is said of Christ in Scripture. But then, how should Scripture be used in constructing such Christologies? For Ezigbo,

> The mosaic of pictures of Jesus represented in the Bible should *only* function as *elastic parameters* for testing the adequacy of the representations of him that emerge from within African Christians' experiences and contexts. Therefore, the biblical representations of Jesus Christ must not repress the possibility of some new christological expressions.[107]

There are two major problems with this claim for us to consider.

First, Ezigbo's idea of an "elastic parameter" seems confusing. To see the problem, let us say that elasticity refers to an inherent ability of deformable materials, which enables them to recover their original shape once the force(s) causing the deformation has been removed.[108] Then let us take a parameter to mean a limiting or variable factor that determines outcome, which means that a parameter conditions rather than it being conditioned.

---

105. See Ezigbo, *Re-imagining African Christologies*, 201–6.
106. Ezigbo, 63.
107. Ezigbo, 63. Emphasis added.
108. For discussions on elasticity, see Sneddon and Berry, "Classical Theory of Elasticity," or Bron, "Elasticity."

So, if a thing is a parameter, it cannot at the same time be elastic (i.e. being reshaped or conditioned by some force). The idea of an elastic parameter therefore is as nonsensical as that of a round square or as dubious as that of an expandable boundary. If a person wants to add more land beyond the bounded area, while still remaining within the boundary lines, all they have to do is to shift the boundary lines. This clearly raises the question: is there actually a boundary line? The problem with this way of thinking when applied to doing Christology is that there cannot be any wrong christological claims or constructions.

The second problem is that, it is not quite clear how the biblical representations of Jesus Christ can repress some new christological expression. Although the idea has been shown to be logically incoherent, but if we grant that the Bible should function as an elastic parameter for testing the adequacy of any new christological expression, then we must also grant that this elastic parameter will always press against the new christological expression. If the expression keeps resisting the pressing of the elastic parameter, then the latter may reach breaking point since being elastic does not mean having a limitless expandability. For the adequacy of a Christology to be tested by Scripture suggests an ontological status for Scripture as the word of God rather than a mere functional status as some elastic parameter. The implication is that Scripture then becomes the primary source of our understanding of Christ rather than a mere instrument for testing a new understanding we are generating from our experiences. This is not to say that our experiences have no place in doing Christology, but that such experience must be informed and authorized by Scripture. But Ezigbo seems to view the scriptural witness about Christ as providing only a controlling, rather than an authorizing function in Christologizing (see the discussion in chapter 3 on revelational control versus authorization).[109] While a position like this may still uphold a very high view of Scripture, it clearly amounts to a very weak use of it.

A final problem with Ezigbo's christological model is the fact that it seems to veer toward a reductionist Christology, which is suggestive even in the title "Revealer Christology." It circumscribes Christology to the revelation of true divinity and humanity in Christ and the purposes of that revealing. Ezigbo tries as much as possible to avoid discussion on the ontological constitution

---

109. Richard Hays makes a similar case in *Moral Vision of the New Testament*, 160.

of Christ and the critical issue of defining the conditions under which divinity and humanity coexist in one person without confusion, mixture, division, and separation, as Chalcedon articulates. He avoids this discussion as though it will make his Christology un-African so to speak. Instead, he claims that discussing the ontological constitution of the hypostatic union should be avoided because, (1) it leads to distortions and heresies, and (2) even the New Testament writers did not go in that direction.[110] However, if discussions about the nature of the hypostatic union would lead to heresies, how does avoiding the discussion stop such heresies from being believed? It seems asserting (1) above is tantamount to saying something like (3) we should not drive cars because it leads to auto accidents. But this does not seem like the only or even the best solution to the problem of auto accidents. Perhaps, what is needed is more training in and mastery of good driving skills and habits (e.g. defensive driving). Similarly, what if improved familiarity with the discussions is what is actually needed? Similarly, with respect to (2), we may posit an equivalent claim as follows, (4) we should not discuss African Christology (something Ezigbo does) simply because the New Testament writers did not go that way. This is a bigger problem because if both (2) and (4) are taken seriously, then any form of Christologizing beyond mere repetition of what is written in the Bible would be impossible. Therefore, avoiding discussion about the nature of the existence of both divinity and humanity in the one divine-human person of Christ is inescapable for any christological reflection whether or not it is claimed to be a non-Western Christology.

Decolonization as De-Missionarization: The Final Word

To summarize, this chapter overviewed the practice of global theology/Christology in general, and its exemplification in the wider African contexts where liberation, inculturation, and reconstruction models have been the dominant approaches. For more specificity, we explored the Guest and Revealer Christologies of Udoh and Ezigbo respectively from the Nigerian context. One of the key features that both Guest and Revealer Christologies share in common, as seen in the discussion above, is a critical attitude toward

---

110. Hays, 201.

the so-called missionary Christology discussed earlier in this chapter. In the Guest Christology of Udoh, this missionary Christology is accused of starting with the claim that Jesus is Lord, which is then construed as an extension of the superiority of white missionaries. As for Ezigbo's Revealer Christology, the problem with missionary Christology is its being intellectualistic and imperialistic. Obviously, the primary concern here is with the missionaries' deliberate eroding of the cultural identities and practices of African peoples by demeaning, denouncing, and destroying them. We noted the various efforts of many African scholars and theologians, such as Kwame Bediako, to address this problem headlong. It turns out on our reading, that the Christologies of Udoh and Ezigbo are also efforts in that direction, albeit in different ways and to varying degrees.[111]

Generally speaking, a driving agenda in these christological efforts ultimately is to rid African understandings of Christ from the understandings that have been conveyed to African Christians by Western missionaries. This is an agenda that is in tandem with the idea of postcolonialism, that is, as R. S. Sugirtharajah puts it, where "everything is contested, everything is contestable."[112] This contestation is what Kwasi Wiredu also identifies as the process of intellectual decolonization, even with respect to Christian teachings. He says that "Any African who espouses Christianity without critical examination at some point of the truth or falsity of its propositions, or the validity of their supporting arguments, where there are any, must incur the label of being an intellectually colonized African."[113] Since this is not a label that anyone would want to carry as a badge of honor, the contestation continues and this decolonization becomes a kind of "de-missionarization" as well, both of Christology and indeed all of Christianity in Africa. A refusal to demissionarize one's Christology from inherited elements is interpreted by some as intellectual subservience of some sort. For example, Clifton Clark says, "In spite of the advances that have undoubtedly taken place in the area of Christology in Africa, to a large extent there still remains a conscious and/or a sub-conscious desire for theological approval by the western theological

---

111. See Bediako, *Theology and Identity*.
112. Sugirtharajah, "Charting the Aftermath," 8.
113. Wiredu, "Toward Decolonizing African Philosophy," 296.

intelligentsia."[114] This mindset engenders an approach to Christology that seeks to be different in order not to be seen as bowing to Western ways of Christologizing.

But what if the mindset itself is false? What if the problem is not necessarily with the Christology of the missionaries but with their use (or abuse) of that Christology? It seems to me that a rejection of this so-called missionary Christology, which for many includes creedal christological affirmations, amounts to throwing out the dogmatic or theological baby with the cultural or imperialistic bath water. What if one can affirm and appropriate the Christology of the missionaries without at the same time embracing their imperialistic and racially supremacist appropriations of it (where that was actually the case)? These are concerns that neither Udoh nor Ezigbo fully took into account as the discussion above has shown, perhaps due to the realities of missionary encounters in their contexts of southeastern Nigeria. The next chapter paints a different picture of missionary presence in Nigeria, this time around in the northern part of the country. It also presents an approach to christological reflection that is canonical and catholic in its fidelity while at the same time being contextually and conceptually sound.

Conclusion

From our study thus far, we may conclude the following. (1) There is a general low use of or engagement with the text of Scripture for supporting christological proposals in Africa. (2) Closely related to that is absence (or perhaps neglect?) of dogmatic Christology for an understanding of Christ in African contexts. (3) Christological discussions in the rest of Africa (West, East, Central, and Southern) fail to engage the context of North Africa such that it cannot qualify as wholly African, and this is one more reason why describing some Christology as "African" is inaccurate. In addition, such an exercise, as exemplified in the Nigerian context, tends to treat the doctrine of Christ mostly as a means to some end. It also tends toward dissociation from or a redefinition of the doctrine from its historic understanding in the Christian tradition in favor of cultural or contextual particularities and uniqueness. It is as if the fact of being distinctly African necessitates a distinctly African

---

114. Clarke, *African Christology*, 151.

understanding of Christ, an understanding that may even be contradictory to the one conveyed in the creeds of the church.

In addition, the outcomes of most efforts in contextual Christologizing are functional Christologies, informing Tiénou's reference to "our generation's preference for functional Christology."[115] However, Tiénou further states that "the basic Christological question remains: what kind of man must Jesus the Christ have been to do the things he did? Consequently, no functional Christology can be adequate without it being grounded in ontology."[116] The point is that Jesus would have to be a certain kind of being or person for him to be able to carry out certain kinds of functions or actions. In this case, it seems artificial then to limit ontological discussions in Christology to certain regions of the world based on the charge that it is an aspect of Greek-thought or a symptom of Western intellectualism. More so, because we have already seen in chapter 1 that intellectuality or intellectualism is not inherently (i.e. originally) Western. It is equally artificial to presume that functional Christologies only apply to non-Western and Western-minority contexts because both ontological and functional aspects are necessary for a truly global understanding of Christ.

Therefore, the next chapter proposes a global theological analytic approach to Christology based on the idea that, if we are to construct an adequate contextual and globally attentive Christology, more needs to be said and not less than the understanding of Christ that has been received from Scripture and the Christian tradition (e.g. through the missionaries). We now turn our attention to this discussion using the researcher's context of Christian experience in northern Nigeria.

---

115. Tiénou, "Jesus as Guest," 3.
116. Tiénou 3.

CHAPTER 5

Toward a Global Analytic Christology

The previous chapter concluded with the claim that certain pursuits in contextual Christology, particularly as seen in Guest Christology and Revealer Christology, often end up sacrificing or limiting the canonical and catholic principles for contextual concerns. More precisely, we identified an inadequate engagement with Scripture and creedal Christology or tradition. We also noted a tendency toward or a preference for a functional construal of Christ, which results in either an outright dismissal (Udoh) or a cultural minimalization (Ezigbo) of ontological concerns. However, it should be recalled that chapter 2 made a case for the theological use of Scripture in doing Christology, where we pointed out that the idea of Scripture as God's word through which he has shared with humanity some knowledge of himself and of all things relative to him is the most central claim of what it means to do theology theologically. This claim identifies both the ontology of Scripture as God's word and its teleology as a means for humans to share in God's knowledge. This therefore engenders an attitude of submission to Scripture's authority and necessitates its use in contextual theological and christological reflections. Furthermore, we began to point out that the intentional use of one's contextual resources must not be allowed to set the agenda and create new or different christological identities that do not sustain the same christological judgments found in the biblical text. To this end, careful conceptual analysis is of great importance to the task of reflecting on Christ in newer contexts, if indeed such reflection will be about the very same Christ of Scripture, of early Christian tradition, and of other Christians in diverse parts of the world who also believe in and follow him.

In light of the foregoing, this chapter aims at a christological reflection that is exegetically driven or firmly grounded in Scripture, continuous with the great Christian tradition, attentive to present realities faced by the church (precisely, in northern Nigeria), and providing careful conceptual analysis with rigor of argumentation. In a nutshell, these are the principles that have emerged from our discussions in the three previous chapters. Our first goal in this chapter is to succinctly restate these cardinal principles for doing theology/Christology in a way that highlights the distinction, necessity, and benefits of each principle. This discussion will form the first major part of the chapter.

The second major part begins with an articulation of the contextual realities in the author's northern Nigerian setting for christological reflection. The primary issues pertain to the continuing official and unofficial marginalization of and frequent mob violence meted out on local Christians and churches by Muslims who constitute the majority in the region. The choice of this problem for contextual christological reflection in this study should become clear shortly, especially when we provide a synopsis of the principle of contextuality. Next, we inquire into how Christ may be understood and the doctrine performed in this Muslim-dominated context. This concern is addressed in the light of Scripture by engaging two christological passages (one narrative, the other didactic) in order to ground our christological claims in the biblical text. I employ here an exegetical and dogmatic reading of the texts while also deploying analytic tools (where necessary) for conceptual clarity and consistency of claims made.

At the end, this chapter[1] demonstrates that the scriptural and creedal Christ who must be reflected upon and understood is the self-same living and present Christ who must be experienced in one's prevailing ecclesial and social situatedness. The new situation does not have to (and should not) transform the identity of Christ, but the identity of Christ transforms the believers' experience of the new context, which eventually brings about a transformation of the context itself. But first, we begin with the synopsis of the core principles that underlie our proposed approach to Christology.

---

1. A slightly revised version of this chapter has been published as a journal article. See: Isuwa Atsen, "Towards a Global Analytic Christology," *Trinity Journal* 42 NS, No. 2 (2021): 167–184.

A Theological Analytic Contextual Approach to Christology

There are certain critical factors that must be accounted for if Christology (and indeed theology) in a global setting is to avoid being purely contextually relativized and thereby balkanized, as is the case today, particularly with respect to the so-called Western versus the many non-Western theologies (even non-Western versus some other non-Western). This drift toward relativization and balkanization inevitably belies the unity and catholicity of the church thus hindering the possibility of mutual conversations in doing theology, which ideally should be the hallmark of global theologizing. The critical issues therefore that will help stem this drift are the principles of canonicity, catholicity, contextuality, and conceptuality. With regards to the practice of global Christology, the respective concerns are: (1) submission to the *authority* of the canonical texts for our knowledge of Christ and his significance; (2) being in *continuity* with the understanding of Christ in the broader Christian tradition; (3) appropriating our understanding of Christ to address some specific *reality* of our context; and (4) careful attention to the conceptual furnishings that sustain the *identity* of Christ (not just ours) as the one who is the same yesterday, today, and forever (cf. Heb 13:8).

However, one may ask, why these principles and what makes them important and necessary for a global understanding of Christ? What follows is an attempt to spell this out as clearly as possible. In doing this, the following questions will inform much of what is said. (1) How do we know that we are all referring to the *same* Christ, namely, the one who is the same yesterday, today, and forever? (2) Is there a difference between who Christ *is* simpliciter and who he is *for us* as such and such (e.g. as Africans); or relatedly, between understanding Christ in himself and articulating the implications of that understanding to our living situations? (3) Finally, do we have to attach qualifiers to Christology (e.g. Guest, Revealer, etc.) in order to communicate doctrinal truth in particular contexts and for particular constituencies?

Scripture as Canon

One of the most widely used scriptures for contextual Christology is Mark 8:29 where Jesus asked his disciples the question, "Who do you say that I am?" This question is then asked of a given people or context – cultural, economic, political, spiritual, etc. In the African context for example, Mugambi and Magesa state, "From the African Church, a clear and convincing answer is demanded to this question: Who is Jesus Christ for you, Africa? Who do you say that He is?"[2] Clearly, the emphasis is placed on "you" – who he is to *you* (Africa) and who *you* say he is. The emphasis is on every given context articulating their own unique response or answer to that question without an equal attention to whether or not the answer is the right one. In using this verse as a springboard for contextual Christology, most people often fail to note that in the immediate context of the passage, (1) there were wrong responses to the question (e.g. some said he was just one of the prophets); and (2) when Peter gave "his" response to the question, Jesus noted that that answer could not have originated with him but must have come from the Father himself through the Spirit, and this is because human beings were not privy to such knowledge (Matt 16:13–17). What becomes clear then is the fact that we cannot know Christ without the Spirit of the Father making him known through the Scriptures and the church.

Consequently, a Christology that is not demonstrably based on the knowledge of the Father about his Son, part of which he has shared with us in the Scriptures, stands in grave danger of constructing another Christ. This points to the necessity of using Scripture as canon (the rule or standard) for working out right responses to the Jesus question and as the means to receiving God's own answer *for us* (e.g. Africans) to this question. It is in this sense that the principle of canonicity identifies Scripture as the *norming norm* – the authoritative source that norms all other sources (or better still, resources) for our understanding of Christ. Unless Scripture authorizes and is shown to authorize a given Christology, such an understanding of Christ will linger under the shadow of illegitimacy. This is because "*canon is itself an expression of the lordship of Jesus Christ through the Holy Spirit.*"[3] So, instead of construing the scriptural depictions of Christ as culturally-conditioned representations to which we may add our own cultural portrayals of him (as Ezigbo suggested), we ought to see these as the authoritative descriptions of

---

2. Mugambi and Magesa, "Introduction," in *Jesus in African Christianity*, x. See also Stinton who points out that the purpose of her research "is essentially to explore how African Christians today respond to the fundamental question of Jesus Christ, 'Who do you say I am' (Mk 8:29)." Stinton, *Jesus of Africa*, 21.

3. Vanhoozer, *Drama of Doctrine*, 122. Emphasis in original.

the Father, revealing his Son, through his Spirit, to his church – that is, normative descriptions of the identity of Jesus Christ to which *all* cultures and contexts are subordinate. They are normative because they are the inspired and authorized testimonies of eye-witnesses or their close associates passed down to the whole church. This is nothing less than a theologically-driven approach to our understanding of Christ, as opposed to one that is merely sociocultural or historicocritical.

Therefore, when, for an example, Ezigbo says that "all interpretations of Jesus, including the images of him in the Bible, are not only culturally laden but also contextually driven,"[4] what he clearly leaves out is this theological component. But to leave out this component is to fail to see that, "Theology is evangelical [or theological] to the extent that it acknowledges and preserves the priority of the Word and Act of God over that of human beings."[5] This does not mean that Ezigbo and other theologians in Africa like him, who want to distance themselves from Byang Kato's much maligned concept of "biblical Christianity in Africa," have a low view of Scripture.[6] But this simply points to the fact that whatever high view of Scripture they hold has not translated into a right theological use of the Bible.

It is for this reason that the idea of theological interpretation as exegetical and dogmatic reasoning (spelled out in chapter 2) is much needed for doing contextual Christology. Such theological exegesis of the Bible is clearly lacking in the works of both Udoh and Ezigbo. The question then is, what would Christology in the Nigerian Christian context look like if it is immersed in and allowed to emerge from an intentional theological reading of the Bible, such an intentional theological reading that does not merely reflect the interests of the interpretive community but primarily reflects the theological interests of the texts themselves? We will occupy ourselves in the present

---

4. Ezigbo, "Rethinking the Sources," 70. He also makes a similar claim elsewhere when he said that "the forms of Christianity that are expressed in the New Testament are clothed in the thoughts, cultures, religious aspirations, religious experiences, and theological questions of the earliest Christian communities." Ezigbo, "Jesus as God's Communicative," 49.

5. Vanhoozer, *Drama of Doctrine*, 239.

6. Ezigbo says quite expressly, "I classify the sources of Christian Christology into two tiers. The Bible belongs to the first tier (in its capacity as the inspired sacred writing) and functions as the final authority in assessing our understandings of Jesus Christ. The Christologies that contradict scriptural teaching about Jesus Christ have failed the primary test of Christian identity." Ezigbo, "Jesus as God's Communicative," 55.

chapter with actually showing this in practice. In the meantime, we turn our attention to the next principle, which relates to Webster's dogmatic reasoning (as discussed in chapter 2).

Tradition as Guide

Catholicity is the second principle that should be seen to inform the work of constructive contextual Christology. This principle considers creedal Christology, being part of the early church's rule of faith, as *normed norm* – crystallized understandings of the Christ through the operations of the Holy Spirit in the life of the early church (i.e. judgments expressed in concrete forms) that should continue to guide contemporary expressions in the global ecclesia. In other words, as distributaries of the one stream of faith in the one Christ who is the same yesterday, today, and forever (i.e. same across contextual space and time), contemporary global churches are to affirm the christological deliverances of the early church as scripturally-consistent truth claims, embrace them as normative for our own readings of Scripture today, and providing guidance in the subsequent work of constructing contextual Christologies. This construal is usually not embraced by many global theologians, who seem to prefer one of two alternatives: either a downgrade or an outright disregard of creedal Christology.

The first alternative advances what we shall call an exemplar view of creedal Christology for doing contextual Christologies. On this view, creedal Christology is construed as just another contextual Christology and taken to be on the same level with other contextual Christologies (e.g. African or Latin American).[7] Ezigbo, for example, classifies the sources of Christology into two tiers or levels. He puts the Bible at the top level (and rightly so) and then claims that the "Christologies of the classical ecumenical councils and the contemporary contexts of local Christian communities belong to the second tier. African Christology should *learn* from the Christologies of the earliest ecumenical councils."[8] But, one may ask, learn what? Ezigbo identifies two

---

7. In the African context, Bediako was the one who advanced and popularized this view or attitude towards the theological deliverances of the early church. He argues that African theologians should learn from those early Christian theologians who hellenized the gospel in the second century. See Bediako, *Theology and Identity*.

8. Ezigbo, "Jesus as God's Communicative," 55. Emphasis added.

lessons, neither of which are theological. He calls them the lesson of contextualization (an example to follow) and that of the danger of imperial romance (an example not to follow).[9] The former claims that the ecumenical councils employed culturally-conditioned concepts (e.g. *homoousios*) to explicate the person of Christ, and African theologians should do same; while the latter focuses on the influences of political forces of the Roman Empire in shaping the decisions of the councils with largely negative consequences (e.g. the use of force and violence to silence dissenters like the Copts).

The second alternative goes a step further to say that creedal Christology should be completely disregarded in contextual Christologizing because it is completely meaningless and irrelevant to newer contexts of the Christian faith such as that of Africa, Latin America, and Asia. Andrew Mbuvi, for example, argues that "if Christologies were from the very beginning the products of the encounter of the gospel message with different cultures, *then one wonders whether there is need to revisit the creeds themselves*, given the more recent Christian encounters within African, Asian, and Latin American cultures."[10] In addition, he thinks that "beginning the presentation of the gospel message, as most Western missionaries did in sub-Saharan Africa, with the assumptions of the Chalcedonian Creed, created a 'biased' perspective about how to understand the person and work of Jesus Christ."[11] Therefore, he reads the cultic language in 1 Peter for explicating Christ "in light of some pre-Christian cultic religious practices of the Akamba of Kenya,"[12] without any reference to or assumptions of creedal Christology in the framework. At the end of his essay, he notes that the creeds should be treated as sealed documents as this hinders the development of other elements of Christology. He then suggests that if one is attentive to African christological concerns when reading Scripture directly, the creeds are inevitably relegated to irrelevance as the "issues central to the Chalcedonian Council (the relationship of the divinity and humanity of Jesus) hardly ever show up."[13]

---

9. Ezigbo, 39–40.
10. Mbuvi, "Christology and *Cultus*," 161. Emphasis added.
11. Mbuvi, 141.
12. Mbuvi, 149.
13. Mbuvi, 160.

The problem with these alternative views however, as I noted elsewhere,[14] is that they are theologically and ecclesiologically deficient. First, the claim that Chalcedon is just another contextual Christology errs on the side of dogmatic ranking in which Scripture is the norming norm, followed by creedal Christology as normed norm, and finally, subsequent constructive christological reflections of individual theologians as *theologoumenon* (theological opinion). Therefore, instead of "jumping over" Chalcedon and straight to the New Testament portrayals of Jesus as K. K. Yeo suggests,[15] we should be sustaining and incorporating Chalcedon's biblical judgments in our cultural or contextual understandings of the Christ. In so doing, we will be deploying, in the words of John Webster, "a theological (rather than socio-cultural) understanding of tradition."[16] To construe Chalcedon as merely contextual and then make that the premise on which it is jettisoned amounts to throwing away the dogmatic baby with the cultural bath water. In addition, these alternative views seem to suggest that the out-workings of the Spirit in the church within a different culture and time (i.e. the development of the Creeds) are of no consequence to today's global church. In spite of the church's contextual diversities, does Scripture not tell us that it is one because (among other things) we have *one* Lord and *one* faith (cf. Eph 4:5)? It seems then that we should take into account the theological claims about the one Lord Jesus Christ in the Christian tradition, if today's disciples in the global church are to follow the same Lord in the same Way (the faith and not the manner) that the community of Jesus from inception has followed. It is in this sense therefore that contextual Christology needs to be continuous with creedal Christology.

However, this does not mean that contextual Christologies should merely repeat unimaginatively the understanding of Christ captured in the creeds. As Vanhoozer notes, "The church cannot rest content with identical repetitions. The church is not called to play the same scene over and over but to take the gospel into new situations. To be faithful in its witness, the church must constantly be different. Indeed, at times it must even *improvise*."[17] The question then is how? How can the church carry on with the same understanding of

---

14. Atsen, Review of *Jesus without Borders*, 131–33.
15. Yeo, "Biblical Christologies," 167–69.
16. Webster, "Theologies of Retrieval," 584.
17. Vanhoozer, *Drama of Doctrine*, 128.

Christ that has been passed on in the Christian tradition while being different at the same time? An adequate response to this question necessitates a careful attention to the complex principle of contextuality to which we now turn.

Context as Theater

In the *Drama of Doctrine*, Kevin Vanhoozer construes theology as giving direction to the church for fitting participation in the divine drama through canonical scientia and sapiential improvisation in new contexts. In this framework, the canon is the script to be performed by the local church in a new theater (context) and in the light of past performances (e.g. Nicaea and Chalcedon). This picture is in agreement with one of the oft repeated claims by missiologist and intercultural theologians that every theology is contextual or context-specific. The truth of this claim is surprisingly straightforward since theology as a human enterprise is undertaken by theologians who live, think, and write in particular moments in time and space. This claim would have been trivial if it had not taken the church and Christian theology hundreds of years to recognize it on a wide scale. This is particularly pertinent to the situation engendered by the nineteenth-century Western missionary movement whereby missionaries helped entrench a devaluing of other cultures (especially African) and a concurrent identification of Western ways with the Christian Way. The negative impact this has had on missionary work has led to a new understanding of missiology as "the scholarly interdiscipline that affirms both the mission of the church and the value of culture."[18] The perception though among many theologians in the West, while changing gradually, remains to a large extent that of superiority over non-Western theological discourse.[19] Quite often, theological institutions in non-Western societies are treated condescendingly[20] as the works of Western theologians are identified simply as theology (with universal applicability), while those of non-Western theologians are affixed regional qualifiers (e.g. African, Asian, or Latin American).[21]

---

18. Tizon, *Whole and Reconciled*, 2.
19. See Tiénou, "Christian Theology," 37–51.
20. Tiénou, 47.
21. Consequently, the temptation for non-Western theologians is to disregard Western theological works and carve out our unique ways of doing theology. Mofokeng for example

However, if we take all theological reflections to be contextual as noted above, then contextuality is, in principle, inescapable or inherent to every theological reflection. Rather than the pretentious claim to some universal theology, which is usually a pretext for theological hegemony, every theologian ought to be more consciously and intentionally contextual. This is what non-Western theologians have brought to the fore of the shared consciousness of the global ecclesia. It must be noted however that being self-consciously contextual in theology poses certain dangers to the theological enterprise. First, there is the danger of over-contextualization or what Hiebert describes as "an uncritical contextualization"[22] – a situation whereby one's culture or elements in the culture are construed to be identical with Christ or the Christian faith. This is the error of Christendom and Western Christianity and African theologians perpetuate this error when they show more allegiance to their African identity over their Christian identity.[23] The claim to an authentic African Christology therefore falls into this trap as theologians make every effort to identify authentically African elements, usually from Africa's pre-Christian religious traditions, and then Christologize with them.

There are three major problems with this way of doing contextual Christology in Africa. First, it fails to take into account the complexity of what it actually means to be African and seems to simply work with the assumption that the ancestral is what is authentically African. But Anthony Appiah has shown quite powerfully that African identity is complex and cannot be simplistically identified with just the ancestral element, but must be understood in the sense of contemporary Africa or what we may call "Africa as it is."[24] Appiah states quite poignantly:

> All aspects of contemporary African cultural life—including
> music and some sculpture and painting, even some writings

---

wants to present his Black Theology and Black Christology in a way that it will not be seen as "undergoing the test for approval and acceptability into the fold of legitimate Theologies." Mofokeng, *Crucified among the Crossbearers*, 4.

22. Hiebert, "Beyond Anti-Colonialism," 272.

23. In making this same point, Mukoma Wa Ngugi notes with respect to literary works that "Often, scholars from the Global South relate to each other through ideological constructs from the West. Thus, we triangulate theory, whether political or literary, through the West. Even liberationist concepts and theories such as deconstruction or hybridity end up trapped in the same dialectic from which they are trying to break free." Ngugi, "Breaking Out of the Prison," 39.

24. I first heard the phrase used in this sense by Dr. Tite Tiénou in a private conversation.

with which the West is largely not familiar—have been influenced, often powerfully, by the transition of African societies *through* colonialism, but they are not all in the relevant sense *post*colonial. For the *post* in postcolonial like the *post* in postmodern is the *post* of the space-clearing gesture. . . . and many areas of contemporary African cultural life—what has come to be theorized as popular culture, in particular—are not in this way concerned with transcending, with going beyond, coloniality. Indeed, it might be said to be a mark of popular culture that its borrowings from international cultural forms are remarkably insensitive to—not so much dismissive of as blind to—the issue of neocolonialism or "cultural imperialism."[25]

We will return to this issue shortly. But we must note at this point that if this attitude is true of popular culture in contemporary Africa, how much so should it be of Christian theology in Africa given the catholicity of the faith?

Second, and closely related to this first problem, is the rather ironic problem of irrelevance. The recovery of the ancestral may no longer speak meaningfully to the modern African. In this case, the contextual Christologies that are constructed from Africa's ancestral or primal religious traditions end up being as irrelevant to the modern African Christian as it has been claimed about Western Christologies. Veli-Matti Kärkkäinen makes the same point when he says, "Many African Christologies that are authentically African, based on the history and beliefs of past cultures, are no longer relevant to urbanized, modernized Africans, many of whom have received a Western education and are influenced by Western mass media."[26] Consequently, Kärkkäinen calls for "a genuine, relevant African Christology for the third millennium [that] needs to avoid both a traditionalist attempt to preserve African culture in a mindless fashion and a reformist neglect of African roots."[27]

Third, even if we grant that the ancestral is authentic to being African, this line of reasoning seems to suggest that there are only two options for the African Christian theologian, either African authenticity or Westernization.

---

25. See Appiah, *In My Father's House*, 149.
26. Kärkkäinen, *Christology*, 255.
27. Kärkkäinen, 255.

But Tite Tiénou argues that there is a third option, and that option is being Christian, which is not necessarily African or Western.[28] He calls for an allegiance to God the Father of Jesus Christ as opposed to an unreserved allegiance or giving priority to the ancestral past.[29] He writes:

> And as African Christians exert their right to be different, they should also have the courage to stand firmly for the fact that their allegiance to "God the Father of our Lord Jesus Christ" will necessarily entail a distancing from some elements of indigenous cultures. Rejecting aspects of the traditional heritage certainly does not in itself make them un-African. . . . African Christians have a contribution to make by refusing to be trapped in the sterile debate which argues for either westernization or indigenous authenticity. How? By focusing the discussion on Africa's current problems and opportunities as it faces the future.[30]

But what does this Christian focus on Africa's current problems and future opportunities involve? How does it affect contextual Christology in an African setting such that this Christology also remains catholic?

First, it will involve the contemporary situations of African local churches (the real problems of real churches) as the genuine ground of contextual Christologizing. This entails the rejection of African Christian theologizing as a purely academic exercise because "as long as theological development in Africa is left in the hands of an academic elite, it has little chance of being genuinely and significantly African."[31] Tiénou contends that it is the problems being faced by a living local church within the present realities of its cultural

---

28. Kevin Vanhoozer makes a similar point when he calls for a diasporadic consciousness for doing theology. "To do theology and to read the Bible with diasporadic consciousness is to recognize that one must never be too at home in any one culture. Whatever their passports, Christians are really resident aliens (1 Pet. 2:11). The people of God must never define themselves primarily in terms of their culture, nationality, or ethnicity." Vanhoozer, "One Rule to Rule," 125.

29. Tiénou, "Which Way for African Christianity," 9.

30. Tiénou, 9.

31. Tiénou, "Problem of Methodology," 92. Vanhoozer makes the same point when he says, "Being biblical is ultimately an ecclesiastical rather than academic project" (Vanhoozer, "Drama-of-Redemption Model," 154). The point here is not that academic theological work should be stopped, because even this book as well Tiénou's and Vanhoozer's works belong to that category. But what we mean here is that academic theological work should take its bearing from the ecclesia such that theological reflection is done in conversation with and attention on the church or the concrete experiences of particular believers.

context that should inform how contextual theology should proceed. This should yield what he calls prescriptive theology, a theology that

> seeks to solve problems faced by Christians in their specific contexts. Its essential focus is not on systems of ideas. In that sense, prescriptive theology is neither specifically African nor un-African. But if one helps solve problems which are specific to African Christians in their contexts, the prescriptive theology used will be African.[32]

Such prescriptive theology or Christology will not be necessarily functional as one may assume because the problem it may be solving for a particular local church is that of clearly defining how Christ is both God and Man at the same time. This will be seen below in our treatment of Philippians 2:5–11.

Finally, and as already established in the first two principles, the way to being catholic in contextual Christologizing is in being biblical and dogmatic. This means articulating the judgments established from Scriptures and the Christian tradition in concepts that resonate with contemporary African Christians.[33] David Yeago has demonstrated that Paul's claim about the identity of Christ in Philippians 2 and that of the Nicene Creed actually make the same judgments even though they employed different concepts. Concepts, he says, are instrumental to judgments and not vice versa. To read the Bible rightly

> is to inquire attentively into what the texts say and how they say it, in search of unifying common judgements which may be rendered in very diverse ways, attempting to redescribe or re-render those judgements so as to do justice to the significance of their various articulations across the range of the canon.[34]

---

32. Tiénou, "Problem of Methodology," 189.

33. There are those who erroneously think that such engagement simply means seeking Western approval. Clifton Clarke for example says, "In spite of the advances that have undoubtedly taken place in the area of Christology in Africa, to a large extent there still remains a conscious and/or a sub-conscious desire for theological approval by the western theological intelligentsia." Clarke, *African Christology*, 151. But the first two principles we discussed above demonstrated why this is an important step.

34. Yeago, "New Testament and the Nicene Dogma," 96.

To be able to do this in the context of Nigerian Christianity will better serve the church than a contextual Christology that seems to prioritize the African pre-Christian cultural and religious heritage over Scriptures and the Christian tradition. Doing this will entail what Vanhoozer calls faithful improvisation with the script of the Bible within new contexts, and the controlling adjective suggests that there is bad improvisation which must be avoided. "Improvising well requires both training (formation) and discernment (imagination)."[35] For purposes of our project, this will involve making the same christological judgments as the biblical authors and church fathers but using different conceptual terms and cultural categories (where available).

To be able to do this well, without distorting or even denying some aspect of Jesus's true identity, the tools of analytic theology will come in handy. The next section therefore focuses on the use of analytic tools for potential fruitful work in the task of global Christologizing in general, particularly in the African (Nigerian) context.

Conceptual Analysis as a Tool

The final principle is conceptuality and it focuses on the need for careful and rigorous conceptual analysis of the different contextual concepts being appropriated to express the christological judgment derived from Scripture and the Christian tradition. The key question for contextual Christology on this point is: do the concepts employed actually convey the very same christological judgments communicated by the biblical texts and the creeds? In other words, how do we know that we are still speaking of the same Christ that the early church spoke about when we employ such contextual concepts like guest and ancestor? What are the conditions that we must obtain before we can say that the identity of the Christ has been sufficiently sustained in some contextual Christology? Analytic theology – drawing from analytic philosophical devices as chapter 3 demonstrates – has the tools to better serve contextual Christology in this regard. It serves as a good example of the important role(s) that philosophy plays in doing theology.[36] It is for this

---

35. Vanhoozer, *Drama of Doctrine*, 337.

36. This point touches on the old debate on the relationship between faith and reason or between theology and philosophy, a debate that is almost as old as Christianity itself.

reason that we recommend it for doing theology in the African, particularly, the Nigerian context.

Tersur Aben makes a similar proposal when he says that African theologians must let their work address and clarify Christian teaching "which constitute dogmas and form Christian tradition. In clarifying church dogmas, African theologians would need to employ the rules of propositional logic in stating what they understand Christianity as teaching."[37] The point is that (again as shown in chapter 3) the method of analytic theology can help us in making finer distinctions with respect to not only philosophical and theological (i.e. canonical and catholic) conceptual categories, but also contextual ones. In this sense then, the principle of conceptuality intersects all the other three principles. This becomes clear when we focus our attention on one of the most crucial distinctions that needs to be made in doing contextual Christology, and that is distinguishing between who is Jesus Christ simpliciter (ontologically) and who is Jesus to or for us as such and such (functional)?

The first question focuses on the person of Christ and points to his identity as being "fully God and fully man" or the God-man – a descriptor affirmed by the early church and traceable from the biblical narrative about Jesus.[38] The most critical issue here is how Jesus Christ is the same as one who is at once fully God and fully human without division in his person. The possibility of sustaining sameness of the self over time and spheres is a critical desideratum for any response to the identity question. What exactly makes Christ the self-same Word who was in the beginning as God (John 1:1) and at a point in time became human (John 1:14)? How or under what conditions does he remain the same even after such a radically transformative event as the incarnation has taken place? We may respond to this question in two different but non-contradictory ways. Ontologically, there is a dual substantiality in Christ as Nicene-Chalcedonian Christology explicates – that, he is consubstantial with the Father as to his divinity and consubstantial with us

---

Diverse theories and practices have been advanced by important individuals such as Tertulian, Augustine, Aquinas, Luther, Calvin, Barth, etc., with several approaches across the spectrum ranging from tension to synthesis and everything in between. For a more recent discussion of this subject, see Wilkens, *Faith and Reason*.

37. Aben, *African Christian Theology*, 187.

38. For a discussion on how the ontological and the narratival identity of Jesus compliment rather than contradict each other, see Vanhoozer, "Christology in the West," 23–27.

as to his humanity. In this sense, Christ then has (or must have) a substantial self that endures through change (e.g. from eternal begottenness to incarnation, death, resurrection, etc.) and unifies his consciousness as an indivisible person who remains the "*I*" in "*I* and the Father are one" (John 10:30) or in "before Abraham was, *I* am" (John 8:58), and also the "*me*" in "My God, my God, why have you forsaken *me*" (Mark 15:34). The second way to respond would be narratively. This is to say that the story of Christ is such that he shares the same eternal aims and actions with the Father and also shares the same story with us of birth, life, death, and life after death. Richard Bauckham calls this a personal identity, which is unique to an individual on the basis of their story or history. With respect to God, Bauckham says that besides his name, "God's identity is known to Israel from the recital of his acts in history and from the revelation of his character to Israel."[39] He then goes on to show that the New Testament identifies Christ with the one God of Israel, thus including Jesus in the unique divine identity. If we ask then, who is the gospel narrative about or whose story is it? The answer one must give is that, it is the story of the man who was God in the beginning and the God who is man forever as told in the Scriptures.

Ultimately then, from both an ontological and a narrative point of view, the most important judgment is that of the full divinity and full humanity of Christ as a single person, such that we can no longer speak of his divinity without his humanity or of his humanity without his divinity.[40] He can only be identified by both at the same time, which means that "the God-man" becomes a rigid-designator that always picks out the Christ, such that any local term or concept we employ to speak about Christ must convey this same identity.[41] Contextual Christologies therefore would do well to begin with this identity of Christ rather than try to redefine (or even constrict) his identify

---

39. Bauckham, *Jesus and the God of Israel*, 7–8. For a similar point, see also Vanhoozer, "Does the Trinity Belong"; Cook, *Christology as Narrative Quest*; and Yadav, "Christian Doctrine as Ontological Commitment."

40. Although Richard Bauckham wants to contrast between narrative explanation as focusing on "*whoness*" and ontological explication as a preoccupation with "*whatness*," even he had to admit that the two categories are not unrelated. Bauckham, *Jesus and the God of Israel*, 7. Apparently, the only way to show that one approach must be favored over the other is to demonstrate that they are contradictory in terms of their aim and objective, which we have argued above that that is not the case.

41. For a standard and rigorous discussion about the idea of rigid and non-rigid designators, see Kripke, *Naming and Necessity*.

based on cultural descriptors. This was seen in Enyi Ben Udoh's claim that in Nigerian cultural understanding, God cannot be a man and man cannot be God, a claim that contributed to his rejection of the lordship of Christ. As most contextual Christologies tend to do, Udoh isolates from and then prioritizes Jesus's humanity over his divinity rather than proceed from Jesus's singular identity as the God-man.

The second question dwells on the way that Jesus Christ functions (or is perceived to function) in and for any given context or culture, at any given time, and among any given people. In this sense, Jesus Christ who is one "thing" (the God-man) is at the same time many "things" to many cultures, times, and peoples or functions (perhaps, as liberator, ancestor, guest, revealer, healer, etc.), thus, the utility of functional Christologies. Consequently, we may think of the identity or ontological component as a christological constant and the functional element as a variable.[42] While it may appear as if Jesus takes up a new identity when he enters a new sociocultural context, logically speaking, it is not a new identity per se but a new understanding of his significance. Therefore, in so far as the distinction between the identity and functions of Christ is not blurred, as is often the case in many contextual Christologies, creedal Christology remains necessary for any form of global Christologizing today, and analytic tools can help us sustain this distinction.

However, it may be argued by some that the employment of analytic theology/philosophy for doing theology in Africa is a strange approach that is foreign to Africans and may be a re-subjection of the African mind to Western imperialistic and intellectualistic ways. In this sense, the African is not only forced to play second fiddle in theological discourse, but is also faced with unhelpful and irrelevant conceptual categories that are unintelligible. In response to these concerns, first, we must note the discussion in chapter 1 about the very idea of what is and what is not Western. At this point though, let us consider Tite Tiénou's submission that African philosophy and African theology share the same roots and history. To show how

---

42. While it is true that Jesus Christ functions as Lord and Savior to all peoples of all cultures, the ramifications of this function are often experienced differently based on what people need saving from. For example, aside from the universal need for salvation from the guilt of sin, there are particular needs for salvation from certain contextual manifestations of sin such as social injustices, demonic oppressions, physical and mental sicknesses, etc. This is what informs the different expressions of Jesus as Lord and Savior. In this sense therefore, the function can still be construed as something that varies from place to place and over time.

this is the case, he provides a helpful synopsis of Leo Apostel's four stages of development of African philosophy, which are reminiscent of the different approaches to African theology earlier outlined in this chapter. He describes the four stages as follows:

> In Stage I, Westerners view African cultures as childlike; they are to be corrected and brought to the level of the West. This display of an attitude of superiority inevitably leads to reaction. The reaction takes place in Stage II. This second stage is properly the beginning point of the quest for an African philosophy. As Africans and some Westerners react against Western ethnocentrism, they tend to assert qualitative differences between African and Western philosophies. The goal is for Africans to achieve cultural autonomy. In this second stage, the search is for ethnic, tribal or traditional philosophies. In time Stage III is reached. Stage III, as a reaction against the assumptions of Stage II, is actually more of a critique than a formulation of philosophies. In Stage III, the critics claim that there is no philosophy that is proper to cultures or nations but only philosophies created by individuals. Stage IV in turn would be a synthesis between stage II and III. According to Apostel, Stage IV is yet to come.[43]

At the end of his detailed discussion of these stages, Tiénou concludes that "African philosophy is no longer defined in opposition to Western philosophy. Yet African thinkers take traditional worldviews seriously. Today, the question is not: How African is this or that philosophy? Rather the question is: How may Africans contribute to philosophy? This has implications for other disciplines."[44] The implication for present purposes is that analytic philosophy (and theology) cannot be said to be un-African because (1) logic does not play favorites and is not essential to any culture; and (2) African philosophers are already contributing (whether others recognize it or not) to discourse in the field of analytic philosophy.[45] If it is true then that African philosophy and African theology share the same roots, then this irenic phase

---

43. Tiénou, "Right to Difference," 26.

44. Tiénou, 30.

45. See for example Appiah, *In My Father's House*; Wiredu, *Cultural Universals and Particulars*; and Eze, *On Reason*.

of African philosophy that is witnessing appropriations of analytic philosophy may suggest to us that the interaction of African theology and analytic theology should be expected. In fact, the appropriation of analytic theology for doing theology in Africa may just contribute to ongoing efforts in the fourth stage of the development of African theology.

On the question of the foreignness of analytic theology for African theology and thus its unintelligibility, this concern thrives on an error we may call here the fallacy of familiarity (i.e. the African mind can only understand what is familiar to it). David Tonghou Ngong argues that the kind of theological discourse in Africa that uses *only* familiar African idioms

> stifles the African Christian imagination. . . . It presupposes that Africans do not respond to what is not familiar to them and thus fail to challenge African Christians to new perspectives that are sometimes wrongly characterized as un-African. This . . . does not only limit the range of African theology, it also undermines the dignity and wellbeing of Africans.[46]

The African mind, like any other mind, has the capacity for comprehending the unfamiliar and must not be characterized as capable of thinking in only certain ways but not others. That will be "endorsing an essentialistic [racist] view of how Africans think."[47] As to the possibility of analytic theology being unhelpful or too abstract and only ends up producing mere exotic academic theologies with no use for African Christianity, one must admit that this is a real and present danger in analytic theology. However, this problem is not inherent to analytic theology per se, but is relative to the analytic theologian whether in Africa or anywhere else for that matter. The idea here is that it is possible to do analytic theology in an unhelpful way and it is also possible to do it in a helpful way.[48] It is only when the exercise refuses to give attention to the treatment of concrete issues being faced by the local churches of Africa today that it will end up being merely abstract, intellectualistic, and

---

46. Ngong, *Holy Spirit and Salvation*, 6.
47. Ngong, 2. See also Appiah, *In My Father's House*, 3–15.
48. Thomas McCall rightly points out that "unless analytic theology is merely 'armchair theology' . . . it will be grounded in the Christian Scriptures, it will be informed by the great tradition of doctrinal development, it will be 'christologically normed' and it will be culturally engaged." McCall, *Analytic Christian Theology*, 22.

unhelpful for the African context. McCall's call is apt at this point, "we need more Western theologians who have the humility and patience to learn from their global colleagues *and* more theologians from Africa, Asia and Oceania who are able to employ analytic skills and tools in a helpful way."[49]

Conclusion

We have noted in this chapter the four principles of canonicity, catholicity, contextuality, and conceptuality (as a collective) that should guide the task of global Christologizing. The next chapter attempts to put these principles to work in reflecting christologically on the experience of Christians and churches of northern Nigeria amid both subtle and vicious attacks from the Muslim majority in the region. It is important to note at this point, that while the principles are arranged in what may be considered as an order of priority for theological reflection, it is not necessarily the case that one must begin with the text of Scripture. The starting point of any Christology could (and quite rightly so) be a specific problem of understanding Christ or his significance within a particular ecclesial context. Even though it is possible that a specific contextual element or problem that is used to trigger christological reflection might also be prioritized over and above canonical claims – a practice that is typical of classical liberation theology and some other contextual theologies as shown in the previous chapter – it is not logically necessary that this has to be the case. Where christological reflection is occasioned by contextual realities (as was the case in both the New Testament and the creeds), Christology becomes, from the very beginning, a little less abstract and irrelevant or unrelatable even when the christological judgments of Scripture and the creeds are given their rightful theological place in such Christologies. This is how the next chapter will proceed.

So far, we have outlined four key principles that will bolster the practice of contextual Christology in a global mode with particular reference to the Nigerian (and in some sense African) context. The principles of canonicity, catholicity, contextuality, and conceptuality were discussed and potential problems were also addressed, where necessary. The next questions to consider are, how will these four principles interact in actual practice? What

---

49. McCall, 158. Emphasis in original.

understanding of Christ would emerge in a global context, say northern Nigeria, where all four principles are taken into account? The next chapter addresses these questions and more. But first, we will seek to understand the experience of Christians and churches of northern Nigeria as the primary context of our reflection – a context of hate, marginalization, and violence by the Muslim majority. While this is not unique or essential to northern Nigeria and indeed Africa, the choice of this problem is informed by the fact that this is the most immediate predicament that threatens the very existence of the church in northern Nigeria. This is in keeping with earlier points made that contextual christologizing needs to focus on the real problems faced by local churches in contemporary Africa rather than occupy itself with some pre-Christian and precolonial cultural/religious resources. It is time therefore to explicate the present reality of Islamic dominance in northern Nigerian from both current and historical perspectives.

CHAPTER 6

Christ in the Context of Violence

Since the first crisis in the city of Jos, which took the majority Christian population by surprise, violence continues to be unleashed on the city from time to time. Jos has always been viewed by other Christians in the far-north cities of northern Nigeria as the bastion of Christianity in the region, a place where persecuted Christians from these other cities have always fled to for refuge. Since the late 1980s, Christians in the far-north cities of northern Nigerian such as Kano, Kaduna, Zaria, Bauchi, Borno, etc. have become much acquainted with incessant attacks by Muslims on their very existence.[1] This has been the case because Muslims are in the majority in those cities, and now that their population in Jos has grown significantly, this perceived Christian city is also not spared. That would be the first of several attacks that would take place in the years to follow both in the city and the surrounding rural areas of Jos.

This is the present reality of Christians and churches of northern Nigeria, that of hateful treatment and deadly violence from the majority Muslim population of the region. Patrick Sookhdeo aptly captures the situation as follows:

> More often than not, Christians have been the targets of Muslim-initiated violence, perpetrated by groups ranging from gangs of young people to fully armed Islamist militias. Attacks by Muslims in the last ten years have killed thousands of Christians. The climate of intimidation and fear that these repeated conflicts

---

1. Higazi, "Jos Crisis," 2.

engender adds to an existing situation of anti-Christian discrimination and marginalization in the North.²

The situation continues to grow worse as evidenced by the establishment of full shari'a laws in some northern states, the rise of the deadly Islamist terrorist group Boko Haram, the denial of land permits for church buildings, the refusal to teach Christian religious knowledge in public schools and forcing Christian children to sit in Islamic religious knowledge classes, stopping the promotion of Christian workers in civil/public service, etc. It is therefore unsurprising that the 2022 World Watch List of Open Doors USA ranked Nigeria seventh out of fifty countries where it is most dangerous to follow Jesus.³ What the World Watch List map fails to indicate is that, without any exception, all the troubled areas where Christians and churches continuously experience danger to their social well-being and physical existence are in the northern part of the country. A brief historical and sociopolitical description of Nigeria's northern region will enable us see how the problem is deeply rooted in and pervasive throughout the region.

Rough estimates put Nigeria's population at 50 percent Muslim and 50 percent non-Muslim (this includes both Christians and adherents of traditional religions). While southern Nigeria has a majority Christian population, northern Nigeria is predominantly Muslim. Most of the Christians in northern Nigeria are in the Middle Belt region. According to Yusufu Turaki, since precolonial and in colonial times, northern Nigeria has been "divided into two [sub] regions: the far north and the Middle Belt to the south."⁴ While the far north was conquered by the Islamic Jihad of the Fulani Sokoto Caliphate in the west and the Kanem-Bornu Sultanate in the east, the many ethnic groups of the Middle Belt region (and a few minority ethnic groups in the far north) resisted these jihadists and continued to practice their various indigenous religions. Most of them would later embrace Christianity in response to already ongoing missionary activities within their domain. So, the peoples of the Middle Belt kept Islamic domination at bay in precolonial times. However, when the British colonial administrators arrived on the scene and took over from the Royal Niger Company in 1900, the situation changed in favor of the

---

2. Sookhdeo, Foreword to *Tainted Legacy*, 7.
3. Open Doors, "World Watch List."
4. Turaki, *Tainted Legacy*, 24.

now predominant Muslim Hausa-Fulani in the west and Kanuri/Shuwa Arabs in the east of northern Nigeria. "When the British colonial masters saw that these ethnic groups had no centralised authority, administrative machinery or constituted judicial institutions, they subordinated them to the rule of the Muslim Hausa-Fulani or Kanuri."[5] This is the "Indirect Rule" policy of the British colonial system in northern Nigeria. There are three major factors or components in this arrangement.

First, it was simply a matter of administrative convenience. The British administrators found the already established governing structures of both the Sokoto Caliphate and Kanem-Bornu Sultanate to be beneficial to their economic exploitation through taxation and for keeping the peace through the local judicial and law enforcement systems. The over 200 ethnic groups of the Middle Belt region and the few in the far north had less sophisticated governing systems given their sizes.[6] The second factor was racial.

> The British considered themselves superior to all non-white peoples and the Arabs were considered superior to the darker-skinned peoples. Therefore, the Fulani were considered to be superior to the darker skinned "Negroes." The British officials were the overseers (the residents and district officers), and the Fulani were considered "natural rulers" who could look after their racially less distinguished subjects, the non-Muslim traditionalists.[7]

As noted above, these non-Muslim adherents of indigenous religions would later embrace the missionary witness of the Christian gospel, which takes us to the third factor for the British subordination of non-Muslims under Muslim control of northern Nigeria. The third component was religious. This component had a political undercurrent to it involving both Islam and Christianity. The British colonial administrators were advised by their anthropologist and ethnographers to give preferential treatment to Islam over

---

5. Turaki, 33.

6. Turaki describes these ethnic groups as "segmented societies" which operated like "mini republics (or tribes) that lacked a common ethnic identity, authority or legitimacy. Each one was a confederacy of communities and villages based upon lineage and kinship systems. Each lived on its own and was independent of others because the sense of tribal affinity and unity excluded all those who did not belong." Turaki, 31.

7. Turaki, 30.

missionary Christianity because, "They believed that Islam had integrated better into African life than missionary Christianity had, on the grounds that Islamic practices appeared to resemble those of African culture much more closely, especially with regard to polygamy and folk religion."[8] Therefore,

> while Islam was well positioned, Christianity was kept at the periphery, because the British rulers (and the Muslim leaders) viewed Christian missions and African converts with suspicion. They saw Christianity as both "detribalising" (that is, as making Africans less African), and as destabilising (because African Christians sought more freedoms than their non-Christian compatriots did). The socio-political implications of this negative view put Christianity at a disadvantage in post-colonial society.[9]

Consequently, the minority ethnic groups of the far north and of the Middle Belt that successfully (even if temporarily) resisted Islamic Jihad before colonialism and later embraced Christianity during colonial times were put at a disadvantage by the colonial system in northern Nigeria. This situation, in many instances has led to conversion by coercion of some people, usually chiefs or district heads of these ethnic minorities.[10] Whenever and wherever Muslims are not in control or begin to sense that their control may be in jeopardy, they get agitated and unleash mayhem on Christians and other non-Muslims in the region. At the slightest provocation, whether real or simply made up, a Muslim mob can kill Christians and destroy their property with no or very little restraint from law enforcement agencies, which usually comes after the damage has been done. The examples are simply too numerous to recount here; these include situations like that of Christianah Oluwatoyin Oluwasesin, a Christian teacher who caught a student cheating during an exam and seized the Qur'an in which he had written the answers. The Muslim students in the class incited other Muslims in the school and

---

8. Turaki, 43.

9. Turaki, 47.

10. Among the Afizere people, for example, Abok Musa Nyam reports that Islam was used as a political weapon by the Islamic oligarch of northern Nigeria. They forced "the chiefs in non-Moslem areas to convert to Islam if they were to remain in the good books of the then Northern Nigerian Government. Thus, through coercion and/or intimidation after persuasion had failed, the Adagwom Izere, Alhaji Yakubu himself (1960) became a Moslem with his three District Heads." Nyam, *Afizere (Jarawa) People*, 57.

the neighborhood by accusing her of desecrating the Qur'an. They attacked her, stripped her naked, beat her up, and lynched her with no one to help her.[11] When the Miss World Beauty Pageant was scheduled to hold in Nigeria, Muslim mobs came out to protest this and went about killing Christians for no reason. The Guardian reported it as follows, "During three days of rioting in Kaduna, ostensibly triggered by Muslim rage at Nigeria's hosting of Miss World, 58 churches were attacked and at least 215 people were killed."[12] Similarly, when the Danish cartoonist Kurt Westergaard published satirical cartoons of the Prophet Mohammed in a Danish newspaper Jyllands-Posten, protests erupted in northern Nigeria claiming many Christian lives and church buildings.[13] The list goes on and on. Christian churches have experienced and endured suicide bombing during Sunday worship, gun attacks during prayer meetings, and general intimidation and marginalization. To be a Christian in this environment is to embrace this experience.

The key question for reflection then is, what understanding of Christ is relevant for this context and how may such an understanding transform this experience of Christians in northern Nigeria? The two sections of this chapter that follow will reflect on the person and works of Christ in this particular context using two specific passages of Scripture (Matt 14:22–33 and Phil 2:6–11). This reflection will also be done in light of the wisdom of the church catholic and with the rigor and clarity of analytic thinking.

Encountering the Son of God in an African Windstorm

In Matthew 14:22–33, we have the story of Jesus walking on water (as it is popularly known), which provided his disciples with an opportunity to encounter him in a way they had not previously. This is a remarkable story with a clear beginning, an eventful middle, and a climactic ending. In it, the divine identity of Jesus is not only demonstrated and declared, the lives of the disciples were also saved by Jesus amid some harsh conditions on the lake. We will use this story of Jesus to show that the churches and Christians

---

11. Blake, "Christian School Teacher Brutally Murdered."
12. Astill, "Truth behind the Miss World Riots."
13. BBC News, "Nigeria Cartoon Protests Kill 16."

of Nigeria's northern region, who are constantly being buffeted by the opposing winds of Islamic hate, marginalization, and violence, can find much needed comfort and wisdom for the present as well as hope for the future. This should lead to the continued worship of Jesus Christ as the Son of God.

It should be noted at this point that we are making a metaphorical, or better still an allegorical, association between the natural storm the disciples of Jesus faced on the lake and the political storm that the Christians and churches of northern Nigeria are facing today.[14] The image of Jesus that should become clear at the end of this section is that of a miracle worker, the deliverer of his followers, and ultimately one who is worthy of worship. We will now consider the story in some detail and weave along some dogmatic and analytic considerations as we address the problem stated above.

Plot and Structure

Jesus had just finished feeding the five thousand (Matt 14:13–21) and wanted to have some time by himself with the Father – perhaps, exactly what he wanted to do in the first instance when he withdrew to a solitary place (cf. Matt 14:13) after hearing about the beheading of John the Baptist (Matt 14:1–12). Therefore, he made his disciples go without him on the boat while he stayed back and prayed from evening into the early hours of the next day. Meanwhile, his disciples were still in the boat and were unable to reach the shore because they were being buffeted by the waves and the wind was against them. Jesus shows up walking on the lake as he approached them, causing a great deal of fear among the disciples because they thought he was a ghost. But Jesus reassured them that it was he and confirmed it by letting Peter also walk on the water. He then had to save Peter from sinking in the water when Peter began to doubt. At the end, Jesus and Peter climbed into the boat, and

---

14. According to Craig Carter,
    The allegorical approach views the text as having more than one meaning, but not an unlimited number of meanings and certainly not mutually contradictory ones. But if one believes (as many evangelical biblical scholars do) that the only thing standing between us and interpretive chaos is the singe-meaning theory, one naturally would be loath to give it up lest the whole enterprise of biblical interpretation degenerates into the expression of individual opinions as to meanings of texts with no way to adjudicate among them.
    Carter, *Interpreting Scripture*, 6.

immediately the opposing wind died down. This lead the disciples to worship Jesus and proclaimed, "Truly you are the Son of God."

In considering this text, John Nolland notes that "A concentric structure seems likely, with vv. 22–23 corresponding to vv. 31–33 as separation and reunion, v. 24 to v. 30 as situations of danger and danger again, and vv. 25–26 to vv. 28–29 as first miracle and second miracle. V. 27 is in the centre."[15] In this center of the story, we find Jesus declaring to his frightened disciples, "Take courage! It is I. Don't be afraid." Many commentators have noted here the striking echo of God's self-naming found in the Old Testament with Jesus's ἐγώ εἰμι ("It is I," literally: I am).[16] It seems rather obvious that Jesus was making here a self-declaration of his true identity, which has been demonstrated by his earlier feeding of the five thousand, his presently walking on water, and the shortly to be performed act of stilling the waves and the wind. Therefore, we are going to reflect upon and appropriate this story as follows: the absence of Jesus (22–24), the presence of Jesus (25–31), and the worship of Jesus (32–33).

The Absence, Presence, and Worship of Jesus

We first see in this story Jesus letting his disciples go without him and letting them struggle all on their own against the waves and the wind for hours in the dark of the night. Craig Keener points out how this "suggests that just because disciples face difficulties does not mean that Jesus is not the one who sent them (14:22, 24; cf. 10:17–39)."[17] On the verge of exhaustion and despair, Jesus shows up in a way that clearly identifies him as someone who is not merely human, thus the disciples' conclusion that this must be some kind of spirit on the water. His self-declaration to them both confirmed this not-merely-human identity of Jesus to the disciples and dispelled their fears. His encounter with Peter was a confirmation of this declaration, and then the way he stopped the wind brought the story to its intended climax. "Remarkably the danger ceases simply by the presence of Jesus in the boat. No word need

---

15. Nolland, *Gospel of Matthew*, 597.

16. Nolland thinks that in context, the phrase simply has an emphatic function. However, he concedes that "perhaps ἐγώ εἰμι takes both roles simultaneously." Nolland, 601.

17. Keener, *Gospel of Matthew*, 406.

be spoken (cf. 8:26). Their solemn recognition of his identity (θεοῦ υἱὸς in 14:33) affirms what the reader has known all along."[18]

Christians and churches of northern Nigeria have been praying and continue to pray for God's mighty deliverance from the spontaneous, unpredictable, and fierce attacks of their Muslim neighbors. However, they are not alone in their prayers because the opening of this story "presents Jesus as a man of prayer (14:23),"[19] one who is definitely praying for his church today through the Spirit (cf. Rom 8:26–27; Heb 2:17) as he probably was also praying for his disciples at that time during their hours of danger on the lake. This should bring comfort to all Christians facing persecution. The fact that he could not be with his disciples in the boat while at the same time praying on the mountain points to his humanity; and this too should be comforting to us, that he knows and suffered our human limitations as a human being himself. However, the persecuted Christian can find hope for the future in the fact that, though *fully* human, Christ is not *merely* human. Thomas V. Morris clarifies this distinction when he says,

> To be a human being is to exemplify human nature. An individual is *fully human* just in case he fully exemplifies human nature. To be *merely human* is not to exemplify a kind-nature, a natural kind, distinct from that of humanity; it is rather to exemplify humanity without also exemplifying any ontologically higher kind, such as divinity.[20]

But, by (1) showing up on the lake like a ghost, (2) referring to himself as "I am," and (3) stilling the waves and the wind without a word, Jesus exemplifies an ontologically higher kind (i.e. a divine nature). Because deep waters are often a symbol for (primeval) chaos in Scripture (see, Ps 46), Jesus demonstrates his supremacy over them by walking calmly on the water as the divine Son of God. This point was not missed by the disciples who responded to the encounter they witnessed by worshipping him.

Similarly, the Christians of northern Nigeria can hope to encounter this divine Son of God in the midst of their own windstorm; they can trust him

---

18. Cabrido, *Portrayal of Jesus*, 187–88.
19. Keener, *Gospel of Matthew*, 406.
20. Morris, *Logic of God Incarnate*, 66. Emphasis added.

to show up and put an end to it. The fact that he has not put an end to it now does not mean that he does not want to or is not able to. It simply means it is not yet his time to do so, as Keener rightly notes, "Jesus has authority to settle totally any crisis when he is ready to do so (14:32)."[21] The disciples would have been wondering why Jesus made them go on in the boat without him in the first place. With his miraculous feeding of the five thousand still fresh on their minds (14:13–21), they would have been thinking that if only Jesus was there with them in the boat, their worries and woes would be over. This seemingly intentional absence of Jesus in the disciples' hour of desperation is often the experience of northern Nigerian Christians. Due to this reality, some Middle Belt non-Christians and Christians whose faith is weak have, in a move reminiscent of Christianity being blamed for the fall of Rome, blamed the Christian faith for making it possible for Muslims to be winning whenever they attack the people of the Middle Belt. Such people complain that while in precolonial times our forebears prevailed against the Hausa-Fulani Islamic jihad because of their traditional systems of warfare and the supernatural powers for protection they obtained from indigenous religious practices, Christianity has phased out our traditional practices in general, but especially with respect to warfare, and has also condemned the use of spiritual powers from traditional religions.[22] How do we respond christologically to a charge like this?

First (and going back to our primary text), we may wish to reiterate that the absence of Christ from the struggles of his disciples on the lake was only temporary. He eventually showed up at the time he knew was right. So, while the disciples were exhausted, they were not consumed. Jesus the God-man has both the divine power and human affinity to his people to be present with them in their time of trouble and to deliver them. The perception or experience of his absence is simply the middle of the story and not necessarily where it ends.[23] Northern Nigerian Christians can rest assured in this hope

---

21. Keener, *Gospel of Matthew*, 407–8.

22. It is in this sense that Abok Musa Nyam, for an example, writing about the Afizere people complained against Christianity and called it "The greatest foreign impact that nearly destroyed Afizere culture and traditions." Nyam, *Afizere (Jarawa) People*, 49.

23. While the Passion narrative may seem more central to this idea of Jesus sharing with us in our suffering and showing himself to be the Son of God, this story is preferred in light of its pre-Passion and pre-resurrection context. This is important because it is in the middle of Jesus's

and be comforted by it, that Christ always makes his presence known eventually. However, this comfort and hope do not necessarily constitute a basis for Christian passivity in the face of danger, which takes us to our second point.

The second thing to note in the passage is that while hoping, perhaps, that Jesus would come and rescue them from the waves and the wind, the disciples in the boat never stopped rowing and doing all they could to stay alive. In a similar sense, the Christians in northern Nigeria do not have to do nothing besides prayer as they wait for Jesus's manifest presence on the scene to bring deliverance from these Islamic attacks. The situation calls for some form of improvisation in the interaction of text and context. The outcome is what we will call here a phronetic use of violence for self-defense.[24] In Matthew 10:16 Jesus instructs his disciples to be as wise as serpents but as harmless as doves when they find themselves facing persecution, because in the world, they are like sheep among wolves. First, by describing his followers as sheep and the people of the world who persecute them as wolves, Jesus underscores the fallenness of the world; this in turn makes it necessary that we take seriously the eschatological tension between the already and the not yet. While it is true that we have been called to be perfect like our Father is perfect (Matt 5:48) since we have been perfected, the world itself is not yet a perfect place and we will have to deal with some imperfections (e.g. some "wolves"). Similarly, Paul admonishes in Romans 12:18 that we are to live at peace with all people as long as it depends on us; and the caveat here is that there is a point where it no longer depends on us – a point where the attacker (or wolf) is bent on killing and maiming and bloodletting. In such a situation, what might the disciple of Jesus do?

Jesus's second point then is priceless. He teaches both shrewdness on the one hand and harmlessness on the other. It is interesting that the word translated as "shrewd" or "wise" by many English versions is the Greek word

---

earthly divine-human life rather than at the beginning (incarnation) or at the end (exaltation) during which some divine manifestation may be thought necessary unlike in the middle.

24. It may be argued that rowing against the waves and wind to stay alive is not the same thing as using violence against human beings, which could lead to their death; also that when it comes to the use of violence or otherwise, the most relevant NT text to consider is the Sermon on the Mount. Actually, I have addressed this concern in more detail elsewhere and repeating it here is not necessary for purposes of this project. Therefore, for a more philosophically and theologically nuanced treatment of the issue, see, Atsen, "Self-Defense and a Phronetic Use of Violence."

φρόνιμοι (*phronimoi*) from the root *phronismos*, which means practical wisdom. Bruner comments that Jesus's "portrait of sheep amid wolves teaches disciples their vulnerability, but his portrait of snakes says, 'Don't be stupidly vulnerable.' The canniness of snakes is proverbial. Disciples are not asked to imitate everything in snakes: their stealth or poisonous attacks, for example; only their intelligence."[25] For this reason Jesus introduces the harmlessness of a dove as the quality to be possessed along with a serpent-like shrewdness or wisdom. This wisdom is not a rule, method, or formula, but some act of prudence, which means that it will most likely be something different in different contexts, even when certain factors remain constant. The most important factor is the kind of person the disciple has become or is becoming rather than a fixed kind of action that must be carried out at all times and in all places. This picture counters naïve pacifism while at the same time excludes crusading tendencies.

Christians in northern Nigeria therefore may, as a community of believers, articulate a phronetic or nuanced approach to restraining mob violence by Muslims in order to defend their families – the emphasis is on restraining because a properly Christian self-defense must be done in a way that harm is avoided, or where that is not possible it is highly limited or greatly minimized such that it is not life threatening. It must not only be the case that we made all efforts to preserve life, but it must also be seen to be the case. Where all such efforts to preserve life fails and an attacker is killed, the community of Christians would need to mourn and lament the taking of such life.[26] George Tinker highlights this concern as follows:

> Violence cannot be perpetrated, a life taken, in a Native American society, without some spiritual reciprocation. I am so much a part of the whole of creation and its balance, anything I do to perpetrate an act of violence, *even a necessary act of violence* like hunting or harvesting, must be accompanied by an act of spiritual reciprocation intended to restore the balance of existence. . . . The ideal of harmony and balance requires that

---

25. Bruner, *Matthew*, 474.

26. George Tinker notes that in Native American tradition, "The total destruction or conquest of an enemy was never a military objective. Indeed, the killing of an enemy was not usually accorded the same high honor as 'counting coup,' or touching an enemy in battle without being touched in return." Tinker, *Spirit and Resistance*, x.

all share a respect for all other existent things, a respect for life and avoiding gratuitous or unthinking acts of violence.[27]

This is where a phronetic use of violence is most critical; such an attitude means that reprisal and premeditated attacks are unjustified on whatever grounds.[28] Rather, in the course of defending themselves Christians must set free those they capture, treat those who are wounded, and where possible return both groups to their homes. Such action at the end of the day will be a greater display of the love of Christ to the enemies much more than mere pacifist nonviolent nonresistance.

The final (and perhaps, most important) point to note is what comes at the very end of the story – Jesus was recognized and worshipped as the Son of God (Matt 14:33). The identification of the man Jesus with the one true God of Israel here is quite remarkable. Critical commentators often argue that the worship of Jesus as God was a latter development in the history of the church and that it was more a matter of superstitious tradition and politics than faith in something factual.[29] However, even before his death and resurrection, Jesus's disciples already encountered and recognized him as divine. The fact that they worshipped him and declared him to be the Son of God at the end of the story underscores the fundamental telos of encountering Jesus (i.e. experiencing and reflecting on him). It is meant to lead to the understanding and worship of the Christ as the Son of the living God – he shows up in the storm and in the darkest night to both demonstrate and declare his true identity to his faithful followers.

This narrative should give the Christians of northern Nigeria confidence in the fact that Jesus Christ will eventually bring deliverance to them (whether in this age or at the end of the age) in order to further confirm among them who he already is – the Son of God. In fact, it is obvious that Christ has already been a source of deliverance for the minority ethnic groups of northern Nigeria through the witness of the missionaries that worked among them.

---

27. Tinker, 19–20.

28. Sadly, this has sometimes been the case among some Christian communities in northern Nigeria. Based on the Dallas News online article cited earlier in this work, the attack on Dogo Nahawa was a reprisal by the Muslims in response to an earlier reprisal attack by the Christians which itself was a reprisal to a much earlier attack by the Muslims. This often is the problem with reprisal attacks – they result in more reprisals.

29. See Erhman, *How Jesus Became God*.

We noted earlier that the colonial administrators basically subjugated these minority non-Muslim ethnic groups under the hegemony of the majority Muslim Hausa-Fulani chiefs or governing structure, which was due to racial and religious biases of the colonialists as well as their political and administrative expediency. With this arrangement in place, it was only a matter of time before the Hausa-Fulani Muslim majority began to impose Islam on these ethnic minorities. However, Christ showed up through the missionaries. The missionaries served primarily among these ethnic minorities of northern Nigeria, partly because the colonial authorities banned or restricted them from preaching among the Muslims in order to keep the peace, but also because the gospel message bore more fruit among these non-Muslim ethnic groups.[30] The activities of the missionaries included building schools and hospitals and teaching God's word thus empowering the ethnic minorities in a way that enabled them to weather the storm of both colonial and Islamic oppression.

Therefore, it was not surprising that the activities and teachings of the missionaries were disturbing to the colonial authorities who instituted and sought to sustain the superiority of Muslims over non-Muslims. For example, the British Governor General in Nigeria, Sir Frederick Lord Lugard remarked,

> Racial distinction should be accepted as the true basis of African education. . . . I am informed that they [some missionaries] preach the equality of Europeans and natives, which, however true from a doctrinal point of view, is apt to be mis-applied by people in a low stage of development, and interpreted as an abolition of class distinction.[31]

Indeed, Lugard was right because the knowledge of the gospel and the education that these ethnic minorities received elevated their status in modern society, which further raised some concerns among the colonialists. Turaki reports that "K. V. Elpinstone, the Resident of Kabba Province in 1912, complained: 'I have no hesitation in saying that the native converts are a constant source of trouble . . . being literate and being in very intimate relationship

---

30. Turaki, *Tainted Legacy*, 127–36.
31. Quoted in Turaki, *British Colonial Legacy*, 81.

with white men are the cause of this trouble.'"[32] Therefore, "Many British colonial officers hated to see Africans being converted to Christianity. They called the converts insulting names such as 'mission boys,' 'black white men,' 'half baked,' 'rebels,' 'hot heads,' 'detribalised,' 'denationalised,' 'anglicised,' and 'Christianised.'"[33]

Such pejoratives notwithstanding, the presence of Christ through the missionary witness among these ethnic minorities of northern Nigeria was providential as it staved off the forceful advance and domination of Islam over these peoples. Even now, in spite of the prevailing violence – itself a sign of frustration with the continuing growth of the Christian faith – Christians and churches of northern Nigeria are witnesses to the preserving power of Christ. This should and does evoke worship in the hearts of the people, and such worship is the proper end of christological experience and reflection. To worship Jesus is to come to an understanding of his full identity as one who is not only fully human but also fully divine. However, the worship of Jesus and proclaiming him as the Son of God is arguably the most disagreeable and most offensive claim of Christianity among northern Nigerian Muslims. This claim has often led to some contentious arguments between Christians and Muslims in the region and has generated a great deal of hate toward Christianity and Christians from their Muslim neighbors. They question quite straightforwardly how God can have a son when he does not have a wife. While Islam in general believes in *Isa* (Jesus) as a great prophet, it finds the claim of his divinity nonsensical and considers the worship of Jesus as an aberration of early Christianity.[34]

Given these challenges, how might Christ be confessed in this context as the Son of God, without at the same time being offensive to Muslims? How do we explain this concept to a Muslim or Muslim convert in northern Nigeria in a way that is relatable and acceptable? What conceptual furnishings within that context might be beneficial to this endeavor? Quite interestingly, we might be able to get help from John of Damascus, who himself had lived and worked in a harsh and unjust Muslim environment in his native Syria,

---

32. Turaki, *Tainted Legacy*, 136.
33. Turaki, 136.
34. See Akyol, *Islamic Jesus*, 169.

which was ruled by the Umayyad Dynasty following the Muslim conquest.[35] Sidney Griffith reports that John of Damascus "was at home in the world of Islam, and arguably he was also the first Christian thinker to seriously take account of Islam's challenge to Christianity."[36] Because John was also an astute expositor and a staunch defender of Nicene-Chalcedonian Christology, he seems the most fitting figure in the tradition to draw from on this matter.

First, John of Damascus considers Islam to be a heresy or "a deceptive superstition"[37] as opposed to a distinct religion in its own right that we take it to be today. Now, while this may not be helpful for peaceful dialogue, it is perhaps the most effective insight for addressing misconceptions about Christ in an environment replete with Islamic notions of him. The Damascene describes Mohammed (the founder of Islam) as a false prophet who rose among the Ishmaelites[38] "having chanced upon the Old and New Testaments and likewise, it seems, having conversed with an Arian monk, devised his own heresy."[39] Clearly, John of Damascus considers Islam to be, at its very core, a christological heresy of the Arian sort. This is a very useful and explosive theological consideration to take into account when speaking about Christ in a Muslim-dominated context. Mustafa Akyol notes that some Islamic scholars make a distinction between the concepts of Jesus as *the Son of God* and that of Jesus as *God the Son*. The former may be acceptable to Islam (and Judaism too) if, and only if, it is understood as "sonship to God in the monotheist Hebrew context—in the Old Testament sense of being chosen and beloved by

---

35. Historical accounts have it that the grandfather of John of Damascus known as Mansur ibn Sarjun was "the person who negotiated with the Muslim commander the surrender of the city and who opened the Eastern Gate (*al-Bab al-Sharqi*) of Damascus to the Muslim troops." Sahas, *John of Damascus on Islam*, 2.

36. Griffith, "Mansur Family and Saint John," 30. Griffith further notes that John's original name was Mansur ibn Sarjun ibn Mansur, but he would later take up the name John most likely "on becoming a monk in Jerusalem." Griffith, 32.

37. Sahas, *John of Damascus on Islam*, 68. Here, Sahas also argues that, due to the ambiguity of the word employed, it may be difficult to conclude definitively that John of Damascus did not consider Islam to be a separate religion. He thinks that the terminology does allow for a wide range of consideration.

38. This is John's preferred name for Muslims so as to trace the people's ethnic, idolatrous, and pre-Islamic origins, about whom he further wrote: "They are descended from Ishmael, who was born to Abraham of Agar, and for this reason they are called both *Agarenes* and *Ishmaelites*. They are also called *Saracens*, which is derived from Σάρρας κενοί, or *destitute of Sara*, because of what Agar said to the angel: 'Sara hath sent me away destitute.'" John of Damascus, *Writings*, 153.

39. John of Damascus, 153.

God,"⁴⁰ rather than the sense of being begotten by God, which is offensive to Islam given its emergence "in a cultural context in which people believed in deities having carnal relations."⁴¹ The latter concept of God the Son is completely rejected and this logically entails a rejection of the Trinity. It seems that the influence of Arianism on Islamic Christology as suggested by John of Damascus is unmistakable, which informs the theological and christological disagreements between Christianity and Islam.

Second, John of Damascus's approach to engaging with the understanding of Christ in Islam is by way of disputation and finding parallels or common grounds with respect to the claims about Jesus in both the Bible and the Qur'an. The most potent parallel for the Damascene is the claim in the Qur'an that Jesus is the Word of God and a Spirit of God. It is in this respect that he counters a charge by Muslims that Christians are "*Hetaeriasts*, or *Associators*, because, they say, we introduce an associate with God by declaring Christ to [be] the Son of God and God."⁴² In response, John argues as follows:

> As long as you say that Christ is the Word of God and Spirit, why do you accuse us of being Hetaeriasts? For the word, and the spirit, is inseparable from that in which it naturally has existence. Therefore, if the Word of God is in God, then it is obvious that He is God. If, however, He is outside of God, then, according to you, God is without word and without spirit. Consequently, by avoiding the introduction of an associate with God you have mutilated Him. It would be far better for you to say that He has an associate than to mutilate Him, as if you were dealing with a stone or a piece of wood or some other inanimate object.⁴³

Because Muslims believe that the Qur'an as the word of God was given to Mohammed from heaven, it is uncreated. Therefore, John of Damascus thinks that they are logically forced to affirm that Christ as the Word and Spirit of

---

40. Akyol, *Islamic Jesus*, 168.

41. Akyol, 168.

42. John of Damascus, *Writings*, 155. Emphasis in original. Mustafa Akyol also expresses this criticism by noting that "The Qur'an rejects the title 'Son of God' not only for Jesus, but for anybody. For it finds the very idea of divine begetting deeply disrespectful to God. 'God has no son and there is no other god accompanying Him,' declares one of the Qur'anic verses that condemn the notion." Akyol, *Islamic Jesus*, 167.

43. John of Damascus, *Writings*, 156.

God is also uncreated, which would entail that Christ is coeternal with God. Islam however does not affirm this entailment but instead, in a quasi-Arian move, "puts Jesus somewhere between human beings and God—somewhere, one could suggest, on the same level with the angels."[44]

Furthermore, Akyol notes that Islam's vehement rejection of divine begetting is informed by the pagan religious context within which it (Islam) emerged and sought to correct – a context in which belief in deities having carnal relations to reproduce more deities was replete. Thus, this idea of sonship to God is offensive to Muslims. "In contrast, however, sonship to God in the monotheist Hebrew context—in the Old Testament sense of being chosen and beloved by God—would not be offensive to Islam."[45] This would have been an acceptable solution if (and only if) the New Testament portrays Jesus as the "Son" of God in this sense, a portrayal that Akyol erroneously claims when he says that

> theological tension between Islam and mainstream Christianity does not necessarily exist between Islam and the New Testament gospels. For in the gospels, Jesus is repeatedly called Son of God, but never God the Son. The latter term was established in church councils, as an interpretation of the New Testament, and at the expense of the various "heretics" who had differing interpretations.[46]

The problem with this claim is that it fails to account for the early worship of Jesus in the Gospels as seen in the Matthew story we have discussed in this section. The fact that the disciples in the boat worshipped Jesus while acknowledging him to be the Son of God shows that there is more to their understanding than Islam is willing to admit.

As we will see in the next section, with help from David Yeago, the church councils' interpretation of the New Testament does not introduce any new judgments into the New Testament as Islam purports, but simply affirms the implicit judgment of the New Testament about the Son's begottenness. It is this same judgment that the early church explicates and preserves in and through

---

44. Akyol, *Islamic Jesus*, 165.
45. Akyol, 168.
46. Akyol, 169.

different terms and concepts. The next section, to which we now turn, will dwell on this and other related discussions in more detail.

Confessing Jesus Christ as Lord of and in All Contexts

The primary text for reflection in this section is Philippians 2:6–11, a passage that many commentators consider as the most important part of the book of Philippians.[47] It is widely recognized as a hymn of the early church in honor of Christ; not a hymn in the modern sense, but in a creedal, confessional, and doxological sense. Gordon Fee thinks of it as a narrative that "begins with Christ's pre-existence, followed by his incarnation, including his death on the cross, and concludes with his (assumed) return to heaven as exalted Lord of heaven and earth."[48] Paul appropriates this hymn or "creed" or narrative in his epistle so as to drive home an earlier call he made in verses 1–2 for unity among the believers in Philippi – a unity that should be anchored in and fueled by mutual self-giving and the priority of the "other," thus devoid of selfish-ambition and vain-conceit (vv. 3–4). He then presents the humble self-sacrifice of Christ as the most excellent example of such prioritizing of others over oneself that all believers should follow.

Therefore, verse 5 in the Greek text begins with an emphatic "this"[49] and literally reads: "This, which also was in Christ Jesus, think in you (or among yourselves)!" But what is the referent of *this*? It is the particular way of thinking already spelled out in verses 3–4 seen above, which Paul now identifies as the very same way of thinking that was operational in Christ leading to his incarnation and death. Different translations render it as this "attitude" or "mindset" or simply "mind." It is *this* same way of thinking (or attitude or mindset) that Paul now commands believers to take up in them as well. The obvious question that follows at the end of verse 5 is, how was this thinking or attitude or mindset operational in Christ? And it is in the course of making explicit how this attitude was operational in Christ that the hymn articulates

---

47. Hawthorne, *Philippians*, 76. Its importance is highlighted both by its style and content: "Like threads in a beautiful tapestry, the lines in this poem are carefully woven together to form a complete picture." Hansen, *Letter to the Philippians*, 123.

48. Fee, *Paul's Letter to the Philippians*, 194.

49. Fee, 199.

for us an ontologically rich understanding of Christ as the God-man, and explicating this understanding will benefit from the analytic theological approach.[50] It is obvious at this point that verse 5 rightly serves as a connection between verses 1–4 and 6–11. Therefore, we will now consider the text of 6–11 and see how it enriches a global understanding of Christ.

Divine Self-Emptying and Human Self-Humbling

The first part of the hymn is verses 6–8 in which the divine existence, incarnation, and perfect obedience of Christ to death are captured. Christ is presented in verse 6 to have been in the *form* (μορφῇ) of God, which the NIV renders as "being in very nature God,"[51] yet he did not think of that sameness of identity (i.e. in form or nature) as something he is unable to let go. The idea of Christ being in the form of God, according to Gerald Hawthorne, is not limited to mere appearance as the word may seem to suggest. This notion would not be consistent with the context of the hymn since it cannot apply to the second use of the word in verse 7. Therefore, Hawthorne rejects suggestions that μορφῇ simply refers to God's glory, God's image, a mode of being, and a divine condition/status. Instead, while acknowledging the elusiveness of the word's meaning, he goes with its usage in earliest Greek texts where it expresses "the way in which a thing, being what it is in itself, appears to our senses."[52] To say then that Christ was in the form of God is to say that Christ shares in the "essential nature and character of God."[53] This understanding is further confirmed by the reference to his equality with God as stated in the second part of the verse.

---

50. It must be noted that the analytic theological task is not simply the search for propositional restatements and conceptual conundrums to feast on, but a genuine and noble desire to demonstrate the clarity and consistency of the scriptural claims about the person and function of Christ. The task is critical if one acknowledges that the understanding of Jesus as God-man is the most fundamental claim of Scripture and of the Christian tradition generally speaking. The consequence of this claim is that we must then think and speak of Jesus's divinity and humanity at once; that we cannot isolate one (with no reference to the other) in order to understand it well, as doing so will simply lead to distortions and confusions about the singular divine-human hypostasis of Christ. The analytic theological task simply serves this purpose.

51. Hawthorne notes that this is "a difficult phrase to interpret, if for no other reason than that the word μορφῇ occurs only here and in v 7 in the NT." Hawthorne, *Philippians*, 81.

52. Hawthorne, 83.

53. Hawthorne, 84.

Furthermore and as noted above, David Yeago points out that this same understanding or judgment about Christ is what Nicene dogma both expresses with and preserves in the concept of *homoousios*, as opposed to claims that the concept is merely Greek-thought imposed on or "distantly deduced *from* Scripture."[54] One may say then that Nicene Christology, which was further clarified via elaborations in the Chalcedonian statement, represents an exercise in drawing a picture of Jesus by simply tracing out the original picture on a translucent paper. The portrayal(s) of Christ in Scripture is the original, and the new context in which Christ is being expressed is the translucent paper. In this sense, the texture of contextual paper should not be too thick as to block or blur the original scriptural image of Christ from being seen clearly and traced out correctly.[55] In the northern Nigerian context for example, the Hausa Bible – by far the most widely used Bible in the region – translates the word *form* as "*siffa*" or "*sura*," which simply means shape or image, also likeness or nature. The word connotes the likeness of a thing that is based on its intrinsic makeup or structure, and this, in contradistinction to the likeness that is based on mere appearance or outward features. This second sense of likeness is usually expressed with a different word "*kamani*," (e.g. in Matt 17:2 where Jesus was transfigured); thus, the Hausa saying: "*kama da wane ba ta wane*," which can be translated as "similarity is not the same as identity" (lit: to look like someone or something is not the same as being that person or thing). This same idea is encapsulated in Leibniz's Law of Identicals as follows: for any entity X and for any entity Y, if X is identical to Y; then for any property A, if A is true of X then A must be true of Y. In this sense therefore, we can say that the likeness of Jesus to God is based not just on mere appearance, but on his intrinsic or essential identity to God, and this thought is the referent of *morphe*, *homoousios*, and *siffa*.

This intrinsic or essential identity of Christ to the God of Israel is what he (Christ) did not think to himself as something he needed to tightly hold on to, or use for his own advantage. Instead, he willingly gave it up according to verse 7, "but made himself nothing [lit: emptied himself], taking the

---

54. Yeago, "New Testament and Nicene Dogma," 3. Emphasis in original.

55. In this sense, tracing is to an image what translating is to a word or term. In both instances, the original is being reproduced in a new way without losing either its explicit claim or implicit judgment.

very nature of a servant, being made in human likeness" (NIV). The idea that Christ emptied himself (ἑαυτὸν ἐκένωσεν) has generated several discussions both for and against the notion of a kenotic Christology – the claim that "God the Son in some way limited or temporarily divested himself of some of the properties thought to be divine prerogatives."[56] Oliver Crisp suggests that both ontological (the Word abdicates his divine properties at the incarnation) and functionalist (the Word does not exercise certain divine properties at the incarnation) kenosis fail for three reasons. (1) God cannot have contingent properties so that at any point he ceases to have the divine properties, he ceases to be God. (2) Jesus did not cease to have a human nature post-resurrection, which would suggest that he is still in a state of limitation or divesture of the divine properties. (3) kenoticism fails to obtain if we are to affirm *extra calvinisticum* – that is, the idea that the divine "attributes had to be exercised by the Word in order that the second person of the Trinity (a) remain divine and (b) retain his divine role of upholding the cosmos in being while incarnate."[57] Therefore, a notion of divine self-emptying that is consistent with Chalcedon involves Christ's humility of "taking on" rather than "giving up" something, an idea that is clearly expressed in the second part of verse 7 "taking the very nature of a servant, being made in human likeness." Crisp calls this divine *krypsis* (self-concealment), a state in which Christ remains fully God but yields to his full humanity through which his divinity is concealed (unless otherwise revealed) without being limited or divested necessarily. So he empties himself by adding to himself and operating with the form or nature (of a slave and of man), which is less than his original form (of God).[58] Cyril of Alexandria puts it much better when trying to explain the sense in which the Word became flesh:

> He did not *change* himself into flesh; he did not endure any *mixture* or blending, or anything else of this kind. But he submitted himself to being emptied . . . and did not disdain the poverty of human nature. As God he wished to make that flesh which was held in the grip of sin and death evidently superior to sin and death. He made it his very own, and not soulless as some have

---

56. Evans, "Introduction," in *Exploring Kenotic Christology*, 4.
57. Crisp, *Divinity and Humanity*, 142.
58. See the discussion in Hawthorne, *Philippians*, 86.

said, but rather animated with a rational soul, and thus restored flesh to what it was in the beginning.[59]

If as God Christ *emptied himself* by becoming man, then verse 8 tells us that as Man he *humbled himself* by becoming obedient unto death: "And being found in appearance as a man, he humbled himself and became obedient to death—even death on a cross!" (NIV). Having added human nature to himself as his means of self-emptying, Christ then subjected himself to the humiliation of human experience, the worst being death in a most humiliating manner. To further highlight Jesus's example as one who sought out the interest of others rather than being self-seeking, his act of self-humbling is expressed as obedience or submission to "another" – a total obedience to God and in service to humanity.

> This service entailed a positive response to the fundamental though inarticulate demand of the human race: "Ransom us from death by your death!" To this demand Jesus's answer was not only, "I have come to do your will, O God" (cf. Heb 10:7), but also, "I have come to seek and save that which is lost (Luke 19:10), to serve and to give my life a ransom for many" (Mark 10:45).[60]

So, Hawthorne concludes that Jesus's full surrender to death "was his ultimate *yes* to God and man, his ultimate act of obedience to God in his self-giving service to people."[61]

Besides the means and outcome of Jesus's self-humbling, one other entailment to draw here is the sameness or singularity of agency with respect to both acts of self-emptying (v. 7) and self-humbling (v. 8), even when there is a clear identification of two distinct "*morphes*" (divine and human). The self-same individual who acted *qua* divine agent by emptying himself also acted *qua* human agent by humbling himself without at the same time necessitating or instantiating two acting agents. The potential for confusion here is not a trivial one, more so in a context challenged by Islamic christological claims (better still, counter-claims) as seen above. On this note, John of Damascus

---

59. St. Cyril of Alexandria, *On the Unity of Christ*, 54–55.
60. Hawthorne, *Philippians*, 89.
61. Hawthorne, 89.

is again helpful. He addresses such christological confusions and counterclaims with a robust explication of Nicene-Chalcedonian Christology, and we should do no less in the present Muslim-dominated context of northern Nigeria. This is the understanding that informs the discussion that follows.

Chalcedon recognized the scriptural judgment of the singularity of agency in Christ, expressing the same with the concept of hypostasis or persona, while the notion of nature or essence was employed to identify the distinction of forms (divine and human). The characterization advanced by Boethius on the idea of person is very helpful and has remained influential in contemporary discussions. He gives the definition of person as "The individual substance of a rational sort."[62] The way Boethius arrived at his "rational sort" qualification is by eliminating such things that have no self-consciousness like a stone (non-living), a tree (living but non-sentient), or a horse (sentient but non-rational[63]). A person therefore is a distinct, unified center of self-awareness or self-consciousness.[64] We may add here that a person is also the answer to the "*who* question" – that is, a person is the kind of entity about whom a story can be told, precisely because a person does things. We learn about what a person is like by observing what a person says and does.

Furthermore, the idea of an individual for Boethius points to the fact that "person cannot anywhere be predicated of universals, but only of [concrete] particulars and individuals; for there is no person of man as animal or genus; only of Cicero, Plato, or other single individuals are single persons named."[65] To see the point more clearly we need to contrast this way of talking about person with his qualification of nature as "the specific difference that gives form to *anything*."[66] So while nature (divine or human) is kind-specific, person is individual- or self-specific. For Boethius, "nature is a substrate of person, and that person cannot be predicated apart from nature."[67] In other words,

---

62. Boethius, "Contra Eutychen," 100.

63. The choice of non-rational rather than irrational is informed by the fact that the point here is not on the ability to reason but on *the having* of that ability whether it is functional or not. This avoids the slippery slope of excluding those in, say, a vegetative state from being persons, which would be quite odd a thing to say.

64. This way of characterizing person is also consistent with social trinitarianism, at least as construed by Moreland and Craig, *Philosophical Foundations*, 583.

65. Boethius, "Contra Eutychen."

66. Boethius, 98. Emphasis added.

67. Boethius, 99.

although person is kind-neutral it is not nature-neutral; instead, persons are the possessors of nature so that it is not possible to say anything that is nature-free of any person. Thus, when a certain nature is predicated of any person it is understood to be the nature of that particular person in a "personal" rather than a generic sense. Consequently, the singular individual who existed in the form of God was already a person, albeit divine, and does not need to add another person to himself in order to become a human person. Actually, he cannot do that since he would not be one and the same person anymore. Instead, he only needs to take on a different form (a human form or nature) into his already existing person in order to become at once a divine-human individual without mixing and confusing the forms or separating and dividing the person.

These fine distinctions and explanations are not merely academic but hold a practical implication for the life of the church. Perhaps, directly relevant to the general context of the text under consideration, this raises a question about Christian discipleship, precisely in relation to following the example of Christ. It is not uncommon for some Christians in northern Nigeria to question the possibility of fully imitating Christ since he was not only human but also divine and could do what we cannot do. It is as if by virtue of his being divine, Christ had an enhanced humanity that is inaccessible to us and by which he lived a perfect human life. In this sense therefore, it would not be possible for believers to follow the example of Christ in the true sense of it, given the limitations of our humanity and the added burden of it being a fallen humanity as opposed to the perfect humanity of Christ. Some, like Udoh, seem to suggest that as long as Jesus is first understood as a preexistent divine person, his full humanity (i.e. with respect to our humanity) would have to be in a state of compromise. This is why Udoh insists on the historicity of Jesus as noted in the previous chapter and gives priority to a Christology from below. However, whether one begins from above or from below, the most important thing is the firm recognition of Christ as the God-man without mixture and confusion of the two forms (natures) or division and separation of the one individual. He is not only like us in our full humanity and in solidarity with us in our "de-humanity," but he is also the Holy One among us and our Immanuel (cf. Matt 1:23). This is why the rejection of the lordship of Christ by Udoh in order to preserve and project the full humanity of Christ is not only unnecessary, but also erroneous since the human nature of Christ was assumed into his person and not into his divine nature.

Furthermore, and perhaps more crucial for present purposes, we may acknowledge a certain uniqueness the humanity of Christ has in comparison to our humanity. This uniqueness, according to Karl Barth, is simply the fact that his humanity stands in relation to his divine person or divinity. Jesus, he says, "is the creaturely being who not only exists from God and in God but absolutely for God instead of for Himself."[68] This uniqueness is not necessarily *sui generis* for Barth but the expression of true humanity such that to be truly human is to stand in true relation to the divine Other. As one who exemplifies this relation perfectly, Jesus himself then functions as "the divine Counterpart of every man" so that every human is confronted by this divine Other (Christ). Barth further notes that "Since Jesus as the Bearer of the divine uniqueness and transcendence is like man, God is revealed to man, and in this confrontation with God man is revealed to himself."[69] So, godlessness (being without God) makes humans "non-human," which is an ontological impossibility because "man is as he is with God and therefore not without him."[70] The point is that by virtue of his humanity standing in relation to his divinity, Jesus exemplifies for us the fact of our need of God in life. To be fully human then is not to be without any reference to God, but actually to be in God and to live for God rather than for ourselves. In this sense therefore, Jesus is not an impossible example for us as humans to follow simply because he is both fully God and fully man. Instead, he is the perfect example for us to follow or what Larry Hurtado describes as the "Lordly example to the readers who acclaim him now."[71] As we stand in relation to him as our divine Other, we draw strength from his Spirit to help us live in conformity to the mindset or attitude that was in him. On this note, Hurtado is again helpful when he points out that "it is not strict *imitatio* but rather *conformitas* that the passage promotes, by which the believers are called to see in Jesus' action not only the basis of their obedience but also its pattern and direction."[72]

---

68. Barth, *Church Dogmatics* III/2, 133.
69. Barth, 138.
70. Barth, 139.
71. Hurtado, "Jesus as Lordly Example," 126.
72. Hurtado, 125.

In the final part of the passage (vv. 9–11), the exaltation of Jesus is narrated, thus his vindication and confirmation as Lord of all. To call him the Lordly example is to say that his divine-human life of self-emptying and self-humbling is not merely an exemplar for local or contextual Christian living, but that it also has a universal or cosmic effect. What this involves and entails is the focus of the next and final section of this chapter.

The Exaltation and Lordship of Christ

If as God Jesus Christ emptied himself by becoming human, and as Man he humbled himself by obeying to the point of death, then as the God-man, he was exalted to the highest place and given the greatest name by God the Father. While he was the subject in verses 6–8 carrying out the acts of self-emptying and self-humbling, in verse 9 Jesus is the object of the Father's actions:[73] "Therefore God exalted him to the highest place and gave him the name that is above every name," meaning this was not a case of self-exaltation. This exaltation consists of two things: a place (the highest) and a name (the most powerful). That the place Jesus has been exalted to is described as the highest place simply means that there is no other place or position or status that is higher than this one, which by implication is a way of stating the restoration of Jesus's initial status of full equality with God. It was this same status that in verse 6 he did not think of as something to contend for, but *concealed* it through his incarnation. The verb used here to describe this maximal exaltation of the Christ is ὑπερύψωσεν, which according to Hawthorne is not comparative (i.e. "Christ is now someone greater than he was before the incarnation, or possesses a status superior to that which he had in his preexistent state"[74]), but superlative (i.e. given a status that is matchless by any other existing status). "Interestingly this verb, ὑπερυψοῦν, is used in the LXX OT to describe Yahweh as the one who is 'exalted far above all gods' (Ps 96 [97]:9; cf. Dan 3:52, 54, 57–88)."[75] This idea that Christ is exalted to his preexistent status that is no less than that of Yahweh is further substantiated by what ensues from these actions of God just described above.

---

73. Hawthorne calls this shift (and rightly so) "a radical change in the hymn." Hawthorne, *Philippians*, 90.

74. Hawthorne, 91.

75. Hawthorne, 91.

God's dramatic act of exalting Jesus inevitably instantiates (or will instantiate) a response from all other beings that are below this status as seen in verses 10–11: "that at the name of Jesus every knee should bow, in heaven and on earth and under the earth, and every tongue confess that *Jesus Christ is Lord*, to the glory of God the Father." The response here is basically that of acknowledgement and it involves the acts of kneeling (demonstrable submission whether willfully or otherwise) and confessing (open declaration or proclamation). The act of submission relates to the power of the name of Jesus, being the most powerful name, while the act of open declaration pertains to his highest status now identified with the term κύριος or Lord. The allusions of this christological title to its LXX usage in reference to Yahweh as well as its subversive NT and early Christian usage with reference to the Roman Emperor are widely acknowledged in diverse studies and commentaries.[76] Therefore, to use this title for Jesus is to portray him as God and Ruler of the entire universe, thus highlighting not only his divinity but also his cosmic significance. This is seen in the fact that all beings in the entire cosmos – angels, humans (both dead and living), and demons – will acknowledge Christ as Lord. To acknowledge the lordship of Christ is not limited to just humans, let alone some ethnic groups or particular cultures that find this idea agreeable to their cultural sensibilities; rather, it is an acknowledgment of what is the case whether it is culturally acceptable or not. Indeed, while "Some will do it gladly; others because they cannot resist."[77] Ultimately, all will acknowledge Jesus Christ as Lord at the parousia, but his followers gladly begin to do so in the here and now.

Consequently, allegiance to Jesus emerged from this understanding of the Christ and this acknowledgment of his lordship. The fact that this emerged from a religious context described by Larry Hurtado as "exclusivist monotheism" means that the evidence was quite compelling to the earliest followers of Christ.[78] He was seen to be identical with the one true God of Israel who is believed to have exalted him (Jesus) to the highest place, given him the most powerful name, and takes all the glory for the reverencing of Jesus (v.

---

76. For detailed discussion about this issue, see Capes, *Old Testament Yahweh*; Hurtado, *Lord Jesus Christ*; Thurston and Ryan, *Philippians and Philemon*, 84–85; Wright, *Paul and the Faithfulness of God*, 701.

77. O'Brien, *Epistle to the Philippians*, 245.

78. Hurtado, *Lord Jesus Christ*, 52.

11). The radical implication of this idea is the fact that Christology therefore began to shape – and indeed should continue to shape– the whole project of reading, not only the Gospel narratives, but all of Scripture. It was in this sense that the Old Testament was read and understood in the light of Jesus Christ as the Lord God of Israel. It is in this sense that allegiance to Jesus is not seen as allegiance to another other than to the one true God, and this trumps any other form of allegiance that includes: (1) a Jewish reading of the *Tanak* that preserves a non-christological monotheism, (2) a Greek commitment to culture that simply uses Christ to advance cultural ideals, and (3) a Roman submission to imperial power in the acknowledgment of the emperor as lord of all. It was the absence of this unreserved allegiance to Jesus as Lord that entrenched the Aryan exaltation of "whiteness" and Western ways over other cultures such that the image of Jesus simply became a tool in that project as rightly noted by Enyi Ben Udoh in chapter 4.

Similarly, the kind of global Christology that tends toward replacing allegiance to Western cultures with uncritical commitment to some non-Western culture only perpetuates the error. Instead, global Christology ought to be driven by unreserved allegiance to the person and work of Jesus Christ such that his story redefines, or better still, redeems our cultures. In this sense, it will be impossible to say like Udoh that we reject the lordship of Christ as the starting point of an African Christology. Instead, we should be able to say that we reject the illegitimate use of the story of Jesus Christ, particularly his lordship, as an excuse for the lordship or superiority of another culture or people and thereby refocus our allegiance to Christ alone. The primary preoccupation of a global Christology therefore will not be the search of some cultural or contextual expression of the story of Christ (as important as that maybe), but the continued exaltation of the Christ and a direct submission to him within these diverse contexts. John Mbiti is quite helpful on this note when he pointed out that in the African context,

> It is not difficult to make contact with traditional thought-forms, in considering the title of Lord (κύριος) as applied to Jesus. Some of our peoples refer to God as Lord, or Master. The immediate

background here is naturally the political set up, especially in societies which had traditional rulers (like chiefs and kings).[79]

For example, the idea of lordship in the dominant Hausa culture of northern Nigeria connotes ownership, rulership, deserving service, having authority, and commanding respect as one who is over a house, farm, community, or region. This is expressed by the Hausa words *ubangiji* meaning lord or *maigida* (lit: head or owner of house). If this title with its attendant concept is applied to Jesus Christ vis-à-vis the whole world or all of creation, then he is identified as the owner and ruler of the universe deserving of our obeisance. The corollary of this portrayal is an affirmation of the divinity and worship of Jesus as evident in Philippians 2:9–11,[80] or at the very least, his exalted status above all else. Mbiti again notes this point when he says that "the Lordship of Jesus can be fitted into the African concept of his person and position. He would indeed shine through as the Lord of lords, since Africa knows also of other lords besides God."[81] In this sense, the canonical idea of lordship is both catholic and contextual, through which Jesus is identified (as in the New Testament) with the one true God, the supreme being, and Maker of heaven and earth.

Conclusion

This chapter proposed attention to the theological use of Scripture (reading the canonical text with dogmatic lenses) along with conceptual analysis for doing global Christology. The northern Nigerian context of hate and violence by the Muslim majority against Christians and churches (other non-Muslims too) of the region was the sociocultural context of reflection using the text of Matthew 14:22–33. Similarly, Philippians 2:5–11 was used as the primary text for christological reflection in the ecclesial context of northern Nigerian Christians, where the example of Jesus for his followers as humans was considered in light of his full humanity along with his full divinity as Lord.

What should be evident from this is that the scriptural and creedal Christ to be reflected upon and understood is the self-same living and present Christ

---

79. Mbiti, "Some African Concepts of Christology," 59.
80. Bauckham, "Worship of Jesus," 136.
81. Mbiti, "Some African Concepts of Christology," 59.

who must be experienced in one's prevailing ecclesial and social situatedness. The new social or ecclesial situation does not need to determine the identity of Christ before he is able to identify fully with us and be seen to be among us. The determination or identification of Christology via potentially neverending contextual qualifiers (e.g. Guest, Revealer, African, Akan, Liberation, Asian, Latin-American, etc.) seems unnecessary and many times unhelpful because they often err on the identity question. The search for some distinctly contextual (e.g. Nigerian or African) as opposed to a so-called Western understanding of Christ continues to drive many approaches to global Christology.[82] In contrast, this chapter addresses present realities in a given context (in our case, northern Nigeria) through (1) the exegetical and dogmatic reading of Scripture, and where necessary, and (2) the analysis of important concepts that help to make and preserve the same christological judgments we find in Scripture and the Christian tradition.

The next and final chapter of our study provides a recap of the entire project, draws final implications and conclusions from previous chapters, and makes some recommendations for the task of global Christologizing and theologizing in general. We now turn our attention to this final task of our project.

---

82. See for example the approaches advanced in Green, Pardue, and Yeo, *Jesus without Borders*.

CHAPTER 7

Summary and Conclusion

Summary

We began this study by presenting the art of weaving as a metaphor for doing theology, particularly when it comes to the task of reflecting on the person and work of Christ in different contexts. The major problem that informed this way of thinking about christological discourse is the pervasively non-theological reading of Scripture in constructive contextual Christologies and the use of local concepts that in some instances fail to advance the same judgments about Christ from the biblical texts and the Christian tradition broadly construed. As such, this study proposed the theological interpretation of Scripture as exegetical and dogmatic reasoning for christological reflection, as well as the theological use of analytic tools for careful conceptual analysis so as to speak about the same Christ of Scripture and tradition in a new global context. It is to these ends that we made a case for theological interpretation of Scripture in chapter 2 and characterized the work of analytic theology in chapter 3 as a way of introducing the disciplines and commending them for a global Christology.

However, we noted at different points in the study (precisely in chapters 1 and 4) how these approaches may be considered by some as Western and on that basis insist on their non-inclusion for constructive Christology in non-Western contexts. This way of thinking was neutralized from the point of view of Bernal's history of Western civilization as having its roots in Africa and Asia, and also from the point of Thiong'o's globalectics approach to engaging literature. But more importantly, from a theological point of view, we argued for continuity with the scriptural and catholic portrayal of Jesus Christ in a contemporary context. In chapter 4, we analyzed some constructive Christologies of two evangelical theologians in Nigeria and noted (among other problems) this lack of continuity with catholic Christology in the case of Udoh, and a disconcerting view of Scripture as elastic parameter for Christology in Ezigbo. While not being representative of all contextual Christologies, these problems apparently continue to plague many of these constructive endeavors.

Consequently, we set out in chapter 5 to reflect about the person and works of Christ in a way that weaves together at once the principles of canonicity, catholicity, contextuality, and conceptuality. The context for reflection was the experience of Christians and churches of northern Nigeria amid hate, marginalization, and incessant violence from the dominant Muslim majority. We used two christological passages of Scripture to inform our reflections, one from the Gospel narratives and the other from the more didactic epistles of Paul. From Matthew 14:22–33, we reflected on the Christ who eventually delivers his followers from their troubles even if he may seem absent for a season. He is able to deliver because he is the eternal Son of God who as such is worshipped. We also noted Paul's appropriation of the Christ hymn (or "creed" or narrative) in Philippians 2:5–11, where he uses it to drive home an earlier call that he had made in verses 1–2 for unity among the believers in Philippi. This unity should be anchored in and fueled by an attitude of mutual self-giving and the priority of the "other" devoid of selfish ambition and vain conceit (vv. 3–4). Paul identifies this attitude as having been in Christ Jesus when he emptied himself as God to become human and humbled himself as a human being to die in obedience to the Father's plan of salvation. Here, we explicated the conditions for the full divinity and full humanity of Christ so as to establish the fact that his "Lordly" example is a fully human example that is possible for us to emulate.

What chapter 5 demonstrated was not necessarily a new Christology that is unique to the northern Nigerian context, but a Christology that seeks above all to be canonical and catholic while being contextually and conceptually relevant to the real concerns of Christians in northern Nigeria. This is not necessarily a comprehensive Christology or a proposal for a new christological model so to speak, but simply illustrative of an approach to global Christologizing that is truly global as opposed to being merely contextual while laying claim to "global voices." At this point therefore, we are ready to draw final conclusions and make some general recommendations from the study.

Conclusions and Recommendations

The attitude of Christ that we are confronted with in Philippians 2:5–11 seems like the perfect attitude that should both motivate and regulate the practice of global theologizing and, in our case, Christologizing – an attitude that would engender doing theology as a logically coherent conversation in a catholic space. The task is a complex one because the threads necessary for the work are multiple and the required skills for weaving them together take several years of apprenticeship and immersion in the Word, the Spirit, and the church (i.e. the company of master weavers both past and present). This study is a step in this direction as well as a modest attempt to illustrate (however imperfectly) what christological reflection might look like when carried out in this manner.

The goal, as should have become clear by now, is not the generation of some new contextual Christology that is essential and indigenously African, even if this is what many Western theologians want to see coming from the African and other non-Western contexts. It is in this sense that Kirk R. MacGregor thinks, rather erroneously, that "as the number of African Christians swelled and theological analysis intensified, many Africans started to feel Jesus asking them as Africans, 'Who *do you* say I am?' This question has sparked an entire generation of African Christians—women and men, educated and illiterate—to develop an indigenous African Christology."[1] However, this way of viewing the "Who do you say I am?" christological question has been shown in chapter 5 to be inconsistent with the intentions of Jesus within the context of the passage it is found. Jesus was not saying that all cultures and peoples should formulate their own unique answer to the question and that all claims about who Jesus is are equally right and theologically sound. Furthermore, we have seen in this study that the construction of a unique Christology for the whole of Africa – an indigenous African Christology – is not only ill-informed, but practically impossible. Indeed, the same can be

---

1. MacGregor, *Contemporary Theology*, 276.

said of the quest to construct a national (e.g. a Nigerian) Christology due to the cultural, economic, and religious diversity of the nation.

Some however have pursued (and continue to pursue) an "authentic indigenous Christology" at the level of their own ethnic group. These approaches however end up constructing what at best amounts to a kind of ethno-Christology, which is akin to Paulin Hountondji's characterization of similar approaches to doing philosophy in Africa as ethnophilosophy.[2] These ethno-Christologies, as was the case with Udoh's Guest Christology, end up solving a new problem by resurrecting old problems (e.g. Arianism) largely due to their inattention to dogmatic Christology. In this vein, what this study has advanced instead is the appropriation of biblical and dogmatic Christology in order to address real issues that real local churches face in contemporary African societies. If in the course of this endeavor, some unique Christology or some new dimension to our understanding of Christ emerges, this will be embraced without having to construe it as an authentic indigenous Christology. That Jesus Christ is Lord also means that he is Lord over all cultures and it is in this sense that Christology defines and conditions every aspect of Christianity. This points to the fact that the gospel of Christ will contradict every human culture in some way and thereby serve as a Lordly corrective to the manifest effects of the fallen nature of all cultures – Western and non-Western or those of the Global North and of the Global South alike.

With respect to the relation of analytic theology and the theological interpretation of Scripture for a global Christology, perhaps the greatest area of tension has been that between a narrative account of the identity of Christ advocated by many theological interpreters of Scripture and the focus on ontology and metaphysical explication preferred by most analytic theologians. This concern will definitely require further research and reflection. However, the claim that this study posited is that the two approaches are not necessarily contradictory as some may seem to imply. The two approaches are clearly different and therefore lead to different outcomes, but they both contribute to a fuller understanding of Christ – an understanding that includes primarily who he is, but also what he is. While the first helps us to identify

---

2. See Hountondji, *African Philosophy*, 34. Hountondji coins this word as a referent to Placide Tempels' *Bantu Philosophy*, which he describes, rather poignantly as "an ethnological work with philosophical pretensions" that is addressed, not to Africans, "but to Europeans, and particularly to two categories of Europeans: colonials and missionaries." Hountondji, 34.

Christ as identical to the God of Israel based on the fact that he shares the same story with him as narrated in the Old and New Testaments, the second approach helps us see that beyond the story there is also a shared divine essence or nature by which the man Jesus is identified with the one true and eternal God. Therefore, rather than the prevalent dismissal of the tradition, particularly with respect to creedal Christology as mere Greek-thought that is non-biblical and unintelligible to contemporary modes of thinking, we can seek to understand it through the use of analytic tools.

This study also rejects the notion that this ontological nature of creedal or dogmatic Christology is foreign to non-Western cultures because these cultures do not have ontology as a category of thought. We saw that ontological thinking or claims are often expressed in sayings or proverbs that clearly have ontology or the metaphysics of identity as their underlying assumption. For example, the saying that "no matter how long a log of wood floats in the river, it will never become a crocodile" is in the final analysis an ontological claim. It is not just about the story of the log of wood, even though that is important, but what is more important is that there is something in the internal make up of a log of wood that is essentially different from what it means to be a crocodile even if there is some similarity in the way they both float on water. It is the same with the Bambara proverb that says: "No matter how much the world changes, the cat will never lay eggs." Just as these cultures have such basic understanding of ontology expressed in proverbs, the basic ontology of the hypostatic union of divinity and humanity in Christ as expressed in the creeds can be understood by Christians in non-Western contexts if it is not kept away from them. To do global Christology well will mean incorporating these dogmatic christological claims along with reading the stories of Christ in the biblical text as authoritative for whatever image of Christ we seek to project in some new context of world Christianity.

From the foregoing, we may say that a potential area for further research obviously would be the possibility of greater seamlessness in the process of weaving the diverse threads that this study has brought together. This seems like an important desideratum to be pursued more intentionally. One aspect of this pursuit would be to further compare and contrast between a theo-dramatic approach to theology and an analytic approach with the aim of showing some other ways how they might cohere. Another aspect is definitely the relation of context and dogma or what we may describe as the un-forecloseable quest to, in the words of Byang Kato, "contextualize without compromise."[3] Kato's charge to this effect is worth restating, "Let Christianity truly find its home in Africa, by adopting local hymnology, using native language, idiom and concepts to express the unchanging faith. But always let our primary goal be that Jesus Christ might have the foremost place."[4]

While this study has presented the interaction of the canon of Scripture, ecclesial dogma about Christ, prevailing contextual realities, and careful conceptual analysis as the way to achieve this quest, the possibility of some other way – perhaps, one that might even be better – cannot be foreclosed. That being said, Christian theologians from diverse contexts around the world would do well to ground their work in these key principles and join in weaving a common (catholic) christological tapestry.

---

3. Kato, "Christianity as an African Religion," in *Biblical Christianity*, 38.

4. Kato, 38. While some may quibble with Kato's notion of the faith as "unchanging," it must be noted that he clearly indicated in this essay that the form of the faith (i.e. practice) can and indeed should change in a new context without contradiction to the beliefs that have been passed on in Scripture and through the early church.

Bibliography

Aben, Tersur A. *African Christian Theology: Illusion and Reality*. Jos: ACTS, 2008.
Abraham, William J. "Systematic Theology as Analytic Theology." In *Analytic Theology: New Essays in the Philosophy of Theology*, edited by Oliver D. Crisp and Michael C. Rea, 54–69. New York: Oxford University Press, 2009.
Adam, A. K. M. *What is Postmodern Biblical Criticism?* Minneapolis: Fortress Press, 1995.
Adeyemo, Tokunboh, ed. *Africa Bible Commentary: A One-Volume Commentary Written by 70 African Scholars*. Grand Rapids: Zondervan, 2006.
Aguilar, Mario I. "Postcolonial African Theology in Kabasele Lumbala." *Theological Studies* 63, no. 2 (2002): 302–23.
Akyol, Mustafa. *The Islamic Jesus: How the King of the Jews Became a Prophet of the Muslims*. New York: St. Martin's, 2017.
Allen, Diogenes, and Eric O. Sprinsted. *Philosophy for Understanding Theology*. 2nd ed. Louisville: Westminster John Knox, 2007.
Anatolios, Khaled. *Retrieving Nicaea: The Development and Meaning of Trinitarian Doctrine*. Grand Rapids: Baker Academic, 2011.
Appiah, Anthony. *In My Father's House: Africa in the Philosophy of Culture*. New York: Oxford University Press, 1992.
Aquinas, Thomas. *The Summa Theologica, Vols. 1–22*. Translated by Fathers of the English Dominican Province. London: Burns Oates & Washbourne, 1947.
Asselt, Willem van. *Introduction to Reformed Scholasticism*. Grand Rapids: Reformed Heritage Books, 2011.
Astill, James. "The Truth behind the Miss World Riots." *The Guardian*. 29 November 2002. Accessed 24 November 2018. https://www.theguardian.com/world/2002/nov/30/jamesastill.
Athanasius of Alexandria. *On the Incarnation*. Lexington: Fig Books, 2012.
Atsen, Isuwa Y. Review of *Jesus without Borders: Christology in the Majority World*, edited by Gene L. Green, Stephen T. Pardue, and K. K. Yeo. *Trinity Journal* 38 NS, no. 1 (Spring 2017): 131–33.

———. "Self-Defense and a Phronetic Use of Violence: Christian Response to Muslim-Mob Attacks in Northern Nigeria." *International Journal of Public Theology* 15, 4 (2021): 496–512, doi: https://doi.org/10.1163/15697320-01540016.

Audi, Robert. "Cumulative Case Arguments in Religious Epistemology." In *Oxford Studies in Philosophy of Religion*, edited by Jonathan L. Kvanvig, 1–16. Oxford: Oxford University Press, 2017.

Bahemuka, Judith M. "The Hidden Christ in African Traditional Religion." In *Jesus in African Christianity: Experimentation and Diversity in African Christology*, edited by J. N. K. Mugambi and Laurenti Magesa, 1–16. Nairobi: Initiatives, 1989.

Baird, William. "An Overview of Historical Criticism." In *A History of Biblical Interpretation: The Enlightenment through the Nineteenth Century*, edited by Alan J. Hauser and Duane F. Watson, 93–119. Grand Rapids,: Eerdmans, 2017.

Baker-Hytch, Max. "Analytic Theology and Analytic Philosophy of Religion: What's the Difference?" *Journal of Analytic Theology* 4 (May 2016): 347–61.

Barnes, Leonard. *African Renaissance*. Indianapolis: Bobbs-Merrill, 1969.

Barth, Karl. *Church Dogmatics*. 4 Vols. Edited by G. W. Bromiley and T. F. Torrance. Edinburgh: T&T Clark, 1936–1977.

Bartholomew, Craig G., and Heath A. Thomas, eds. *A Manifesto for Theological Interpretation*. Grand Rapids: Baker Academic, 2016.

Bauckham, Richard. *Jesus and the God of Israel: God Crucified and Other Studies on the New Testament Christology of Divine Identity*. Grand Rapids: Eerdmans, 2008.

———. "The Worship of Jesus in Philippians 2:9–11." In *Where Christology Began: Essays on Philippians 2*, edited by Ralph P. Martin and Brian J. Dodd, 128–39. Louisville: Westminster John Knox, 1998.

BBC News. "Nigeria Cartoon Protests Kill 16." BBC News. Last updated 19 February 2006. Accessed 24 November 2018. http://news.bbc.co.uk/2/hi/4728616.stm.

Beale, G. K., and D. A. Carson, eds. *Commentary on the New Testament Use of the Old Testament*. Grand Rapids: Baker Academic, 2007.

Bediako, Kwame. *Jesus and the Gospel in Africa: History and Experience*. Maryknoll: Orbis Books, 2004.

———. *Theology and Identity: The Impact of Culture upon Christian Thought in the Second Century and in Modern Africa*. Oxford: Regnum Books, 1999.

Beely, Christopher A. *The Unity of Christ: Continuity and Conflict in Patristic Tradition*. New Haven: Yale University Press, 2012.

Bernal, Martin. *Black Athena: The Afroasiatic Roots of Classical Civilization*, Vol. 1, *The Fabrication of Ancient Greece 1785–1985*. New Brunswick: Rutgers University Press, 1987.

———. *Black Athena: The Afroasiatic Roots of Classical Civilization*, Vol. 2, *The Archaeological and Documentary Evidence*. New Brunswick: Rutgers University Press, 1991.

Bevans, Stephen B. "Contextual Theology." An essay for use by participants of the 2010 Study Week of the Southwest Liturgical Conference, Houston, Texas, January 2010.

Blake, Daniel. "Christian School Teacher Brutally Murdered by Extremists in Nigeria." *Christian Today*, 5 June 5 2007. Accessed 24 November 2018. https://www.christiantoday.com/article/christian.school.teacher.brutally.murdered.by.extremists.in.nigeria/11021.htm.

Billings, J. Todd. *The Word of God for the People of God: An Entryway to the Theological Interpretation of Scripture*. Grand Rapids: Eerdmans, 2010.

Blomberg, Craig L. "The Historical-Critical/Grammatical View." In *Biblical Hermeneutics: Five Views*, edited by Stanley E. Porter and Beth M. Stovell, 27–47. Downers Grove: IVP Academic, 2012.

Bock, Darrel L. "Single Meaning, Multiple Contexts and Referents: The New Testament's Legitimate, Accurate, and Multifaceted Use of the Old." In *Three Views on the New Testament Use of the Old Testament*, edited by Stanley N. Gundry, Kenneth Berding, and Jonathan Lunde, 105–51. Grand Rapids: Zondervan, 2008.

Boethius. "Contra Eutychen." In *The Theological Tractates. The Consolation of Philosophy*. Translated by H. F. Stewart, E. K. Rand, and S. J. Tester. Loeb Classical Library 74. Cambridge: Harvard University Press, 1973.

Boff, Leonardo. *Jesus Christ Liberator: A Christology for Our Time*. Translated by Patrick Hughes. Maryknoll: Orbis Books, 1978.

Bongmba, Elias Kifon. "Christianity in North Africa." In *The Routledge Companion to Christianity in Africa*, edited by Elias Kifon Bongmba, 25–44. New York: Routledge, 2016.

Bron, W. E. "Elasticity." In *Encyclopedia of Physics*, edited by Rita G. Lerner and George L. Trigg. 2nd ed. New York: VCH, 1990.

Bruner, Frederick Dale. *Matthew: A Commentary*. Vol. 1, *The Christbook: Matthew 1–12*. Grand Rapids: Eerdmans, 2004.

Bujo, Bénézet. *African Theology in Its Social Context*. Translated by John O'Donohue. Maryknoll: Orbis Books, 1992.

Burnett, Amy Nelson. "The Educational Roots of Reformed Scholasticism: Dialectic and Scriptural Exegesis in the Sixteenth Century." *Dutch Review of Church History* 84 (2004): 289–317.

Burnett, Richard E. *Karl Barth's Theological Exegesis: The Hermeneutical Principals of the Römerbrief Period*. Tübingen: Mohr Siebeck: 2001.

Busari, Stephanie. "Nigeria: Scores Killed, Homes Burned in Plateau State Attacks." CNN Africa, 25 June 2018. Accessed 24 November 2018. https://www.cnn.com/2018/06/25/africa/nigeria-attacks-intl/index.html.

Byerly, T. Ryan. *Introducing Logic and Critical Thinking: The Skills of Reasoning and the Virtues of Inquiry*. Grand Rapids: Baker Academic, 2017.

Cabrido, John Aranda. *The Portrayal of Jesus in the Gospel of Matthew: A Narrative-Critical and Theological Study*. Lewiston: Mellen, 2012.

Capes, David B. *The Divine Christ: Paul, the Lord Jesus, and the Scriptures of Israel*. Grand Rapids: Baker Academic, 2018.

———. *Old Testament Yahweh Texts in Paul's Christology*. Tübingen: Mohr Siebeck, 1992.

Carter, Craig A. *Interpreting Scripture with the Great Tradition: Recovering the Genius of Premodern Exegesis*. Grand Rapids: Baker Academic, 2018.

Carson, D. A. *Jesus' Sermon on the Mount and His Confrontation with the World: An Exposition of Matthew 5 – 10*. Grand Rapids: Global Christian Alliance, 1999.

Childs, Brevard S. *Biblical Theology of the Old and New Testaments: Theological Reflection on the Christian Bible*. Philadelphia: Fortress, 1993.

———. *The New Testament as Canon: An Introduction*. Philadelphia: Fortress, 1985.

———. *Introduction to the Old Testament as Scripture*. Philadelphia: Fortress, 1979.

Clarke, Clifton R. *African Christology: Jesus in Post-Missionary African Christianity*. Eugene: Pickwick, 2011.

Collins, John J. *The Bible after Babel: Historical Criticism and Its Postmodern Critics*. Grand Rapids: Eerdmans, 2005.

Cook, Michael L. *Christology as Narrative Quest*. Collegeville: Liturgical Press, 1997.

Cortez, Marc. *Embodied Souls, Ensouled Bodies: An Exercise in Christological Anthropology and its Significance for the Mind/Body Debate*. New York: T&T Clark, 2008.

Crisp, Oliver D. *Analyzing Doctrine: Toward a Systematic Theology*. Waco: Baylor University Press, 2019.

———. "Analytic Theology as Systematic Theology." *Open Theology* 3 (2017): 156–66.

———. *Divinity and Humanity: The Incarnation Reconsidered*. Cambridge: Cambridge University Press, 2007.

———. "On Analytic Theology." In *Analytic Theology: New Essays in the Philosophy of Theology*, edited by Oliver D. Crisp and Michael Rea, 33–53. New York: Oxford University Press, 2009.

———. *God Incarnate: Explorations in Christology*. London: T & T Clark, 2009

———, ed. *A Reader in Contemporary Philosophical Theology*. New York: T & T Clark, 2009.
Crisp, Oliver D., and Fred Sanders, eds. *The Task of Dogmatics: Explorations in Theological Method*. Grand Rapids: Zondervan, 2017.
Crisp, Oliver D., and Michael C. Rea, eds. *Analytic Theology: New Essays in the Philosophy of Theology*. New York: Oxford University Press, 2009.
Crisp, Oliver D., James M. Arcadi, and Jordan Wessling. *The Nature and Promise of Analytic Theology*. Leiden: Brill, 2019.
Crummey, Donald. "Church and Nation: The Ethiopian Orthodox *Täwahedo* Church (from the thirteenth to the twentieth century)." In *The Cambridge History of Christianity, Vol. 5: Eastern Christianity*, edited by Michael Angold, 457–87. Cambridge: Cambridge University Press, 2006.
Davies, Brian. *Thomas Aquinas's Summa Theologiae: A Guide and Commentary*. New York: Oxford University Press, 2014.
De Lubac, Henri. *Medieval Exegesis, Vol. I: The Four Senses of Scripture*. Translated by Mark Sebanc. Grand Rapids: Eerdmans, 1998.
———. "Spiritual Understanding." Translated by Luke O'Neill. In *Theological Interpretation of Scripture: Classic and Contemporary Readings*, edited by Stephen Fowl, 3–25. Cambridge: Blackwell, 1997.
DeWeese, Garrett J. *Doing Philosophy as a Christian*. Downers Grove: IVP Academic, 2011.
Drabinski, John E. *Levinas and the Postcolonial: Race, Nation, Other*. Edinburgh: Edinburgh University Press, 2011.
Dube, Musa W., Andrew M. Mbuvi, and Dora R. Mbuwayesango, eds. *Postcolonial Perspectives in African Biblical Interpretations*. Atlanta: SBL Press, 2012.
Dunn, J. D. G. "The Quest for the Historical Jesus and Its Implications for Biblical Interpretation." In *A History of Biblical Interpretation: The Enlightenment through the Nineteenth Century*, edited by Alan J. Hauser and Duane F. Watson, 300–318. Grand Rapids: Eerdmans, 2017.
Ela, Jean-Marc. *My Faith as an African*. Translated by John Pairman Brown and Susan Perry. Maryknoll: Orbis Books, 1988.
Enns, Peter. "Fuller Meaning, Single Goal: A Christotelic Approach to the New Testament Use of the Old in Its First-Century Interpretive Environment." In *Three Views on the New Testament Use of the Old Testament*, edited by Stanley N. Gundry, Kenneth Berding, and Jonathan Lunde, 167–217. Grand Rapids: Zondervan, 2008.
Erhman, Bart. *How Jesus Became God: The Exaltation of a Jewish Preacher from Galilee*. New York: HarperCollins, 2014.
Essamuah, Casely B., and David K. Ngaruiya, eds. *Communities of Faith in Africa and the African Diaspora: In Honor of Dr. Tite Tiénou with Additional Essays on World Christianity*. Eugene: Pickwick, 2013.

Evans, C. Stephen, ed. *Exploring Kenotic Christology: The Self-Emptying of God.* Oxford: Oxford University Press, 2006.

Eze, Emmanuel Chukwudi. *On Reason: Rationality in a World of Cultural Conflict and Racism.* Durham: Duke University Press, 2008.

Ezeh, Uchenna A. *Jesus Christ the Ancestor: African Contextual Christology in the Light of the Major Dogmatic Christological Definitions of the Church from the Council of Nicaea (325) to Chalcedon (451).* Bern: Lang, 2003.

Ezigbo, Victor I. "Jesus as God's Communicative and Hermeneutical Act." In *Jesus without Borders: Christology in the Majority World*, edited by Gene L. Green, Stephen T. Pardue, and K. K. Yeo, 37–58. Grand Rapids: Eerdmans, 2014.

———. *Re-imagining African Christologies: Conversing with the Interpretations and Appropriations of Jesus Christ in African Christianity.* Eugene: Pickwick, 2010.

———. "Rethinking the Sources of African Contextual Christology." *Journal of Theology for Southern Africa* 132, no. 1 (November 2008): 53–70.

Fanon, Frantz. *The Wretched of the Earth.* Translated by Constance Farrington. New York: Grove Press, 1968.

Fee, Gordon D. *Paul's Letter to the Philippians.* The New International Commentary on the New Testament. Grand Rapids: Eerdmans, 1995.

Flint, Thomas P., and Michael C. Rea, eds. *The Oxford Handbook of Philosophical Theology.* Oxford: Oxford University Press, 2009.

Fowl, Stephen E. *Engaging Scripture: A Model for Theological Interpretation.* Oxford: Blackwell, 1998.

———. "The Importance of a Multivoiced Literal Sense of Scripture: The Example of Thomas Aquinas." In *Reading Scripture with the Church: Toward a Hermeneutic for Theological Interpretation*, edited by A. K. M. Adam, Stephen E. Fowl, Kevin J. Vanhoozer, and Francis Watson, 35–50. Grand Rapids: Baker Academics, 2006.

———. *Philippians.* The Two Horizons New Testament Commentary. Grand Rapids: Eerdmans, 2005.

———, ed. *Theological Interpretation of Scripture: Classic and Contemporary Readings.* Cambridge: Blackwell, 1997.

Frampton, Travis L. "Spinoza and His Influence on Biblical Interpretation." In *A History of Biblical Interpretation: The Enlightenment through the Nineteenth Century*, edited by Alan J. Hauser and Duane F. Watson, 120–50. Grand Rapids: Eerdmans, 2017.

Frei, Hans W. *The Eclipse of Biblical Narratives: A Study in Eighteenth and Nineteenth Century Hermeneutics.* New Haven: Yale University Press, 1974.

———. *The Identity of Jesus Christ: The Hermeneutical Basis of Dogmatic Theology.* Philadelphia: Fortress, 1975.

———. *Types of Christian Theology.* New Haven: Yale University Press, 1992.

Froehlich, Karlfried. *Biblical Interpretation in the Early Church*. Philadelphia: Fortress, 1984.

Gadamer, Hans-Georg. *Truth and Method*. Translated by by Garrett Barnden and John Cumming. New York: Seabury, 1975.

Gasser, Georg. "Toward Analytic Theology: An Itinerary." *Scientia et Fides* 3, no. 2 (2015): 23–56.

Geertz, Clifford. "Thick Description: Toward an Interpretive Theory of Culture." In *The Interpretation of Cultures*, 3–30. New York: Basic Books, 2000.

Goldingay, John. *Reading Jesus' Bible: How the New Testament Helps Us Understand the Old Testament*. Grand Rapids: Eerdmans, 2017.

Graves, Michael, ed. *Biblical Interpretation in the Early Church*. Minneapolis: Fortress, 2017.

Green, Gene L. "The Challenge of Global Hermeneutics." In *Global Theology in Evangelical Perspective: Exploring the Contextual Nature of Theology and Mission*, edited by Jeffrey P. Greenman and Gene L. Green, 50–65. Downers Grove: IVP Academic, 2012.

Green, Gene L., Stephen T. Pardue, and K. K. Yeo, eds. *Jesus without Borders: Christology in the Majority World*. Grand Rapids: Eerdmans, 2014.

Greene, Colin J. D. *Christology in Cultural Perspective: Marking Out the Horizons*. Grand Rapids: Eerdmans, 2003.

Griffith, Sidney H. "The Mansur Family and Saint John of Damascus: Christians and Muslims in Umayyad Times." In *Christians and Others in the Umayyad State*, edited by Antoine Borrut and Fred M. Donner, 29–51. Chicago: University of Chicago, 2016.

Gundry, Stanley N., Kenneth Berding, and Jonathan Lunde, eds. In *Three Views on the New Testament Use of the Old Testament*. Grand Rapids: Zondervan, 2008.

Hägglund, Bengt. *History of Theology*, translated by Gene J. Lund. St. Louis: Concordia, 1968.

Hanks, Peter. *Propositional Content*. Oxford: Oxford University Press, 2015.

Hansen, G. Walter. *The Letter to the Philippians*. The Pillar New Testament Commentary. Grand Rapids: Eerdmans, 2009.

Harrisville, Roy A., and Walter Sundberg. *The Bible in Modern Culture: Baruch Spinoza to Brevard Childs*. Grand Rapids: Eerdmans, 2002.

Hatfield, Gary. "René Descartes." *The Stanford Encyclopedia of Philosophy*, Summer 2016 Edition, edited by Edward N. Zalta. Accessed 1 January 2018. https://plato.stanford.edu/archives/sum2016/entries/descartes/.

Hauser, Alan J., and Duane F. Watson. "Introduction and Overview." In *A History of Biblical Interpretation, Vol. 3: The Enlightenment through the Nineteenth Century*, edited by Alan J. Hauser and Duane F. Watson, 1–72. Grand Rapids: Eerdmans, 2017.

_____. "Introduction and Overview." In *A History of Biblical Interpretation, Vol. 1: The Ancient Period*, edited by Alan J. Hauser and Duane F. Watson, 1–54. Grand Rapids: Eerdmans, 2003.

Hawthorne, Gerald F. *Philippians*. Word Biblical Commentary 43. Waco: Word Books, 1983.

Hays, Richard B. *The Moral Vision of the New Testament: A Contemporary Introduction to New Testament Ethics*. San Francisco: Harper, 1996.

———. *Reading Backwards: Figural Christology and the Fourfold Gospel Witness*. Waco: Baylor University Press, 2014.

Hiebert, Paul G. "Beyond Anti-Colonialism to Globalism." *Missiology: An International Review* 19, no. 3 (July 1991): 263–81.

———. *Missiological Implications of Epistemological Shifts: Affirming Truth in a Modern/Postmodern World*. Harrisburg: Trinity Press International, 1999.

Higazi, Adam. "The Jos Crisis: A Recurrent Nigerian Tragedy." *Friedrich Ebert Stiftung Discussion Paper* 2 (Jan 2011): 2–34. Available online, https://library.fes.de/pdf-files/bueros/nigeria/07812.pdf.

Holmes, Michael W. "From Books to Library: The Formation of the Biblical Canons." In *Scriptures and Its Interpretation: A Global, Ecumenical Introduction to the Bible*, edited by Michael J. Gorman, 115–32. Grand Rapids: Baker Academic, 2017.

Horton, Michael. *The Christian Faith: A Systematic Theology for Pilgrims on the Way*. Grand Rapids: Zondervan, 2011.

Hountondji, Paulin J. *African Philosophy: Myth and Reality*. 2nd ed. Translated by Henri Evans. Bloomington: Indiana University Press, 1996.

Human Rights Watch. "Jos: A City Torn Apart." 18 December 2001. https://www.hrw.org/report/2001/12/18/jos/city-torn-apart.

Hurtado, L. W. "Jesus as Lordly Example in Philippians 2:5–11." In *From Jesus to Paul: Studies in Honour of Francis Wright Beare*, edited by Peter Richardson and John C. Hurd, 113–26. Ontario: Wilfrid Laurier University Press, 1984.

———. *Lord Jesus Christ: Devotion to Jesus in Earliest Christianity*. Grand Rapids: Eerdmans, 2005.

Ijatuyi-Morphé, Randee. *Africa's Social and Religious Quest: A Comprehensive Survey and Analysis of the African Situation*. Lanham: University Press of America, 2014.

Imasogie, Osadolor. *Guidelines for Christian Theology in Africa*. Achimota: African Christian Press, 1983.

Irele, Abiola. Introduction to *African Philosophy: Myth and Reality*, by Paulin J. Hountondji, 7–30. 2nd ed. Translated by Henri Evans. Bloomington: Indiana University Press, 1996.

Jenkins, Philip. *God's Continent: Christianity, Islam, and Europe's Religious Crisis*. Oxford: Oxford University Press, 2007.

———. *The Next Christendom: The Coming of Global Christianity*. New York: Oxford University Press, 2002.
Jennings, Willie James. *The Christian Imagination: Theology and the Origins of Race*. New Haven: Yale University Press, 2010.
Jenson, Robert W. *Canon and Creed*. Louisville: Westminster John Knox, 2010.
John of Damascus. *Writings: The Fount of Knowledge*. Translated by Frederic H. Chase, Jr. New York: Fathers of the Church, 1958.
Johnson, Dru. *Biblical Knowing: A Scriptural Epistemology of Error*. Eugene, OR: Cascade, 2013.
Juel, Donald H. "Interpreting Israel's Scriptures in the New Testament." In *A History of Biblical Interpretation, Vol. 1: The Ancient Period*, edited by Alan J. Hauser and Duane F. Watson, 283–303. Grand Rapids: Eerdmans, 2003.
Kannengiesser, Charles. *Handbook of Patristic Exegesis*. Vol. 1. Leiden: Brill, 2004.
———. *Handbook of Patristic Exegesis*. Vol. 2. Leiden: Brill, 2004.
Kaiser, Walter C., Jr. "Single Meaning, Unified Referents: Accurate Citations of the Old Testament by the New Testament." In *Three Views on the New Testament Use of the Old Testament*, edited by Stanley N. Gundry, Kenneth Berding, and Jonathan Lunde, 45–89. Grand Rapids: Zondervan, 2008.
Kärkkäinen, Veli-Matti. *Christology: A Global Introduction*. Grand Rapids: Baker Books, 2003.
Katongole, Emmanuel. *Born from Lament: The Theology and Politics of Hope in Africa*. Grand Rapids: Eerdmans, 2017.
———. *A Future for Africa: Critical Essays in Christian Social Imagination*. Scranton: University of Scranton Press, 2005.
Kanu, Ikechukwu Anthony. *Towards an Igbo-African Christology: A Cultural Christological Construct in Post-Missionary Africa*. Beau-Bassin Rose-Hill: Lambert Academic Publishing, 2017.
Kato, Byang H. *Biblical Christianity in Africa: A Collection of Papers and Addresses*. Theological Perspectives in Africa. Achimota: Africa Christian Press, 1985.
———. *Theological Pitfalls in Africa*. Kisumu: Evangel, 1975.
Keener, Craig S. *A Commentary on the Gospel of Matthew*. Grand Rapids: Eerdmans, 1999.
Kelsey, David H. *Proving Doctrine: The Uses of Scripture in Modern Theology*. Harrisburg: Trinity Press International, 1999.
Kim, Elijah J. F. *The Rise of the Global South: The Decline of Western Christendom and the Rise of Majority World Christianity*. Eugene: Wipf & Stock, 2012.
Knighton, Ben. "Issues of African Theology at the turn of the Millennium." *Transformation* 21, no. 3 (July 2004): 147–61.
Kripke, Saul. *Naming and Necessity*. Cambridge: Harvard University Press, 1980.

Kyrtatas, Dimitiris J. "Historical Aspects of the Formation of the New Testament Canon." In *Canon and Canonicity: The Formation and Use of Scripture*, edited by Einar Thomassen, 29–44. Copenhagen: Museum Tusculanum Press, 2010.

Küster, Volker. *The Many Faces of Jesus Christ: Intercultural Christology*. Maryknoll: Orbis Books, 1999.

Lamport, Mark A., ed. *Encyclopedia of Christianity in the Global South*. 2 Vols. Lanham: Rowman & Littlefield, 2018.

Legaspi, Michael C. *The Death of Scripture and the Rise of Biblical Studies*. New York: Oxford University Press, 2010.

Liew, Tat-siong Benny, and Fernando F. Segovia, eds. *Colonialism and the Bible: Reflections from the Global South*. Lanham: Lexington Books, 2018.

Lincoln, Andrew T. *Born of a Virgin? Reconceiving Jesus in the Bible, Tradition, and Theology*. Grand Rapids: Eerdmans, 2013.

Lindbeck, George A. *The Nature of Doctrine: Religion and Theology in a Postliberal Age*. Philadelphia: Westminster Press, 1984.

———. "Postcritical Canonical Interpretation: Three Modes of Retrieval." In *Theological Exegesis: Essays in Honor of Brevard S. Childs*, edited by Christopher Seitz and Kathryn Greene-McCreight, 26–51. Grand Rapids: Eerdmans, 1999.

Locke, John. *An Essay Concerning Human Understanding*. London: William Tegg, 1870.

Luther, Martin. "Disputation Against Scholastic Theology 1517." Translated by Harold J. Grim. In *Luther's Works*, edited by Jeroslav Pelikan. St. Louis: Concordia, 1958.

MacGregor, Kirk R. *Contemporary Theology: An Introduction: Classical, Evangelical, Philosophical, and Global Perspectives*. Grand Rapids: Zondervan, 2019.

MacIntyre, Alasdair. *After Virtue: A Study in Moral Theory*. 3rd ed. Notre Dame: University of Notre Dame, 1981.

Magezi, Christopher, and Jacob T. Igba. "African Theology and African Christology: Difficulty and Complexity in Contemporary Definitions and Methodological Frameworks." *HTS Teologiese Studies / Theological Studies* 74, no. 1 (2018): 1–20.

Magnus, Ukachukwu Chris. *Christ the African King: New Testament Christology*. Frankfurt am Main: Lang, 1993.

Mahler, Anne Garland. "Global South." In *Oxford Bibliographies in Literary and Critical Theory*, edited by Eugene O'Brien. Oxford: Oxford University Press, 2017. https://globalsouthstudies.as.virginia.edu/what-is-global-south.

Maina, Wilson Muoha. *Historical and Social Dimensions in African Christian Theology: A Contemporary Approach*. Eugene, OR: Wipf & Stock, 2009.

Mallinson, Jeffery. *Faith, Reason, and Revelation in Theodore Beza (1519–1605)*. Oxford: Oxford University Press, 2003.

Mana, Kä. *Christians and Churches of Africa: Salvation in Christ and Building a New African Society*. Maryknoll: Orbis, 2004.

Manschreck, Clyde Leonard. *Melanchthon: The Quiet Reformer*. Westport: Greenwood Press, 1975.

Martey, Emmanuel. *African Theology: Inculturation and Liberation*. Maryknoll: Orbis, 1993.

Mazrui, Ali A. *The African Condition: A Political Diagnosis*. New York: Cambridge University Press, 1980.

Mbiti, John S. *African Religions and Philosophy*. 2nd ed. Oxford: Heinemann, 1989.

———. "Some African Concepts of Christology." In *Christ and the Younger Churches*, edited by F. F. Vicedom, 51–62. London: SPCK, 1972.

Mbuvi, Andrew. "Christology and *Cultus* in 1 Peter: An African (Kenyan) Appraisal." In *Jesus without Borders: Christology in the Majority World*, edited by Gene L. Green, Stephen T. Pardue, and K. K. Yeo, . Grand Rapids: Eerdmans, 2014.

McCall, Thomas H. *An Invitation to Analytic Christian Theology*. Downers Grove: IVP Academic, 2015.

———. *Forsaken: The Trinity and the Cross, and Why It Matters*. Downers Grove: InterVarsity Press, 2012.

McCall, Thomas H., and Michael Rea, eds. *Philosophical and Theological Essays on the Trinity*. New York: Oxford University Press, 2009.

Melanchthon, Philip. "Brief Biographical Sketch." In *The Loci Communes of Philip Melanchthon*, translated by Charles Leander Hill, 19–28. Boston: Meador, 1944.

———. *The Chief Theological Topic, Loci Praecipui Theologici 1559*. Translated by J. A. O. Preus. St. Louis: Concordia, 2011.

Michael, Matthew. *Christian Theology and African Traditions*. Eugene: Wipf & Stock, 2013.

Mofokeng, Takatso Alfred. *The Crucified among the Crossbearers: Towards a Black Christology*. Kampen: J.H. Kok, 1983.

Moore, Stephen D., and Fernando F. Segovia, eds. *Postcolonial Biblical Criticism: Interdisciplinary Intersections*. London: T&T Clark, 2005.

Moreland, J. P., and William Lane Craig. *Philosophical Foundations for a Christian Worldview*. Downers Grove: InterVarsity, 2003.

Morris, Thomas V. *Anselmian Explorations: Essays in Philosophical Theology*. Indiana: University of Notre Dame Press, 1987.

———. *The Logic of God Incarnate*. Eugene: Wipf & Stock, 1986.

———. *Our Idea of God: An Introduction to Philosophical Theology*. Vancouver: Regent College Publishing, 1991.

Moyise, Steve. *Jesus and Scripture: Studying the New Testament Use of the Old Testament*. Grand Rapids: Baker Academic, 2010.

Moyo, Dambisa. *Dead Aid: Why Aid is Not Working and How There is a Better Way for Africa*. New York: Farrar, Straus and Giroux, 2009.

Mudimbe, V. Y. *The Idea of Africa*. Bloomington: Indiana University Press, 1994.

———. *The Invention of Africa: Gnosis, Philosophy, and the Order of Knowledge*. Bloomington: Indiana University Press, 1988.

Muller, Richard. "*Ordo docendi*: Melanchthon and the Organization of Calvin's Institutes, 1536 – 1543." In *Melanchthon in Europe: His Work and Influence beyond Wittenberg*, edited by Karin Maag, 123–40. Grand Rapids: Baker Books, 1999.

Mugambi, J. N. K. *From Liberation to Reconstruction: African Christian Theology After the Cold War*. Nairobi: East African Educational, 1995.

Mugambi, J. N. K., and Laurenti Magesa, eds. *Jesus in African Christianity: Experimentation and Diversity in African Christology*. Nairobi: African Initiatives, 1989.

Nanlong, Marie-Therese. "Jos: When Mayhem Returned!" *Vanguard*, 6 October 2018. Accessed 24 November 2018. https://www.vanguardngr.com/2018/10/jos-when-mayhem-returned/.

Nasimiyu-Wasike, Anne. "Christology and an African Woman's Experience." In *Jesus in African Christianity: Experimentation and Diversity in African Christology*, edited by J. N. K. Mugambi and Laurenti Magesa, 123–135. Nairobi: African Initiatives, 1989.

Newman, Las G. "Theology on the Move: Discerning Global Shifts in Theological Thinking in the Global South." *Canadian-American Theological Review* 5, no. 1 (2016): 66–90.

Ngewa, Samuel, Mark Shaw, and Tite Tiénou, eds. *Issues in African Christian Theology*. Nairobi: East African Educational Publishers, 1998.

Ngong, David Tonghou. *The Holy Spirit and Salvation in African Christian Theology: Imagining a More Hopeful Future for Africa*. New York: Lang, 2010.

Ngugi, Mukoma Wa. "Breaking Out of the Prison House of Hierarchy." *World Literature Today* 87, no. 3 (May 2013): 36–39.

Niebuhr, H. Richard. *Christ and Culture*, 50th anniversary expanded ed. New York: HarperCollins, 2001.

Nkrumah, Kwame. *Neo-Colonialism: The Last Stage of Imperialism*. New York: International Publishers, 1965.

Nolland, John. *The Gospel of Matthew: A Commentary on the Greek Text*. The New International Greek Testament Commentary. Grand Rapids: Eerdmans, 2005.

Norman, Ralph. "Abelard's Legacy: Why Theology Is Not Faith Seeking Understanding." *Australian eJournal of Theology* 10 (May 2007): 1–10.

Norris, Richard A. Jr. *The Christological Controversy*. Philadelphia: Fortress, 1980.

———, trans. and ed. *The Theological Controversy*. Philadelphia: Fortress, 1980.
Novikoff, Alex J. "Anselm, Dialogue, and the Rise of Scholastic Disputation." *Speculum* 86, no. 2 (2011): 387–418.
Nyam, Abok Musa. *The Afizere (Jarawa) People of Nigeria*. Jos: National Museum Press, 1988.
Nyamiti, Charles. *Christ as Our Ancestor: Christology from an African Perspective*. Gweru: Mambo Press, 1984.
O'Brien, Peter T. *The Epistle to the Philippians*. The New International Greek Testament Commentary. Grand Rapids: Eerdmans, 1991.
O'Collins, Gerald, and Daniel Kendall. *The Bible for Theology: Ten Principles for the Theological Use of Scripture*. New York: Paulist, 1997.
Oden, Thomas C. *How Africa Shaped the Christian Mind: Rediscovering the African Seedbed of Western Christianity*. Downers Grove: InterVarsity Press, 2007.
Oduyoye, Mercy Amba. *Hearing and Knowing: Theological Reflections on Christianity in Africa*. Maryknoll: Oribis Books, 1986.
———. "Women and Christology: An African Woman's Christ." A Paper Presented at the EATWOT Continental Consultation from the Third World Women's Perspective, Port Harcourt, Nigeria, 19–23 August 1986.
O'Mahony, Anthony. "Coptic Christianity in Modern Egypt." In *The Cambridge History of Christianity, Vol. 5: Eastern Christianity*, edited by Michael Angold, 488–510. Cambridge: Cambridge University Press, 2006.
Omotola, J. Shola. "Independence Movements." In *The Oxford Encyclopedia of African Thought*. Vol. 2, edited by F. Abiola Irele and Biodun Jeyifo, 1–4. New York: Oxford, 2010.
Open Doors. "World Watch List" Accessed 22 March 2019. https://www.opendoorsusa.org/christian-persecution/world-watch-list/.
Ott, Craig, and Harold A. Netland, eds. *Globalizing Theology: Belief and Practice in an Era of World Christianity*. Grand Rapids: Baker Academic, 2006.
Palmer, Timothy. "Jesus Christ: Our Ancestor?" *TCNN Research Bulletin* 42 (2004): 4–17.
Papandrea, James L. *The Earliest Christologies: Five Images of Christ in the Postapostolic Age*. Downers Grove: IVP Academic, 2016.
Papineau, David. *Philosophical Devices: Proofs, Probabilities, Possibilities, and Sets*. Oxford: Oxford University Press, 2012.
Pardue, Stephen T. "Introduction: An Invitation to Discuss Christology with the Global Church." In *Jesus without Borders: Christology in the Majority World*, edited by Gene L. Green, Stephen T. Pardue, and K. K. Yeo, 1–9. Grand Rapids: Eerdmans, 2014.
Pearse, Meic. *Why the Rest Hates the West: Understanding the Roots of Global Rage*. Downers Grove: InterVarsity Press, 2004.

Perreiah, Alan. "Humanistic Critiques of Scholastic Dialectic." *Sixteenth Century Journal* 13, no. 3 (1982): 3–22.

Pieper, Josef. "Scholasticism." *Encyclopædia Britannica Online*. Accessed 26 December 2017. http://www.britannica.com/EBchecked/topic/527973/Scholasticism/68413/Enduring-features.

Plantinga, Alvin. *Warranted Christian Belief*. New York: Oxford University Press, 2000.

Porter, Stanley E., and Beth M. Stovell, eds. *Biblical Hermeneutics: Five Views*. Downers Grove: IVP Academic, 2012.

Preus, Christian. "Introduction." In Philip Melanchthon, *Commonplaces: Loci Communes 1521*. St. Louis: Concordia, 2014.

Preus, Robert D. *The Theology of Post-Reformation Lutheranism: A Study of Theological Prolegomena*. Saint Louis: Concordia, 1970.

Pseudo-Dionysius. *The Complete Works*. Translated by Colm Luibheid. New York: Paulist Press, 1987.

Quinn, Philip L. "Divine Command Theory." *The Blackwell Guide to Ethical Theory*, edited by Hugh LaFollette, 53–73. Malden, MA: Blackwell, 2001.

Rah, Soong-Chan. *The Next Evangelicalism: Releasing the Church from Western Cultural Captivity*. Downers Grove: InterVarsity Press, 2009.

Ray, Charles A., Jr. "The Beatitudes: Challenging Worldviews." *Theological Educator* 46 (1992): 97–104.

Rea, Michael C. "Introduction." In *Analytic Theology: New Essays in the Philosophy of Theology*, edited by Oliver D. Crisp and Michael Rea, 1–30. New York: Oxford University Press, 2009.

Reed, Rodney L., ed. *African Contextual Realities*. ASET Series. Carlisle: Langham Global Library, 2018.

Reventlow, Hennig Graf. "The Role of the Old Testament in the German Liberal Protestant Theology of the Nineteenth Century." In *Biblical Studies and the Shifting of Paradigms, 1850–1914*, edited by Henning Graf Reventlow and William Farmer, 132–48. Sheffield: Sheffield Academic Press, 1995.

Richards, E. Randolph, and Brandon J. O'Brien. *Misreading Scripture with Western Eyes: Removing Cultural Blinders to better Understand the Bible*. Downers Grove: InterVarsity Press, 2012.

Rodney, Walter. *How Europe Underdeveloped Africa*. Washington, DC: Howard University Press, 1974.

Rouwendal, Pieter L. "The Method of the Schools: Medieval Scholasticism." In *Introduction to Reformed Scholasticism*, edited by Willem van Asselt, 56–71. Grand Rapids: Reformation Heritage Books, 2011.

Rummel, Erika. *The Humanist – Scholastic Debate in the Renaissance and the Reformation*. Massachusetts: Harvard University Press, 1995.

Sahas, Daniel J. *John of Damascus on Islam: The "Heresy of the Ishmaelites.* Leiden: Brill, 1972.
Saint Augustine. *On Christian Doctrine.* Translated by D. W. Robertson, Jr. Upper Saddle River: Prentice Hall, 1997.
Sanneh, Lamin. *Encountering the West: Christianity and the Global Cultural Process: The African Dimension.* Maryknoll: Orbis Books, 1993.
———. *Whose Religion Is Christianity? The Gospel Beyond the West.* Grand Rapids: Eerdmans, 2003.
Scheible, Heinze. "Melanchthon, Phillip." In *The Oxford Encyclopedia of the Reformation.* Vol. 3, edited by Hans Hillerbrand. New York: Oxford University Press, 1996.
Scholtz, Gunter. "The Notion of Historicism and 19th Century Theology." In *Biblical Studies and the Shifting of Paradigms, 1850–1914,* edited by Henning Graf Reventlow and William Farmer, 149–67. Sheffield: Sheffield Academic Press, 1995.
Schreiter, Robert J. *Constructing Local Theologies.* Maryknoll: Orbis Books, 1985.
———, ed. *Faces of Jesus in Africa.* Maryknoll: Orbis Books, 1991.
Schwöbel, Christoph, and Colin E. Gunton, eds. *Persons Divine and Human.* Edinburgh: T&T Clark, 1991.
Sedmark, Clemens. *Doing Local Theology: A Guide for Artisans of a New Humanity.* Maryknoll: Orbis Books, 2002.
Seitz, Christopher R. *Colossians: Brazos Theological Commentary on the Bible.* Grand Rapids: Brazos Press, 2014.
Seitz, Christopher, and Kathryn Greene-McCreight, eds. *Theological Exegesis: Essays in Honor of Brevard S. Childs.* Grand Rapids: Eerdmans, 1999.
———. "The Work and Witness of Brevard S. Childs: Comprehension, Discipline, Obedience." In *Theological Exegesis: Essays in Honor of Brevard S. Childs,* edited by Christopher Seitz and Kathryn Greene-McCreight, 3–6. Grand Rapids: Eerdmans, 1999.
Shorter, Aylward. "Folk Christianity and Functional Christology." *African Ecclesial Review* 24, no. 3 (1982): 133–37.
Shults, F. LeRon. "A Dubious Christological Formula: From Leontius of Byzantium to Karl Barth." *Theological Studies* 57, no. 3 (1996): 431–46.
Smith, Christian. *The Bible Made Impossible: Why Biblicism Is Not a Truly Evangelical Reading of Scripture.* Grand Rapids: Brazos Press, 2012.
Sneddon, I. N., and D. S. Berry. "The Classical Theory of Elasticity." In *Encyclopedia of Physics.* Vol. 3, *Elasticity and Plasticity,* edited by S. Flügge, 1–126. Berlin: Springer, 1958. https://doi.org/10.1007/978-3-642-45887-3.
Sobrino, Jon. *Christology at the Crossroads: A Latin American Approach.* Translated by John Drury. Maryknoll: Orbis Books, 1978.

Sookhdeo, Patrick. Foreword to *Tainted Legacy: Islam, Colonialism and Slavery in Northern Nigeria*, by Yusufu Turaki. McLean: Isaac Publishing, 2010.

Spade, Paul Vincent. "Medieval Philosophy." *The Stanford Encyclopedia of Philosophy* (Spring 2013). Available online, https://plato.stanford.edu/archives/spr2013/entries/medieval-philosophy/.

Speaks, Jeff. "Theories of Meaning." *The Stanford Encyclopedia of Philosophy* (Fall 2017 Edition). Accessed online, https://plato.stanford.edu/archives/fall2017/entries/meaning/.

Spence, Alan. *Incarnation and Inspiration: John Owen and the Coherence of Christology*. London: T&T Clark, 2007.

Spencer, Aida Besancon, and William David Spencer, eds. *The Global God: Multicultural Evangelical Views of God*. Grand Rapids: Baker Books, 1998.

St. Cyril of Alexandria. *On the Unity of Christ*. Translated by John Anthony McGuckin. Crestwood: St. Vladimir's Seminary Press, 1995.

Steinmetz, David C. "The Superiority of Pre-Critical Exegesis." *Theology Today* 37, no. 1 (1980): 27–38.

Stinton, Diane B. *Jesus of Africa: Voices of Contemporary African Christology*. Maryknoll: Orbis Books, 2004.

Strauss, David F. *The Life of Jesus Critically Examined*. Edited by Peter C. Hodgson. Translated by George Eliot. Philadelphia: Fortress, 1972.

Strauss, Stephen J. "Perspectives on the Nature of Christ in the Ethiopian Orthodox Church: A Case Study in Contextualized Theology." PhD Dissertation, Trinity Evangelical Divinity School, 1997.

Sugirtharajah, R. S. "Charting the Aftermath: A Review of Postcolonial Criticism." In *The Postcolonial Biblical Reader*, edited by R. S. Sugirtharajah, 7–32. Malden: Blackwell, 2006.

———. *Exploring Postcolonial Biblical Criticism: History, Method, Practice*. Chichester: Wiley-Blackwell, 2012.

Sung, Elizabeth Y. "'Race' and Ethnicity Discourse and the Christian Doctrine of Humanity: A Systematic Sociological and Theological Appraisal." PhD Dissertation, Trinity Evangelical Divinity School, 2011.

Swinburne, Richard. "Authority of Scripture, Tradition, Church." In *The Oxford Handbook of Philosophical Theology*, edited by Thomas P. Flint and Michael C. Rea, 11–29. Oxford: Oxford University Press, 2009.

Tanner, Kathryn. *Theories of Culture: A New Agenda for Theology*. Minneapolis: Fortress, 1997.

Taylor, John V. *The Primal Vision: Christian Presence Amid African Religion*. Philadelphia: Fortress, 1963.

Tennent, Timothy C. *Theology in the Context of World Christianity: How the Global Church is Influencing the Way We Think about and Discuss Theology*. Grand Rapids, MI: Zondervan, 2007.

Theissen, Gerd. "Das Verschwinden des hermeneutischen Konflikts Zur Rezeption von Paul Ricoeur in der deutschsprachigen theologischen Hermeneutik." *Evangelische Theologie* 73, no. 4 (2013): 258–72.

Thiong'o, Ngũgĩ wa. *Globalectics: Theory and the Politics of Knowing*. New York: Columbia University Press, 2012.

———. *Something Torn and New: An African Renaissance*. New York: BasicCivitas, 2009.

Thomas, George M. "The Cultural and Religious Character of World Society." In *Religion, Globalization, and Culture*, edited by Peter Beyer and Lori Beaman, 35–56. Leiden: Brill, 2007.

Thompson, T. Jack. *Light on Darkness?: Missionary Photography of Africa in the Nineteenth and Early Twentieth Centuries*. Grand Rapids: Eerdmans, 2012.

Thurston, Bonnie B., and Judith M. Ryan. *Philippians and Philemon*. Sacra Pagina. Collegeville: Michael Glazier, 2005.

Tiénou, Tite. "Christian Theology in an Era of World Christianity." In *Globalizing Theology: Belief and Practice in an Era of World Christianity*, edited by Craig Ott and Harold A. Netland, 37–51. Grand Rapids: Baker Academic, 2006.

———. "Gospel and Cultures in the Lausanne Movement." In *The Lausanne Movement: A Range of Perspectives*, edited by Margunn Serigstad Dahle, Lars Dahle, and Knud Jørgensen, 157–70. Eugene: Wipf & Stock, 2014.

———. "Jesus as Guest: A Christology for a Time of Global Fragmentation." A Presentation at the ETS Regional Meeting, Moody Theology Bible Institute, Chicago, Illinois, March 2012.

———. "The Problem of Methodology in African Christian Theologies." PhD Dissertation, Fuller Theological Seminary, School of World Missions, 1984.

———. "The Right to Difference: The Common Roots of African Theology and African Philosophy." *African Journal of Evangelical Theology* 9, no. 1 (1990): 24–34.

———. "Which Way for African Christianity: Westernization or Indigenous Authenticity." *African Journal of Evangelical Theology* 10, no. 2 (1991): 3–12.

Tinker, George E. *Spirit and Resistance: Political Theology and American Indian Liberation*. Minneapolis: Fortress, 2004.

Tizon, Al. *Whole and Reconciled: Gospel, Church, and Mission in a Fractured World*. Grand Rapids: Baker Academic, 2018.

Torrance, Alan J. "Analytic Theology and the Reconciled Mind: The Significance of History." *Journal of Analytic Theology* 1, no. 1 (May 2013): 30–44.

Torrance, Thomas F. *Incarnation: The Person and Life of Christ*. Edited by Robert T. Walker Downers Grove: InterVarsity Press, 2008.

Treier, Daniel. *Introducing Theological Interpretation of Scripture: Recovering a Christian Practice*. Grand Rapids: Baker Academic, 2008.

Treier, Daniel J., and Uche Anizor. "Theological Interpretation of Scripture and Evangelical Systematic Theology: Iron Sharpening Iron?" *Southern Baptist Journal of Theology* 14, no. 2 (2010): 4–17.

Trigg, Joseph. "The Apostolic Fathers and Apologists." In *A History of Biblical Interpretation*. Vol. 1: *The Ancient Period*, edited by Alan J. Hauser and Duane F. Watson, 304–33. Grand Rapids: Eerdmans, 2003.

Troeltsch, Ernst. "The Significance of the Historical Existence of Jesus for Faith." In *Ernst Troeltsch Writings on Theology and Religion*. Translated and edited by Robert Morgan and Michael Pye, 184–200. Louisville: Westminster John Knox, 1977.

Turaki, Yusufu. *The British Colonial Legacy in Northern Nigeria: A Social Ethical Analysis of the Colonial and Post-Colonial Society and Politics in Nigeria*. Jos: Challenge Press, 1993.

———. *Tainted Legacy: Islam, Colonialism and Slavery in Northern Nigeria*. McLean: Isaac Publishing, 2010.

Udoh, Enyi Ben. *Guest Christology: An Interpretative View of the Christological Problem in Africa*. Frankfurt am Main: Lang, 1988.

Vanhoozer, Kevin J. "Analytics, Poetics, and the Missions of Dogmatic Discourse." In *The Task of Dogmatics: Explorations in Theological Method*, edited by Oliver D. Crisp and Fred Sanders, 23–48. Grand Rapids: Zondervan, 2017.

———. *Biblical Narrative in the Philosophy of Paul Ricoeur: A Study in Hermeneutics and Theology*. Cambridge: Cambridge University Press, 1990.

———. "Christology in the West: Conversations in Europe and North America." In *Jesus without Borders: Christology in the Majority World*, edited by Gene L. Green, Stephen T. Pardue, and K. K. Yeo, 11–36. Grand Rapids: Eerdmans, 2014.

———. "Does the Trinity Belong in a Theology of Religions? On Angling in the Rubicon and the 'Identity' of God." In *The Trinity in a Pluralistic Age: Theological Essays on Culture and Religion*, edited by Kevin J. Vanhoozer, 41–71. Grand Rapids: Eerdmans, 1997.

———. *The Drama of Doctrine: A Canonical-Linguistic Approach to Christian Theology*. Louisville: Westminster John Knox Press, 2005.

———. "A Drama-of-Redemption Model: Always Performing?" In *Four Views on Moving Beyond the Bible to Theology*, edited by Gary T. Meadors, 151–99. Grand Rapids: Zondervan, 2009.

———. *First Theology: God, Scripture, and Hermeneutics*. Downers Grove, IL: InterVarsity Press, 2002.

———. "Four Theological Faces of Biblical Interpretation." In *Reading Scripture with the Church: Toward a Hermeneutic for Theological Interpretation*, edited by A. K. M. Adam, Stephen E. Fowl, Kevin J. Vanhoozer, and Francis Watson, 131–42. Grand Rapids, MI: Baker Academic, 2006.

———. "Love's Wisdom: The Authority of Scripture's Form and Content for Faith's Understanding and Theological Judgment." *Journal of Reformed Theology* 5, no. 3 (2011): 247–75.

———. "One Rule to Rule Them All? Theological Method in an Era of World Christianity." In *Globalizing Theology: Belief and Practice in an Era of World Christianity*, edited by Craig Ott and Harold A. Netland, 85–126. Grand Rapids, MI: Baker Academic, 2006.

———. *Remythologizing Theology: Divine Action, Passion, and Authorship*. New York: Cambridge University Press, 2010.

———. "Scripture and Theology: On 'Proving' Doctrine Biblically." In *The Routledge Companion to the Practice of Christian Theology*, edited by Mike Higton and Jim Fodor, 141–59. London: Routledge, 2015.

———. *Is There a Meaning in This Text? The Bible, the Reader, and the Morality of Literary Knowledge*. Grand Rapids: Zondervan, 1998.

Vanhoozer, Kevin J., and Daniel J. Treier. *Theology and the Mirror of Scripture: A Mere Evangelical Account*. Downers Grove: IVP Academic, 2015.

Vanhoozer, Kevin J., Craig G. Bartholomew, and Daniel J. Treier, eds. *Theological Interpretation of the Old Testament: A Book-by-Book Survey*. Grand Rapids: Baker Books, 2008.

Walls, Andrew F. "Demographics, Power and the Gospel in the 21st Century." A Presentation at the SIL International Conference and Wycliffe Bible Translators International Convention, June 2002.

———. "The Gospel as Prisoner and Liberator of Culture: Is There a 'Historic Christian Faith'? In *Landmark Essays in Mission and World Christianity*, edited by Robert L. Gallagher and Paul Hertig, 133–47. Maryknoll: Orbis, 2009.

———. *The Missionary Movement in Christian History: Studies in the Transmission of Faith*. Maryknoll: Orbis, 1996.

Ward, Benedicta. "Bede the Theologian." In *The Medieval Theologians: An Introduction to Theology in the Medieval Period*, edited by G. R. Evans, 57–64. Malden: Blackwell, 2001.

Watson, Francis. *Text, Church and World: Biblical Interpretation in Theological Perspective*. Grand Rapids: Eerdmans, 1994.

Webster, John. *The Domain of the Word: Scripture and Theological Reason*. London: T&T Clark, 2012.

———. "Theology After Liberalism?" In *Theology After Liberalism*, edited by George Schner and John Webster, 52–63. Oxford: Blackwell, 2000.

———. "Theologies of Retrieval." In *The Oxford Dictionary of Systematic Theology*, edited by John Webster, Kathryn Tanner, and Ian Torrance, 583–99. Oxford: Oxford University Press, 2007.

———. "What Makes Theology Theological?" *Journal of Analytic Theology* 3 (May 2015): 17–28.
Weiss, James M. "Humanism." *The Oxford Encyclopedia of the Reformation*, vol. 2, edited by Hans Hillerbrand, 265. New York: Oxford University Press, 1996.
Westphal, Merold. *Whose Community? Which Interpretation? Philosophical Hermeneutics for the Church.* Grand Rapids: Baker Academic, 2009.
Wilkens, Steve. *Beyond Bumper Sticker Ethics: An Introduction to Theories of Right and Wrong.* Downers Grove: InterVarsity Press, 2011.
———, ed. *Faith and Reason: Three Views.* Downers Grove: IVP Academic, 2014.
Wiredu, Kwasi S. *Cultural Universals and Particulars: An African Perspective.* Bloomington: Indiana University Press, 1996.
———. "On Defining African Philosophy." In *African Philosophy: The Essential Readings*, edited by T. Serequerberhan, 87–110. New York: Paragon House Publishers, 1991.
———. "Toward Decolonizing African Philosophy and Religion." In *Inculturation and Postcolonial Discourse in African Theology*, edited by Edward P. Antonio, 291–330. New York: Lang, 2006.
Wolterstorff, Nicholas. "How Philosophical Theology Became Possible within the Analytic Tradition of Philosphy." In Analytic Theology: New Essays in the Philospohy of Theology, edited by Oliver D. Crisp and Michael Rea, 155–69. New York: Oxford University Press, 2009.
Wolvers, Andrea, Oliver Tappe, Tijo Salverda, and Tobias Schwarz. "Concepts of the Global South: Introduction: Voices from Around the World." Global South Studies Center, University of Cologne, Germany. https://kups.ub.uni-koeln.de/6399/1/voices012015_concepts_of_the_global_south.pdf.
Wood, William. "Analytic Theology as a Way of Life." *Journal of Analytic Theology* 2 (May 2014): 43–60.
———. "Trajectories, Traditions, and Tools in Analytic Theology." *Journal of Analytic Theology* 4 (May 2016): 254–66.
Wright, N. T. *Paul and the Faithfulness of God.* Minneapolis: Fortress, 2013.
Wrogemann, Henning. *Intercultural Theology*, vol. 1, *Intercultural Hermeneutics*. Translated by Karl E. Böhmer. Downers Grove: IVP Academic, 2016.
Yadav, Sameer. "Christian Doctrine as Ontological Commitment to a Narrative." In *The Task of Dogmatics: Explorations in Theological Method*, edited by Oliver D. Crisp and Fred Sanders, 70–86. Grand Rapids: Zondervan, 2017.
Yarchin, William. *History of Biblical Interpretation: A Reader.* Grand Rapids: Baker Academic, 2004.
Yeago, David. "The New Testament and the Nicene Dogma: A Contribution to the Recovery of Theological Exegesis." In *Theological Interpretation of Scripture: Classic and Contemporary Readings*, edited by Stephen Fowl, 87–102. Malden, MA: Blackwell, 1997.

Yeo, K. K. "Biblical Christologies of the Global Church: Beyond Chalcedon? Toward a Fully Christian and Fully Cultural Theology." In *Jesus without Borders: Christology in the Majority World*, edited by Gene L. Green, Stephen T. Pardue, and K. K. Yeo, 162–79. Grand Rapids: Eerdmans, 2014.

Yoder, John Howard. *The Politics of Jesus: Vicit Agnus Noster*. Grand Rapids: Eerdmans, 2001.

Young, Frances M. *Biblical Exegesis and the Formation of Christian Culture*. Cambridge: Cambridge University Press, 1997.

———. *From Nicaea to Chalcedon: A Guide to the Literature and Its Background*. 2nd ed. Grand Rapids: Baker Academic, 2010.

Langham Literature, with its publishing work, is a ministry of Langham Partnership.

Langham Partnership is a global fellowship working in pursuit of the vision God entrusted to its founder John Stott –

to facilitate the growth of the church in maturity and Christ-likeness through raising the standards of biblical preaching and teaching.

Our vision is to see churches in the Majority World equipped for mission and growing to maturity in Christ through the ministry of pastors and leaders who believe, teach and live by the word of God.

Our mission is to strengthen the ministry of the word of God through:
- nurturing national movements for biblical preaching
- fostering the creation and distribution of evangelical literature
- enhancing evangelical theological education

especially in countries where churches are under-resourced.

Our ministry

Langham Preaching partners with national leaders to nurture indigenous biblical preaching movements for pastors and lay preachers all around the world. With the support of a team of trainers from many countries, a multi-level programme of seminars provides practical training, and is followed by a programme for training local facilitators. Local preachers' groups and national and regional networks ensure continuity and ongoing development, seeking to build vigorous movements committed to Bible exposition.

Langham Literature provides Majority World preachers, scholars and seminary libraries with evangelical books and electronic resources through publishing and distribution, grants and discounts. The programme also fosters the creation of indigenous evangelical books in many languages, through writer's grants, strengthening local evangelical publishing houses, and investment in major regional literature projects, such as one volume Bible commentaries like the *Africa Bible Commentary* and the *South Asia Bible Commentary*.

Langham Scholars provides financial support for evangelical doctoral students from the Majority World so that, when they return home, they may train pastors and other Christian leaders with sound, biblical and theological teaching. This programme equips those who equip others. Langham Scholars also works in partnership with Majority World seminaries in strengthening evangelical theological education. A growing number of Langham Scholars study in high quality doctoral programmes in the Majority World itself. As well as teaching the next generation of pastors, graduated Langham Scholars exercise significant influence through their writing and leadership.

To learn more about Langham Partnership and the work we do visit **langham.org**

www.ingramcontent.com/pod-product-compliance
Lightning Source LLC
Chambersburg PA
CBHW051540230426
43669CB00015B/2665